Honoring both humanity's passive receptivity before God and its need for active civil engagement, the essayists in this book appropriate a neglected feature of Luther's theology: the two kinds of righteousness. For the Wittenberg reformer, humans are constituted by two dimensions, a vertical one in which Christ's righteousness is imputed to them and a horizontal one in which they are responsible for just and life-giving social relationships. Neither exiling themselves from the wider public nor occupying it through conquest, Christians empowered with Christ's goodness should engage the secular world as full citizens, since their new identity in Christ impels them to make a difference in the public arena. Luther called this approach "our theology." This book helps us to appropriate Luther's theology as our theology as well.

Mark Mattes
Lutheran Bible Institute Chair of Theology
Grand View University

In many expressions of twenty-first century Christian teaching, the only kind of righteousness one hears of is that of human works. This book, grounded in the Lutheran confessions and in the writings of Martin Luther and Philip Melanchthon, provides a healthy antidote to such mistaken instruction. By distinguishing alien and proper righteousness, as did Wittenberg's reformers, this collection of essays by some of the leading scholars at Concordia Seminary, St. Louis, places the gracious, life-giving announcement of God's mercy at the very center of Christian proclamation and opens up new ways for Christians to imagine service to their neighbors. Few books available today will better inform the Christian church and its ministry.

Timothy J. Wengert
Ministerium of Pennsylvania Professor emeritus
United Lutheran Seminary (Philadelphia)

Robert Kolb has spent the last four decades investigating Luther's understanding of God's two kinds of righteousness. God's righteousness in Christ restores His human creatures to saving relationship to their Creator through faith in the divine promise. Set free from self-righteousness, believers live in righteousness in the world, giving themselves to works that serve their neighbors. In this volume, we see the fruits of Kolb's research manifested also in the scholarship of his former students, now colleagues, as they develop the implications of the Reformer's confession of God's twofold work for pastoral ministry, the doctrine of vocation, mission, and ethics. This superb volume makes Luther's theology of the two kinds of righteousness accessible to a wide audience in the church.

John T. Pless
Concordia Theological Seminary
Fort Wayne, IN

the alien +
the proper

*Luther's Two-Fold Righteousness
in Controversy, Ministry, and Citizenship*

the alien +
the proper

*Luther's Two-Fold Righteousness
in Controversy, Ministry, and Citizenship*

Edited by Robert Kolb

Foreword by Michael J. Chan

FIFTEEN-SEVENTEEN PUBLISHING · 1517.

The Alien and the Proper: Luther's Two-Fold Righteousness in Controversy, Ministry, and Citizenship
© 2023 New Reformation Publications

Scripture quotations are from The ESV® Bible (The Holy Bible, English Standard Version®), copyright © 2001 by Crossway, a publishing ministry of Good News Publishers. Used by permission. All rights reserved.

Published by:
1517 Publishing
PO Box 54032
Irvine, CA 92619-4032

Publisher's Cataloging-In-Publication Data
(Prepared by Cassidy Cataloguing Services)

Names: Kolb, Robert, 1941- editor. | Chan, Michael J., writer of foreword.
Title: The alien and the proper : Luther's two-fold righteousness in controversy, ministry, and citizenship / edited by Robert Kolb ; foreword by Michael J. Chan.
Other titles: Lutheran quarterly (Gettysburg, Pa. : 1949) | Concordia journal
Description: Irvine, CA : 1517 Publishing, [2023]
Identifiers: ISBN: 978-1-956658-16-3 (hardcover) | 978-1-956658-17-0 (paperback) | 978-1-956658-18-7 (ebook)
Subjects: LCSH: Luther, Martin, 1483-1546—Criticism and interpretation. | Righteousness. | Christian life. | LCGFT: Essays. | BISAC: RELIGION / Essays. | RELIGION / Christian Theology / General. | RELIGION / Christianity / Lutheran.
Classification: LCC: BR332.5 .A45 2023 | DDC: 230.41—dc23

Printed in the United States of America.

Cover art by Zachariah James Stuef.

David A. Lumpp, "Luther's 'Two Kinds of Righteousness''. A Brief Historical Introduction," Concordia Journal 23 (1997), 27-39. Reprinted with permission of Concordia Journal.

William W. Schumacher, "Civic Participation by Churches and Pastors: an Essay on the Two Kinds of Righteousness," Concordia Journal 30 (2004): 165-177. Reprinted with permission of Concordia Journal.

Charles P. Arand and Joel D. Biermann, "Why the Two Kinds of Righteousness?" Concordia Journal 33 (2007): 116-135. Reprinted with permission of Concordia Journal.

Robert Kolb, "God and His Human Creatures in Luther's Sermons on Genesis: The Reformer's Early Use of His Distinction of Two Kinds of Righteousness," Concordia Journal 33 (2007): 166-184. Reprinted with permission of Concordia Journal.

Timothy E. Saleska, "The Two Kinds of Righteousness: What's a Preacher to Do?" Concordia Journal 33 (2007): 136- 145. Reprinted with permission of Concordia Journal.

Charles P. Arand, "The Ministry of the Church in the Light of the Two Kinds of Righteousness," Concordia Journal 33 (2007): 344-356. Reprinted with permission by Concordia Journal.

Arand, Charles P. Two Kinds of Righteousness as a Framework for law and Gospel in the Apology. Lutheran Quarterly 13 (1999), 417-439. © 1999 Johns Hopkins University Press and Lutheran Quarterly, Inc. Reprinted with permission of Johns Hopkins University Press.

Twofold Righteousness Reader

Foreword by Michael J. Chan. ix

"Our Theology"—Luther's Two Kinds of Righteousness:
   A Personal Reflection
   Robert Kolb. xiii

1. Luther's "Two Kinds of Righteousness":
   A Brief Historical Introduction. 1
   David A. Lumpp

2. Luther on the Two Kinds of Righteousness;
   Reflections on His Two-Dimensional Definition
   of Humanity at the Heart of His Theology 17
   by Robert Kolb

3. Two Kinds of Righteousness as a Framework for Law
   and Gospel in the Apology. 35
   By Charles P. Arand

4. Civic Participation by Churches and Pastors:
   An Essay on Two Kinds of Righteousness. 59
   William W. Schumacher

5. "The Chief Controversy between the Papalists and Us". 75
   Robert Kolb

6. Why the Two Kinds of Righteousness?. 99
   Charles P. Arand and Joel Biermann

7. God and His Human Creatures in Luther's Sermons
    on Genesis: The Reformer's Early Use of His Distinction
    of Two Kinds of Righteousness........................ 125
    Robert Kolb

8. The Two Kinds of Righteousness!:
    What's a Preacher to Do?............................ 149
    Timothy Saleska

9. The Ministry of the Church in Light of the Two Kinds
    of Righteousness 163
    Charles P. Arand

Conclusion 179
    Charles P. Arand

Contributors 189

Apology of the Augsburg Confession (Melanchthon) 193

Subject Index... 195

Scripture Index... 209

Foreword

The critical distinction Luther makes between two kinds of righteousness ("alien" and "proper") is a theological garden that needs constant tending by many loving and diligent hands. When that work is neglected or improperly done, it becomes easy to confuse the two—and often with disastrous results for human beings, the church, and the world. Properly and precisely distinguishing between the righteousness that comes as a divine gift and that which is enacted before other creatures is not simply a matter of academic interest. True human flourishing is at stake.

But take heart, dear reader. You are in good hands. The pages laid out before you were penned with care, rigor, and clarity. While they come from a variety of authors and publications, they have a shared focus on Luther's "twofold righteousness" and the theological insights that follow in their wake (law and gospel, the two kingdoms, etc.). Each author turns this glimmering theological diamond at slightly different angles, offering a picture that, in the final assessment, is both rich and accessible.

Editor Robert Kolb has put us in his debt by opening the book with a personal reflection—written quite appropriately on Palm Sunday, 2022. Characteristically humble and thoughtful, Kolb offers a helpful orientation to the volume that is at the same time interwoven with his own biography as a teacher and a scholar. I would urge readers to consider this opening reflection carefully. As someone who studies, admires, and relies upon Luther from an adjacent field (biblical studies), I depended on this essay to help me comprehend more fully what scholars of Luther might take for granted.

Kolb's essay ends with the hope that the volume will help its readers to address the manifold challenges facing Christian witness and ministry today. For my part I think it can and will accomplish just that. Even though Luther's insights are old, they remain critical and resonant in the current moment.

As noted throughout the book, Luther's insight into "twofold righteousness" is really an explanation of what it means to be a human being in relation to God, our creator, and our fellow creatures. The gift bestowed upon us in the gospel is "alien," insofar as it comes to us from a merciful and benevolent Other. Our true human identity is a gift from the outside. This interpretation of human life stands in stark contrast to the "gospel" according to the "age of authenticity," to borrow a term from the analysis of Charles Taylor.[1] That "gospel" urges its adherents to engage in an internal quest for the authentic self, at the end of which one uncovers a truly American treasure: "my truth."

In such a paradigm, freedom is won by our own hands as the reward for throwing off socially-imposed shackles and for uncovering the true self, buried beneath layers of detritus. Supercharged by a voracious hunger for social media content, exploration of the self has become a market frontier—a vast and seemingly infinite field of monetizable resources. As Jia Tolentino has so powerfully shown, however, it's a "trick mirror."[2]

There may be no theological tradition more well equipped to engage critically with these problematic anthropologies than the Lutheran tradition and "our theology" of righteousness. We must follow the lead of Jeremiah—a true law and gospel preacher—who described Israelite idolatry as a cistern wrought with human hands: it promises to hold lifegiving water but in the end fails to keep its word (Jer 2:13). The age of authenticity offers many promises, especially when it comes to human identity. Like Jeremiah's cisterns, however, these promises leave us thirsting for more and dying in the desert. But this is precisely where the gospel shows up, where the promises of the world have failed us.

This book probes the beating theological heart of Luther's evangelical theology. My prayer is that the Spirit through these essays will rekindle a "first love" (Jer 2:2; Rev 2:4) fire in students of Luther to tend once again to his revolutionary insights.

Michael J. Chan, Ph.D.
Concordia College, Moorhead, MN

Notes

1. Charles Taylor, *A Secular Age* (Cambridge, Mass.: Belknap Press of Harvard University Press, 2007), 473.

2. Jia Tolentino, *Trick Mirror: Reflections on Self-Delusion* (New York: Random House, 2019).

"Our Theology"—
Luther's Two Kinds of Righteousness:
A Personal Reflection

Robert Kolb

The rather strange title of this volume, bringing together two adjectives that do not seem to belong together, rests on attempts to explain two Latin concepts that are not expressed by the English words derived from the original Latin. "Aliena" refers in fact to anything that comes from outside while "propria" refers to what is internally produced. When applied to righteousness, as Luther did when he first formulated his revolutionary concept of human identity or righteousness, they refer to the unconditional gift of the identity of child of God bestowed by the Holy Spirit through our faith in Jesus Christ. That faith determines, as Luther explained in his explanation to the First Commandment in the Large Catechism, our core identity, our righteousness before God. The righteousness or identity established through our love for others and our service to all of God's creation properly comes from our actions, even when they are moved and directed by the Holy Spirit. For Luther, in Latin, the alien and the proper are most distinct and quite inseparable.

Almost forty years ago it fell my lot to teach an elective on the theology of Martin Luther at Concordia College in Saint Paul, Minnesota. Luther's Galatians commentary went onto the required reading list. Luther's own students counted the commentary on Galatians published in 1535 among his best works. The commentary provided readers an edited version of his lectures delivered in

1531. The shadow of the condemnation of the Augsburg Confession's doctrine of justification by grace through faith by the Roman Catholic "Confutation" hung over those lectures. Because of its content and its historical situation, the commentary seemed to me to be an excellent way to get my students into the heart of Luther's thinking. I thought I knew Luther quite well by that time, in my early 40's, and so was surprised to find that in the preface of the printed commentary, he had written,

> This is our theology, by which we teach a precise distinction between these two kinds of righteousness, the active and the passive, so that morality and faith, works and grace, secular society and religion may not be confused. Both are necessary, but both must be kept within their limits.[1]

In reading the reformer's exposition of Galatians with this in mind, it became clear how the distinction of *zweierlei Gerechtigkeit*—it can be rendered either "two kinds of righteousness" as does *Luther's Works*,[2] or "twofold righteousness"—did indeed form and inform Luther's understanding of how God created human creatures to be in a relationship of trust and peace with him and how he restores that relationship.

I do not know how I had missed that in my earlier study as student and instructor. True, only an occasional modern study had highlighted the distinction,[3] and Melanchthon's subsuming the distinction into his topic on justification did not plant it firmly in the minds of Luther's and Melanchthon's students as a category of teaching or topic. My instructors had presumed it in teaching justification, and in my student days theological anthropology was not prominent, as it was becoming in the 1980s. Conversations with colleagues in Saint Paul and then a decade later, when Concordia Seminary called me to join its faculty, with colleagues in Saint Louis enriched my own understanding as they developed further explanations and applications of the fundamental framework for Luther's understanding of what it means to be human.

Melanchthon, too, distinguished between what he preferred to call the righteousness of the law and the righteousness of faith. His *Loci communes* of 1535 defined "new and eternal righteousness and life" as the "gracious remission of sins freely given" or "mercy and freely given acceptance." For the gift of righteousness in God's sight through grace signifies "the giving of the Holy Spirit and eternal life, that is, new and eternal righteousness and life . . ." Melanchthon interpreted John 1:17, "the law was given through Moses, grace and truth were made through Jesus Christ," with these words: "you have heard the law, but this is not what abolishes sin, and it does not get rid of the blindness in the mind, that is, doubts about God and growling before the judging God. It does not deliver true and eternal righteousness, but [exercises] a deadly external discipline over us. That is the eternal and lasting and perpetual righteousness."[4] But that unconditionally bestowed righteousness produces another kind of righteousness, that of "our obedience, that is, the righteousness of a good conscience or works, which God commands us to do, [which] necessarily follow reconciliation."[5] This relationship of the righteousness of the law and the righteousness of faith Melanchthon accentuated in the Apology of the Augsburg Confession.[6]

Somewhere in the 1990s another passage, this one in the work of the "second Martin," Martin Chemnitz, struck me. Chemnitz conveyed what Luther's distinction means with its teaching on "twofold righteousness" in regard to the disputes over justification with Roman Catholics. In his *Examination of the Council of Trent* he wrote,

> For it is regarding the good works of the regenerate, or the new obedience, that there is now the chief controversy between the papalists and us, namely, whether the regenerate are justified by that newness which the Holy Spirit works in them and by the good works which follow from that renewal; that is, whether the newness, the virtues, or good works of the regenerate are the things by which they can stand in the judgment of God that they may not be condemned, on account of which they have a gracious and propitiated God, to whom they should look, on whom they should rely, in whom they should trust when they are dealing with that difficult question, how we may be children of God and be accepted to eternal life.[7]

Chemnitz contrasted the Roman Catholic answer, which Trent presented as grace-wrought good works that the believer can present to God as proof of righteousness, with his own answer as a follower of

Luther and Melanchthon: simply the favor of God, and trust in God's promise to give forgiveness, life, and salvation for Christ's sake to his chosen people.

Luther confessed God first of all as Creator. As described in Genesis 1, his act and mode of creating of the universe and all reality in it *ex nihilo*—out of absolutely nothing—provides also a model, according to Luther, for understanding how he goes about the re-creation of sinners into children of God. His steadfast lovingkindness brought the worlds into being without any conditions through his Word, and with this same steadfast lovingkindness he planned and executed the re-creation of those who doubted his Word and defied his lordship. He accomplished this fashioning of new creatures in Christ (2 Cor. 5:17) through the death and resurrection of Jesus Christ, also without any condition limiting God's love and any contribution required from the human side.[8]

Luther's anthropological axiom of the twofold righteousness is an integral part of a series of hermeneutical rules that governed his interpretation of Scripture. It is coordinate with his view of the two words with which God speaks when he approaches sinners. The first is his plan for human performance, which ends up as the foe of sinners. It is the pronouncement of judgment upon them despite its goodness as the blueprint for the fully human life. The second is his plan for human deliverance through the work of Christ. This plan has come to mortal terms with the law's condemnation of human sin and restores human integrity and identity as child of God to the sinner through the Holy Spirit's delivery of the benefits of Christ.

In addition, the twofold righteousness and the distinction of law and gospel are coordinated with Luther's perception of the two dimensions of human life, commonly designated as "two kingdoms" or in German *zwei Reiche*. The problem with that terminology is that Luther used it in at least three different ways. Sometimes it is roughly equivalent to "church" and "secular government" or, in more modern terminology, "state": at others, it refers to the rule and domain of God and that of Satan. In this sense I have come to use "two kingdoms." However, different from both is what is described in the hermeneutical principle of Luther's recognition that human life takes place in a "realm" of relationship with God and in a quite distinct "realm" of relationships with God's creatures, human and other.[9]

These three interpretive pillars of Luther's theology are inseparably intertwined in all his mature writing. Without the distinction of law and gospel as God's performative address to sinners, the twofold righteousness stands as a glimpse into our humanity without notice of its source and cause as well as of the dynamic involved in God's rescue and restoration of sinners as his children. Without the two kinds of righteousness, concepts of law and gospel can still end up with the position that Chemnitz was rejecting—if one is seeing the gospel as the means by which we produce righteous works that are what in the final analysis do make a difference in how God views us. Luther's insight that even in the final analysis our righteousness is the pure gift of a gracious God from beginning to end preserves the true comfort of the gospel.. A failure to take seriously the two realms or dimensions of human life can let active righteousness seem to count for some merit in God's sight in the vertical realm, before God himself. Therefore, Luther's proclamation of the biblical message depended on all three.

For years I mushed together these three discrete tenets or presuppositions of Luther's thinking. In 2001 my then doctoral student Makito Masaki mustered the courage to tell his advisor that I was confusing the three. He showed me that in the vertical dimension of life, God speaks the law of the first three commandments and demands not only that we fear, love, and trust in him above all things but he also requires our prayer, praise, and attention to his Word. In this dimension he also speaks the gospel that restores our righteousness. In that dimension of life we passively receive that righteousness and actively pray and praise him and devour his Word. In the horizontal dimension of life our identity and motivation are given by the gospel that identifies us in our total passivity as God's born-again righteous children, with the complete passivity of children in the birth process, while the law prescribes the behavior and conduct that pleases the heavenly Father and actively serves his human creatures and his world.

Luther had learned much from Augustine, particularly that God's grace alone delivers from sin. But he also parted company with his ancient forbearer in the faith because Augustine believed that God's grace produces good works in believers that forms the basis of their worthiness in God's sight alongside his merciful forgiveness.[10] Among the many theologians before and after Augustine who accentuated God's grace and mercy, none matched Luther in developing the anthropological implications of the nature of the Creator as sole originator of all that exists, of all that is good, for understanding that our humanity is totally a product of God's creative and re-creative Word. Thus, in Luther's study of Scripture he came upon a foundational insight that the ancient Hebrews, with their sense of what it means that God is Creator out of nothing, had expressed. That is an insight that other cultures, with presuppositions and conceptual frameworks developed apart from that starting point, could not envision.

Jesus taught that God's law distinguishes two ways in which his human creatures are to be what he made them to be, what defines humanity. He did not give a single line of prescription but two. First, we are "to love the Lord your God with all your heart, and with all your soul, and with all your mind." That commandment, he said, takes precedence. Loving God comes only through the gift of God; sinners cannot muster, make, or manage this total love and trust. Adam and Eve were created (passive voice!) with it, and we must be re-created to trust him once he has taken away our sinfulness under the condemnation of death. Then, the second commandment that defines our humanity, informs us, according to Jesus, that we are designed to love the neighbor. In Matthew 22: 34-40 he had sketched the two-sided nature of the human being's righteousness or human identity.

Luther initially used the Latin terms "*aliena*" and "*propria*" for the two kinds of righteousness, for instance, in his 1518 pamphlet, *On Threefold Righteousness*,[11] and in the 1519 treatise *On Twofold Righteousness*.[12] The first treatise had spoken of actions that externally conformed to God's law performed by those outside the faith in Christ alongside the righteousness of faith that is passively received and acted out in praise to God and service to others. Why he did not discuss the righteousness that outwardly conforms to God's plan for human life apart from faith in Christ—what he later termed "civil righteousness"—in the second treatise he did not record. Perhaps his world of only baptized Christians made it unnecessary to discuss that facet of our world, in which civic righteousness is such an important concept. It is certain that he did not abandon the concept.

His designation of righteousness as "*aliena*"—from outside ourselves—later gave way to "*iustitia passiva*" as the term that makes more explicit that God alone establishes our core identity as his children, liberated from sin and all other enemies, liberated to live in trust in him. "*Iustitia propria*"—our own righteousness, that is the righteousness that we perform—became "*iustitia activa*" as the designation of the godly activities that the Holy Spirit produces as we carry out God's commands.

The translation of "*zweierlei Gerechtigkeit*" as "two kinds of righteousness" makes clear that the one righteousness that defines our persons comes from God alone. In receiving it as "the real me" I am completely passive. In contrast, my active righteousness is experienced in my own behavior and the thinking and willing that goes on behind it, under the direction and with the empowerment of the Holy Spirit. The translation of the phrase as "twofold righteousness" emphasizes that there are not two parts of the child of God that can be turned on or off at different times. There is one righteous person, a person defined by God's grace and the death and resurrection of Christ. His death and resurrection have placed the old sinful identity of the person in the Lord's tomb and resurrected the person as a new creature, trusting and hearkening to the Lord. God's declaration that I am righteous in his sight is met by my faith's counter-declaration (though not "counter" in the sense of rejection but in the sense of an affirmative response of agreement). The same faith that throws itself completely on God's love and faithfulness concludes that if God thinks that I am righteous, I want to—and do, though somewhat faltingly— practice being his righteous child. For this reason, although Luther distinguished what later Lutherans would differentiate as justification and sanctification as sharply as they did, he also saw a seamless transition in practice the two. My trust in the fact that God has forgiven me and through his Word made me this new creature leads naturally and willingly to the obedience that carries out the identity that the word of absolution bestows.

Luther's distinction of the two kinds of righteousness sets forth the biblical view what it means to be human. Therefore, it has implications and guidance for the application of all of the Bible to daily life. In this volume some essays sketch the historical aspects of this teaching, and others demonstrate how it helps gain insights into specific issues in the church and in the world today. The essays are presented in the chronological order of their appearance in print so that readers can gain a sense of how this discussion of Luther's anthropology developed. The rendering of each article here reflects the original setting in the place of original publication, so that some articles have footnotes and others have endnotes. Of course, no few contributions to the bibliography treating aspects of the topic of Luther's and Melanchthon's twofold righteousness have appeared in the twenty-five years since the appearance of the first of these essays. Regrettably, these titles cannot be included in this volume.

Such a volume is possible not only because of the authors' initial contributions but also to those who aid in the preparation of the final product. With deep gratitude the editor thanks Melanie Appelbaum of Concordia Seminary Press for assembling the essays into a collection and to Steve Byrnes and Sam Leanza Ortiz of 1517 Publishing for bringing the volume to completion!

We hope that readers will take these insights and work further on the use of this central insight in the Lutheran tradition to the challenges of public witness and ministry today.

Concordia Seminary, Saint Louis
Palm Sunday 2022

Notes

1. *Dr. Martin Luthers Werke* (Weimar: Böhlau, 1883-) [henceforth WA] 40,I:45,24-27; *Luther's Works* (Saint Louis and Philadelphia: Concordia and Fortress, 1958-1986) [henceforth] LW 26:7. For a summary of Luther's definition of "righteousness," and bibliography, see Bengt Hägglund, "Gerechtigkeit. VI. Reformations- und Neuzeit," *Theologische Realenzyklopädie* XII (Berlin: de Gruyter, 1984): 432-434, 440. See also the December 1998 Beiheft issue of *Zeitschrift für Theologie und Kirche* 95, on Luther's understanding of righteousness and justification, particularly as it pertains to the "Joint Declaration on the Doctrine of Justification" (which ignores Luther's distinction of the two kinds of righteousness); see especially Reinhard Schwarz, "Luthers Rechtfertigungslehre als Eckstein der christlichen Theologie und Kirche," *Zeitschrift für Theologie und Kirche* 95, Beiheft 10 (1998): 15-46.

2. LW 31: 297-306.

3. E.g. Paul Althaus, *The Theology of Martin Luther*, trans. Robert C. Schultz (Philadelphia: Fortress, 1966), 224-250.

4. *Melanchthons Werke in Auswahl*, ed. Robert Stupperich 2, 2 (Gütersloh: Bertelsmann, 1953): 372.

5. Ibid., 386.

6. E.g., in Ap IV, para. 147-151 and the discussion leading up to it, where love, as the righteousness of the fulfillment of the law, is contrasted with faith's righteousness, *Die Bekenntnisschrfiten der Evangelische-Lutherischen Kirche*, ed. Irene Dingel (Göttingen: Vandenhoeck & Ruprecht, 2014), 324/325-326/327 (314/315-338/339), *The Book of Concord*, ed. Robert Kolb and Timothy J. Wengert (Minneapolis: Fortress, 2000), 143 (139-149).

7. Martin Chemnitz, *Examen concilii Tridentini*, ed. Eduard Preuss (1861; Darmstadt: Wlssenschaftliche Buchgesellschaft, 1972), 153, English translation: *Examination of the council of Trent, Part I*, trans. Fred Kramer (Saint Louis: Concordia, 1971), 481-482.

8. Johann Haar, *Initium creaturae Dei. Eine Untersuchung über Luthers Begriff der "neuen Creatur" im Zusammenhang mit seine Verständnis von Jakobus 1,18 und mit seinem "Zeit"-Denken* (Gütersloh: Bertelsmann, 1939); Robert Kolb, "Resurrection and Justification. Luther's Use of Romans 4,25," *Lutherjahrbuch* 78 (2011), 39-60.

9. Robert Kolb, "Luther's Hermeneutics of Distinctions: Law and Gospel, Two Kinds of Righteousness, and Two Realms," *The Oxford Handbook of Martin Luther's Theology*, co-edited with Irene Dingel and Lubomir Batka (Oxford: Oxford University Press, 2014), 168-184.

10. Walter Bienert, "'Im Zweifel näher bei Augustin"? – Zum patristischen Hintergrund der Theologie Luthers'. In Damaskinos Papandreeou et al., eds. *Oecumenica et Patristica*. (Stuttgart: Kohlhammer, 1989), 179-181.

11. WA 2: 43-47.

12. WA 2:145-152 , LW 31: 297-306.

Luther's "Two Kinds of Righteousness": A Brief Historical Introduction

David A. Lumpp

An introduction to Martin Luther's writings even in the American Edition can be a daunting experience for students. The fifty-five volumes present a sometimes bewildering array of materials, and students' trepidation grows when they discover that the American Edition provides only a fraction of Luther's collected writings (which, as the Preface to James Kittelson's biography points out, number more than one hundred quarto volumes in its modern edition). Understandably, students seek a unifying theme around which they can organize the material they read in its breadth and diversity. The danger of these attempts, of course, is that one invariably makes a single term or concept bear more weight than it was intended to carry, and one may inadvertently trim evidence to make it fit a thematic conclusion. Luther, as the now vacuous cliché has it, was not a systematician.

Nevertheless, with these caveats in mind, one forages about in Luther himself, hoping to find clues from the reformer's own hand that might sanction the efforts made along these lines. While it is hazardous to focus on any one remark, Luther does give some indication of his theological priorities and his own estimation of what is central. In the longer and definitive *Lectures on Galatians* (delivered in 1531; published in 1535), Luther describes as "our theology" his distinction between two kinds of righteousness: "This is our theology, by which we teach a precise distinction between these two kinds of righteousness, the active and the passive, so that morality and faith, works and grace, secular society and religion may not be confused. Both are necessary, but both must be kept within their limits. Christian righteousness applies to the new man, and the righteousness of the Law applies to the old man, who is born of flesh and blood."[1]

Does the evidence warrant seizing this phrase amid the millions of recorded words of Luther? One can answer affirmatively for several reasons: First, the two kinds of righteousness are indispensable to understanding the nature of Luther's view of the saving work of Jesus Christ;[2] second, the two kinds of righteousness are not separable from (and actually underlie) other distinctions that pervade Luther's theology, such as Law and Gospel, the two governments,[3] his uses of the Law,[4] and his doctrine of vocation; third, the two kinds of righteousness show the futility of using any one motif to capture the breadth of Luther's soteriology;[5] and, fourth, this distinction (in connection with a larger examination of the righteousness of God) is virtually a golden thread that one can use to trace the historical development of Luther's thought both to and well beyond his "evangelical breakthrough" in 1518-1519.[6] In short, the two kinds of righteousness work nicely as a heuristic device around which one can outline Luther's theology in terms of its essential content, its structure, and its internal development.

Toward Clarity

The broad contours of Luther's "rediscovery of the Gospel" are well known and need not be rehearsed here.[7] Although the date has long been in controversy, greater agreement obtains on the nature of the breakthrough itself. In the 1545 *Preface to the Complete Edition of Luther's Latin Writings*, the aging reformer chronicled his discovery in terms of his struggle with the Biblical phrase, "the righteousness of God." In a phrase where quite literally everything hinges upon a preposition, Luther moved from an early "formal" or active view of the *iustitia Dei* as a divine attribute or legal requirement to one that regards it as a passive, evangelical gift.[8]

A great deal has been elided in this sentence, of course—it surveys the development of Luther much as one peers down at a landscape from an airplane. Nonetheless, in what follows we will make three basic points. First, we will sketch the development of Luther's evangelical understanding of the righteousness of God from its early problematic status to its elevated kerygmatic role in his later writings. Second, we will underscore its function in Luther's increasingly forensic notion of justification. Finally, we will highlight the *frölicher Wechsel* or "happy exchange" as a concomitant of Luther's thoroughly incarnational theology and ethics.

Luther's emergent understanding of the two kinds of righteousness came in several phases. One cannot claim simplistically that Luther advanced the righteousness of God from a crude and primitive conception as divine *proprium* to one of *beneficium*. Karl Holl demonstrated convincingly that well before Luther the righteousness of God was understood in the sense of God's giving righteousness (a "genitive of author").[9] Thus, it is not surprising that from 1513 on, the older and so-called early date for Luther's breakthrough, the reformer realized that the righteousness of God was not retributive or punitive; rather, it was the redemptive, divine attribute by which God saves.[10] But this righteousness was consistently construed as a righteousness worked out *in the individual.* This righteousness, possessed by the person, provided a theological foundation for the doctrine of merit from St. Augustine up through the medieval scholastics.[11] For five or six more years, Luther understood justification in largely Augustinian terms. There justification is seen in a "sanative" or medicinal sense as inner renewal: grace is a substance that "heals" the sinner of the disease of sin and produces "works of faith" (*opera fidei*) rather than "works of law" (*opera legis*, which do not justify). This is roughly the position maintained until the summer or early autumn of 1518.[12]

The academic year of 1518-1519 was pivotal for Luther both for his evangelical breakthrough in general and in terms of the present topic. During that year and with the philological assistance of Melanchthon, Luther came to a more forensic view of justification;[13] and he preached two sermons that pertain to God's righteousness. In the fall of 1518, Luther delivered his sermon on the three kinds of righteousness; and in the winter or spring of 1519, he preached the better known sermon on the *Two Kinds of Righteousness.*[14]

In the former, Luther pits civil, alien, and actual righteousness against sin as, correspondingly, civil, inherited (*peccatum essenciale, natale, originale*), and actual.[15] The crucial righteousness with which Luther counters original sin is the righteousness of Jesus Christ,[16] which is the believer's through faith. "This is not the righteousness of the Law, but the righteousness of grace"; it is announced in the Gospel and conferred through Baptism.[17] Significantly, human effort cannot produce this righteousness[18]—thus obviating any of the late medieval *meritum* schemes—and it renders one's salvation sure.[19]

In his sermon the *Two Kinds of Righteousness* of 1519, Luther's distinctions are even cleaner and his soteriology more overtly forensic. With both of these sermons, however, one is hearing Luther in the wake of his self-identified evangelical breakthrough. His celebrated (and controverted) remarks of 1545 implore readers to regard his older efforts "judiciously, yes, with great commiseration" (*cum multa miseratione*) for at the outset of his career Luther was "a monk and most enthusiastic papist" *(papistam insanissimum).*[20] Luther describes his recognition of St. Paul's own connection of Romans 1:17 ("in it the righteousness of God is revealed," where the antecedent of ἐν αὐτῷ is "the gospel" of 1:16) with Habakkuk 2:4. Theologically, this opened the floodgates for Luther, and it makes the comments about his early writings all the more intelligible.

> . . .I began to understand that the righteousness of God is that by which the righteous lives as a gift of God, namely, by faith. And this is the meaning: the righteousness is revealed by the gospel, namely, the passive righteousness with which merciful God justifies us by faith, as it is written, "He who through faith is righteous shall live." Here I felt that I was altogether born again and had entered paradise again through open gates. There a totally other face of the entire Scripture showed itself to me. Thereupon I ran through the Scriptures from memory. I also found in other terms an analogy, as, the work of God, that is, what God does in us, the power of God, with which he makes us strong, the wisdom of God, with which he makes us wise, the strength of God, the salvation of God, the glory of God.
>
> And I extolled my sweetest word with a love as great as the hatred with which I had before hated the word "righteousness of God." Thus that place in Paul was for me truly the gate to paradise.[21]

The sermon on the two kinds of righteousness clarifies several of these insights and begins to apply them in suggestive ways for other theological and ethical topics.[22] The contrasts of the earlier sermons are sharpened to a crucial distinction between alien and proper righteousness, with the former the source and cause of the latter. The following citations, offered seriatim, illustrate the point:

> There are two kinds of Christian righteousness, just as man's sin is of two kinds.
>
> The first is alien righteousness, that is the righteousness of another, instilled [*infusa*] from without. This is the righteousness of Christ by which he justifies through faith. . ... This righteousness, then, is given to men in Baptism and whenever they are truly repentant. . ...
>
> Through faith in Christ, therefore, Christ's righteousness has become our righteousness and all that he has becomes ours; rather, he himself becomes ours. . ... This is an infinite righteousness, and one that swallows up all sins in a moment, for it is impossible that sin should exist in Christ. On the contrary, he who trusts Christ exists in Christ; he is one with Christ, having the same righteousness as he. It is therefore impossible that sin should remain in him. . ...
>
> The second kind of righteousness is our proper righteousness, not because we alone work it, but because we work with that first and alien righteousness. This is the manner of life spent profitably in good works, in the first place, in slaying the flesh and crucifying the desires with respect to the self. . ... In the second place, this righteousness consists in love to one's neighbor, and in the third place, in meekness and fear toward God.[23]

In this sermon, the attention is diverted away from the individual to the person of Christ. As early as the Romans lectures on 1515-1516, Luther asserted that saving righteousness dare never be seen as a personal possession (*iustitia domestica*); instead, it is a possession of Christ (*iustitia aliena*).[24] Hence, it is always *extra nos.*[24] In 1521, in the treatise *Against Latomus*, Luther explicitly declared that righteousness is not a quality or *habitus* of human beings.[25] Righteousness comes exclusively as a gift *propter Christum.*[26]

In terms of the two kinds of righteousness and the distinctions noted above, for Christ's sake righteousness before God is accounted to the one who has been given faith. It is interesting to observe in this connection that roughly until the period of this sermon on the two kinds of righteousness, Luther talked about an infused righteousness. From approximately the early Galatians commentary on, he uses *imputatio* instead of *infusio*.[27] Along with this primary accounting righteous, Christ assumes lordship of the person's life through faith. Christ is supremely active (*Christus actuosissimus*) in the believer;[28] He struggles within the Christian against a constellation of foes, namely, the flesh, the world, death, and the devil.[29]

From the greater accent on the forensic character of justification (even if the dogmaticians' formulation is absent) and from the pervasive accent on the merits of Christ, it is a very short step to the winning language of "exchange." This is already anticipated in 1516 in a letter from Luther to his fellow Augustinian George Spenlein, which is all the more significant because the letter connects the imagery of exchange to an early expression of the two kinds of righteousness.

> Now I should like to know whether your soul, tired of its own righteousness, is learning to be revived by and to trust in the righteousness of Christ. For in our age the temptation to presumption besets many, especially those who try with all their might to be just and good without knowing the righteousness of God, which is most bountifully and freely given us in Christ. They try to do good of themselves in order that they might stand before God clothed in their own virtues and merits. But this is impossible. While you were here, you were one who held this opinion, or rather, error. So was I, and I am still fighting against the error without having conquered it as yet.
>
> Therefore, my dear Friar, learn Christ and him crucified. Learn to praise him and, despairing of yourself, say, "Lord Jesus, you are my righteousness, just as I am your sin. You have taken upon yourself what is mine and have given to me what is yours. You have taken upon yourself what you were not and have given to me what I was not.". . .you will learn from him that just as he has received you, so he has made your sins his own and has made his righteousness yours.[30]

In the sermon on the two kinds of righteousness of 1519, Luther uses similar language:

Therefore a man can with confidence boast in Christ and say: "Mine are Christ's living, doing, and speaking, his suffering and dying, mine as much as if I had lived, done, spoken, and suffered, and died as he did.". . .

. . .everything which Christ has is ours, graciously bestowed on us unworthy men out of God's sheer mercy, although we have rather deserved wrath and condemnation, and hell also. . ..[31]

Moreover, in comments on the Psalms from 1519 to 1521, Luther referred to the "admirable trade" (*admirabili commertio*),[32] and he championed a*mirabilem mutuacionem* or "marvelous exchange" in lectures on Isaiah given from 1527 to 1530.[33]

The *frölicher Wechsel* is developed in The Freedom of a Christian of 1520, even where the terminology itself is not always used (as is often the case in the large Galatians commentary and virtually whenever Luther has occasion to comment on Isaiah 53:6; Galatians 3:13; 2 Corinthians 5:21; and often Romans 6:3-11).[34] Under the terms of the "happy" or "fortunate exchange," Christ assumes and bears the wrath and judgment of God while fallen men and women enjoy all the attendant blessings of salvation.

Of Luther's major writings, these affirmations achieve thematic status in the Galatians lectures of 1531-1535. In these works, of course, the *frölicher Wechsel* or *feliciter commutans* finds its classic formulation, amid the thoroughgoing dialectic that pervades this epistle. To be sure, all the basic contrasts surface in Luther's exposition of Galatians: active and passive righteousness, flesh and spirit, works and faith, Moses and Christ—all rooted, finally, in the most fundamental contrast between Law and Gospel: "By this fortunate exchange [*feliciter commutans*] with us He took upon Himself our sinful person and granted us His innocent and victorious Person. Clothed and dressed in this, we are freed from the curse of the Law, because Christ Himself voluntarily became a curse for us."[35]

The saving righteousness of God is a righteousness *from* God. Such righteousness, while a *donum gratia*, never becomes an ontological possession. Properly speaking, righteousness is found only in Jesus Christ. Yet men and women are now in Christ through the creative power of the Word of God in the declaration of the Gospel and the sacramental washing and regeneration of Holy Baptism. It is not a matter of being potentially righteous, nor is it a matter of God looking at Christians "as though" they are righteous. Luther's accent on the creative Word prevents such misunderstanding. Human beings *are* righteous—authentically and genuinely—but before God their righteousness is never inherent or intrinsic, or, in still more characteristic language, "active" (which, it should be noted, again precludes all vestiges of merit theology). Nor is any kind of ontological mysticism a permissible interpretation, for passive righteousness is extraneous and external (*extranea* and *externa*), and thus always "outside of us."[36]

> . . .it is appropriate to call the righteousness of faith or Christian righteousness "passive." This is a righteousness hidden in a mystery [*in mysterio abscondita*], which the world does not understand. In fact, Christians themselves do not adequately understand it or grasp it in the midst of their temptations. Therefore it must always be taught and continually exercised. And anyone who does not grasp or take hold of it in afflictions and terrors of conscience cannot stand. For there is no comfort of conscience so solid and certain as is this passive righteousness.[37]

The combinations of descriptive adjectives with which Luther nails down his developed understanding of the two kinds of righteousness, coupled with his gradual shift from the language of infusion to imputation, go far to point up Luther's forensic conception of justification. Obviously, forensic justification is developed at length by Melanchthon, the confessional generation, and by the dogmaticians of orthodoxy. However, as Robert Kolb has pointed out, for the most part they did so without recourse to Luther's accent on the two kinds of righteousness. In so doing, while the later generations retain many of the reformer's emphases, their general failure to use the language of passive and active righteousness—wherein God gives Christ's righteousness—potentially allows the Law to retain a determinative position when they characterize the basis of the divine-human relationship.[38]

Applications to Soteriology, Incarnation, and Ethics

Assertions of the non-imputation of sin (both original and residual) and the definitive imputation of Christ's righteousness are sprinkled throughout the Galatians lectures of 1531-1535.[39] In these incontestably mature comments, one sees not only an implicit forensic justification. Most intriguing is the subtle shift—really, only a new and further emphasis—in Luther's use of righteousness language. The accent on the righteousness of God as a passive gift of grace that is ours *extra nos* in the Gospel is a constant from at least 1518-1519 and thereafter. In his fully reformational period,[40] there is a growing focus on righteousness not only in connection with justification per se; indeed, righteousness is an integral component of Luther's understanding of the incarnation.

Taking his cue from those marvelously blunt Pauline texts, which describe not only the gifts that Jesus promises but that go so far as to define Him in His person (such as Life, Blessing, Peace, and, of course, Righteousness),[41] Luther often formulates his "happy exchange" in the language of incarnation as well as conferral. In this way, he is able to depict vividly the extent of God's rescue mission in the Son. This is accomplished—albeit through inversion in connection with 2 Corinthians 5:21—in the following well-known selection from the later Galatians lectures:

> When the merciful Father saw that we were being oppressed through the law, that we were being held under a curse, and that we could not be liberated from it by anything, He sent His Son into the world, heaped all the sins of all men upon Him, and said to Him: "Be Peter the denier; Paul the persecutor, blasphemer, and assaulter; David the adulterer; the sinner who ate the apple in Paradise; the thief on the cross. In short, be the person of all men, the one who has committed the sins of all men. And see to it that you pay and make satisfaction for them."[42]

Luther's distinction between the two kinds of righteousness and his notion of the joyous exchange pertain both to the forgiveness of sins and to the beginning of new life in Jesus Christ in Baptism. Within this exchange, one hears from God that the Law—all of it, in all of its forms—comes to an end in Jesus Christ (Rom. 10:4). The passive righteousness that justifies *coram Deo* enables one to silence the accusation of the Law with the stronger word of the Gospel: "For I am Baptized; and through the Gospel I have been called to a fellowship of righteousness and eternal life, to the kingdom of Christ, in which my conscience is at peace, where there is no law but only the forgiveness of sins, peace, quiet, happiness, salvation, and eternal life. Do not disturb me in these matters."[43] This selection is part of a longer discussion, wherein Luther brings together not only the distinctions between Law and Gospel and active and passive righteousness, but also grounds one's certainty of salvation in Christ's promise and begins preliminary explorations as to the shape of the Christian life. That this immediate context is routinely quoted does not diminish its kerygmatic power:

> Therefore let us learn diligently this art of distinguishing between these two kinds of righteousness, in order that we may know how far we should obey the Law. . ..in a Christian the Law must not exceed its limits but should have its dominion only over the flesh, which is subjected to it and remains under it. When this is the case, the Law remains within its limits. But if it wants to ascend into the conscience and exert its rule there, see to it that you are a good dialectician and that you make the correct distinction. Give no more to the Law than it has coming, and say to it: "Law, you want to ascend into the realm of conscience and rule there. You want to denounce its sin and take away the joy of my heart, which I have through faith in Christ. You want to plunge me into despair, in order that I may perish. You are exceeding your jurisdiction. Stay within your limits, and exercise your dominion over the flesh. You shall not touch my conscience. . .. In my conscience not the Law will reign, that hard tyrant and cruel disciplinarian, but Christ, the Son of God, the King of peace and righteousness, the sweet Savior and Mediator. He will preserve my conscience happy and peaceful in the sound and pure doctrine of the Gospel and in the knowledge of this passive righteousness."[44]

We have seen the relevance of the happy exchange to soteriology and to Luther's theology of the incarnation. At the same time, Luther draws the concept (if not the term itself) into his discussion of ethics in *The Freedom of a Christian* of 1520, arguably his definitive ethical tract. Note well that this was anticipated already in the 1519 sermon on the two kinds of righteousness, when Luther talks about the "second kind" of righteousness.[45] In *The Freedom of a Christian*, the *frölicher Wechsel* is cast in the metaphor of Christ as the bridegroom who through the wedding ring of faith is united with His bride.

> Christ is full of grace, life, and salvation. The soul is full of sins, death, and damnation. Now let faith come between them and sins, death, and damnation will be Christ's while grace, life, and salvation will be the soul's; for if Christ is a bridegroom, he must take upon himself the things which are his bride's and bestow upon her the things that are his. If he gives her his body and very self, how shall he not take all that is hers?. . . By the wedding ring of faith he shares in the sins, death, and pains of hell which are his bride's. As a matter of fact, he makes them his own and acts as if they were his own and as if he himself had sinned; he suffered, died, and descended into hell that he might overcome them all.[46]

Even more poignantly, and in the terms of the two kinds of righteousness, Luther offers the following:

> Who then can fully appreciate what this royal marriage means? Who can understand the riches of the glory of this grace? Here this rich and divine bridegroom Christ marries this poor, wicked harlot, redeems her from all her evil, and adorns her with all his goodness. Her sins cannot now destroy her, since they are laid upon Christ and swallowed up by him. And she has that righteousness in Christ, her husband, of which she may boast as of her own and which she can confidently display alongside her sins in the face of death and hell and say, "If I have sinned, yet my Christ, in whom I believe, has not sinned, and all his is mine and all mine is his,". . ..[47]

This treatise from Luther's pivotal year of 1520 weaves together soteriology, incarnation, and ethics by means of the concept of righteousness. This connection is achieved as Christian people are given Christ's righteousness, respond to the First Commandment through faith, and incarnate their faith and hope in loving service to the neighbor. This is "active" righteousness in the best sense, as it arises freely in response to the passive righteousness conferred by the Gospel.

Although the Christian is thus free from all works, he ought in this liberty to empty himself, take upon himself the form of a servant, be made in the likeness of men, be found in human form, and to serve, help and in every way deal with his neighbor as he sees that God through Christ has dealt with and still deals with him. This he should do freely, having regard for nothing but divine approval.

. . .I will therefore give myself as a Christ to my neighbor, just as Christ offered himself to me; I will do nothing in this life except what I see is necessary, profitable, and salutary to my neighbor, since through faith I have an abundance of all good things in Christ.[48]

For Luther, this incarnate service will usually not take place in ostentatious ways, but in the straightforward manner called for by one's vocation (vocation being then and now perhaps his most radical proposal concerning the nature of the Christian life). Again, Luther makes this last connection with our overall topic explicit:

When I have this righteousness within me, I descend from heaven like the rain that makes the earth fertile. That is, I come forth into another kingdom, and I perform good works whenever the opportunity arises. If I am a minister of the Word, I preach, I comfort the saddened, I administer the sacraments. If I am a father, I rule my household and family, I train my children in piety and honesty. If I am a magistrate, I perform the office which I have received by divine command. If I am a servant, I faithfully tend to my master's affairs.[49]

Luther's evangelical understanding of the two kinds of righteousness did not make quantum leaps after 1518-1519. While there may be some shifts of emphasis, the expressly Gospel terminology is present early on, and Luther adverts to it frequently, most overwhelmingly in his last Galatians lectures. Variety and nuance make this theme a fascinating and fertile area of inquiry, for the reformer never tires of mining this contrast for novel insight, fresh metaphor, and striking kerygmatic application. To the beleaguered student, we can observe that Luther had far more than pedagogical reasons for describing this contrast as "our theology."

Notes

1. The Argument of St. Paul's Epistle to the Galatians," in *Lectures on Galatians—1535, Chapters 1-4,* in *Luther's Works,* 55 vols. (St. Louis and Philadelphia: Concordia and Fortress, 1957-1985), 26:7 (hereafter *LW).* It might not go too far to suggest that this brief "Argument" is the best available introduction to the mature Luther's theology from his own hand.

2. The theme and its development is traced ably and at length by Lowell C. Green in *How Melanchthon Helped Luther Discover the Gospel: The Doctrine of Justification in the Reformation* (Fallbrook, CA: Verdict, 1980).

3. See, for example, Luther's application in the sermon on the *Two Kinds of Righteousness* (cited frequently in the following paragraphs), in *LW* 31:304-305.

4. Timothy J. Wengert has noted that because and as long as Luther spoke in terms of two kinds of righteousness, a righteousness *coram Deo* and a righteousness *coram hominibus,* he would naturally speak in terms of a theological and political use of the Law, and that it would not occur to him to speak in terms of three distinct functions. (We might add that this does not, of itself, speak to or prejudge the issue of whether one finds in Luther a third use in the sense defined by Formula of Concord VI; it does suggest why he arranged the topic as he did.) Wengert further notes that Melanchthon developed the vocabulary of three uses in the third edition of his Colossians commentary in the context of the ongoing dispute over Johann Agricola's antinomianism. Wengert offered these observations at the Sixteenth Century Studies Conference in San Francisco, California, in October 1995.

5. Concurring with Ian D. Siggins and Marc Lienhard, Robert Kolb notes that Luther had no tight, sharply delineated atonement theory; attempts to isolate one theory (e.g., either an exclusively Anselmian vicarious satisfaction or Aulén's *Christus Victor)* invariably neglect some aspect of his thought. See Kolb, "'Not Without the Satisfaction of God's Righteousness': The Atonement and the Generation Gap between Luther and His Students," *Archiv für Reformationsgeschichte,* Sonderband Washington (Gütersloh: Gerd Mohn, 1993), 136-156, especially pp. 137-141.

6. See Green, especially pp. 61-70, 92-95, 165-180, 201-210, 239-250.

7. Along with Green and some of the older works he cites and comments on (e.g., Holl, Boehmer, Schwiebert, Saamivaara), see also Alister McGrath, *Luther's Theology of the Cross: Martin Luther's Theological Breakthrough* (Oxford and New York: Blackwell, 1985), especially for an accessible survey of the late medieval background; Bengt Hägglund, "The Doctrine of Justification" in *Luther: A Profile,* ed. H. G. Koenigsberger (New York: Hill and Wang, 1973), pp. 150-172; and, for an irenic Roman Catholic perspective (in the tradition of Joseph Lortz) on Luther's development up through 1517, see Jared Wicks, *Yearning for Grace: Luther's Early Spiritual Teaching* (Washington, D. C.: Corpus, 1968).

8. See *Preface to the Complete Edition of Luther's Latin Writings*, of 1545; in *LW* 34:336.

9. See Johann Heinz, *Justification and Merit: Luther vs. Catholicism*, Andrews University Seminary Doctoral Dissertation Series, vol. 8 (Berrien Springs, MI: Andrews University Press, 1984), especially pp. 210-211. Karl Holl was well known for his analytic view of justification and for basing his estimation of Luther on the reformer's early writings. For a quick background sketch of some of the different views, see Carl E. Braaten, *Justification: The Article by Which the Church Stands or Falls* (Minneapolis: Fortress, 1990), especially pp. 10-15.

10. See Heinz, pp. 210-211; Green, pp. 49, 51. As early as the *Dictata* of 1513-1515 Luther could describe righteousness in terms of God's mercy, and this becomes routine in later writings. Such comments contributed to the older early datings for the evangelical breakthrough. On the *Dictata*, see Wicks, pp. 41-94.

11. Heinz, pp. 210-211.

12. See Green, pp. 64, 70, 193.

13. Ibid., pp. 117-123, 146-147, 213-227.

14. The precise dates of these homilies are disputed. For purposes of the present essay, I am accepting the date for the more important sermon *Two Kinds of Righteousness* given in the American Edition as Palm Sunday of 1519. In any case, none of the substantive arguments are affected by these particular debates.

15. *Sermon on the Three Kinds of Righteousness*, in *D. Martin Luthers Werke: kritische Gesamtausgabe*, (Weimar: Böhlau, 1883-), vol. 2, p. 44 (Here after *WA*).

16. Ibid., p. 45. Luther cites Col. 3:3; 2 Cor. 5:21; 1 Cor. 1:30; and 1 Cor. 3:11.

17. Ibid.

18. "in hac oportet nos salvos fieri et nulla alia," in ibid.

19. Ibid.

20. *LW* 34:328; *WA* 54:179.

21. Ibid., p. 337.

22. *LW* 31:304-305, for example, Luther works with an implicit distinction between the "two governments" when he addresses the different responsibilities of individuals in their private and public roles.

23. Ibid., pp. 297-299; *WA* 2:145.

24. *Lectures on Romans*, in *LW* 25:136; *WA* 56:158.

25. *Against Latomus, 1521*, in *LW* 32:235. James Kittelson regards this treatise as the closest we come to a primary source treatment of Luther's doctrine of justification. See *Luther the Reformer: The Story of the Man and His Career* (Minneapolis: Augsburg, 1986), pp. 167-168.

26. Regarding Gal. 2:16, in *LW* 26:129-130.

27. Regarding Gal. 2:15-16, in *Lectures on Galatians* of 1519, in *LW* 27:220-221; *WA* 2:490 (*imputetur*). See also Werner Elert, *The Structure of*

Lutheranism, vol. 1, trans. Walter A. Hansen (St. Louis: Concordia, 1962), p. 109. Green observes in a number of contexts that there is no exact, unyielding line of demarcation as one traces Luther's use of vocabulary.

28. *Sermon on St. Matthew's Day*, on Matt. 11:25-30, delivered February 24, 1517; in *LW* 51:29; *WA* 1:140.

29. *Admonition Concerning the Sacrament of the Body and Blood of Our Lord, 1530*, in *LW* 38:131.

30. *To George Spenlein, Wittenberg, April 8, 1516*; in *LW* 48:12-13.

31. *LW* 31:297-299.

32. Regarding Ps. 22:2, in *WA* 5:608.

33. Regarding Is. 53:5-6, in WA 31 II:435.

34. *LW* 31:351; *WA* 7:25 ("Hie hebt sich nu der frölich wechszel und streytt."). See also Kolb, pp. 145-147.

35. Regarding Gal. 3:13, in *LW* 26:284; WA 40:443.

36. Regarding Rom. 1:1, in *LW* 25:136-137; *WA* 56:158.

37. In "Argument. . .of Galatians," *LW* 26:5; *WA* 40:41.

38. This is the burden of much of Kolb's essay. See especially pp. 141-156 (Kolb cites Johann Mathesius, Luther's student and early biographer, as one exception to the general rule). For a brief, interesting examination of atonement language that carries the conversation into classical American Lutheranism, most notably with Adolf Hoenecke and Francis Pieper, see Henry W. Reimann, "Vicarious Satisfaction: A Study in Ecclesiastical Terminology," *Concordia Theological Monthly* 32:2 (February 1961): 69-77.

39. See, for example, *LW* 26:233-234, regarding Gal. 3:6.

40. While there were assuredly developments that took place throughout Luther's career, this essay works with the watershed year of 1520, given the crucial treatises he published in this year, as Luther's point of theological no return vis-a-vis Rome, and therefore as the commencement of his "fully reformational period."

41. Regarding Gal. 3:13, in *LW* 26:282-283.

42. Ibid., p. 280.

43. "Argument of. . .Galatians," in ibid., p. 11.

44. Ibid.

45. *LW* 31:299.

46. *The Freedom of a Christian*, in *LW* 31:351-352.

47. Ibid., p. 352.

48. Ibid., pp. 366-367.

49. "Argument of. . . Galatians," in *LW* 26:11-12.

2

Luther on the Two Kinds of Righteousness; Reflections on His Two-Dimensional Definition of Humanity at the Heart of His Theology

by Robert Kolb

"OUR THEOLOGY," Martin Luther claimed as he wrote the preface to his commentary on Galatians in 1535, consisted of the distinction between two kinds of righteousness:

> This is our theology, by which we teach a precise distinction between these two kinds of righteousness, the active and the passive, so that morality and faith, works and grace, secular society and religion may not be confused. Both are necessary, but both must be kept within their limits.[1]

In making this observation Luther was referring to two kinds of human righteousness, both necessary for the whole and good human life that God had made human creatures to live.

Two Kinds of Divine Righteousness

Luther's theology also rested on a presupposition that there were two definitions for the term "the righteousness of God" as it referred to God's essence. But the Reformer believed that only one of those

definitions corresponded to Paul's usage and to that of the Old
Testament in general. Luther dismissed the predominant medieval understanding of what makes God righteous, or what makes
God God, as he had learned it.[2] God's righteousness has usually
been understood as distributive justice, according to the model of
a Greek judge, who makes the system work by executing the law
and executing human beings—when necessary (or just)—in order
to preserve law and order. Luther indeed had grown up with this
image of God, often depicted in altar pieces which displayed Christ
as judge, with sword in hand. This vision of God's righteousness is
alien to God's true nature and terrified Luther until he discovered
that what makes God God—his most fundamental characteristic—
is not his justice or wrath but rather his steadfast love and mercy.
"To know God aright is to recognize that with him there is nothing
but kindness and mercy. But those who feel that God is angry and
unmerciful do not know him aright."[3] God's righteousness is that
which bestows righteousness upon fallen human creatures.[4] In his
exposition of Psalm 51:14, delivered in Wittenberg in 1532, Luther
commented:

> This term "righteousness" really caused me much trouble. They [the
> scholastic theologians whose works Luther had read as a student] gen-
> erally explained that righteousness is the truth by which God deserv-
> edly condemns or judges those who have merited evil. In opposition
> to righteousness they set mercy by which believers are saved. This
> explanation is most dangerous, besides being vain, because it arouses
> a secret hate against God and his righteousness. Who can love him if
> he wants to deal with sinners according to righteousness? Therefore
> remember that the righteousness of God is that by which we are jus-
> tified, or the gift of the forgiveness of sins. This righteousness in God
> is wonderful because it makes of God not a righteous Judge but a
> forgiving Father, who wants to use his righteousness not to judge but
> to justify and absolve sinners.[5]

This discovery, that God's righteousness or essence is steadfast love
and mercy, played a key role in the formation of Luther's understanding of the biblical message.

Two Kinds of Human Righteousness

Also central to Luther's "evangelical breakthrough" was his discovery of what makes the human creature "righteous" or right, that is, truly human. This involves the distinction emphasized in the preface to the 1535 Galatians commentary cited above. In recalling how he came to understand the entire biblical message Luther focused on his finding a new definition for human righteousness.

This distinction was not a new development in the reformer's thought at this time. A decade later he would reflect on his coming to an understanding of the gospel in the 1510s. At that time his attempt to please God by living the holiest way of life the medieval church knew, the monastic way, had failed. It left him only with "an extremely disturbed conscience." He had come to hate the righteous God who punishes sinners; a secret, perhaps blasphemous anger against God possessed him, and he "raged with a fierce and troubled conscience."

> At last, by the mercy of God, meditating day and night, I gave heed to the context of the words, namely, "In it the righteousness of God is revealed, as it is written, 'He who through faith is righteous shall live.'" There I began to understand that the righteousness of God is that by which the righteous lives by a gift of God, namely by faith. And this is the meaning: the righteousness of God is revealed by the gospel, namely, the passive righteousness with which merciful God justifies us by faith. . . . Here I felt that I was altogether born again and had entered paradise itself through open gates. There a totally other face of the entire Scripture showed itself to me. Thereupon I ran through the Scriptures from memory. I also found in other terms an analogy, as the work of God, that is, what God does in us, the power of God, with which he makes us strong, the wisdom of God, with which he makes us wise, the strength of God, the salvation of God, the glory of God. And I treasured the word that had become the sweetest of all words for me with a love as great as the hatred with which I had previously hated the word "righteousness of God." Thus that passage in Paul was for me truly the gate to paradise.[6]

Luther realized, however, that what made him genuinely right in God's sight had to be distinguished from what made him truly

human—genuinely right—in relationship to other creatures of God.
This distinction is what he labeled "our theology" in 1535.

By differentiating the two dimensions in which human creatures
were created to be human, or righteous, Luther was establishing as
his fundamental hermeneutical principle what Jesus was referring
to when he divided the law into two parts: loving the Lord our God
with all heart, soul, and mind, and loving our neighbors as ourselves
(Matthew 22:37, 39.) When the reformer introduced his readers to
comments he had made on the Epistle to the Galatians in 1531 (as he
edited them four years later), he began by sketching the "argument,"
that is, the central concerns, of the apostle Paul in writing to the
Galatians. According to Luther, Paul's fundamental consideration
in the letter was establishing God's message regarding "faith, grace,
the forgiveness of sins or Christian righteousness." He noted that
there are a variety of definitions for the word righteousness: "righteousness is of many kinds." Luther listed political righteousness,
ceremonial righteousness, the moral righteousness of the decalogue,
all of which, he pointed out, are genuine forms of righteousness.
"Over and above there is the righteousness of faith."[7] Luther defined
"this most excellent righteousness, the righteousness of faith, which
God imputes to us through Christ without works" as a "merely passive righteousness." "For here we work nothing, render nothing to
God; we only receive and permit someone else to work in us, namely,
God. Therefore it is appropriate to call the righteousness of faith or
Christian righteousness 'passive.' This is the righteousness hidden in
a mystery, which the world does not understand. In fact, Christians
themselves do not adequately understand it or grasp it in the midst
of their temptations."[8]

Righteousness in the Two Dimensions or Relationships of Human Life

In developing this contrast between passive righteousness—which
expresses itself in faith—and active righteousness—which expresses
itself in performing the deeds of God's plan for human life—Luther
was bringing to light a fundamental distinction that had escaped
articulation by most theologians since the time of the apostles. This

distinction recognizes and rests upon Christ's observation that human life consists of two kinds of relationship, one with the author and creator of life, the other with all other creatures (Matt. 22:37–39).

Just as the relationship of child to parents differs from the relationship between children and all else that belongs to the family, so the relationship between Creator and creatures is fundamentally not the same kind of relationship as that among his creatures. Parents establish the essential identity of their children; God has made them "responsible" for these children in ways that no sibling or other caretaker—by definition—can be. Parents give the gift of life and determine the genetic identity of their progeny. They shape and form the life of these offspring through their loving care in ways that psychologists perceive to be unique. Siblings, friends, and acquaintances relate to each other in quite different ways than children relate to their parents. These two different spheres of relationship issue from—and express themselves in—God's design for our humanity. Likewise, as our Creator he alone is responsible for our identity. From that identity as his creatures and children proceeds the performance of activities which reflect that identity. Human creatures identify themselves as God's creatures when they live according to that identity which God has given them.

This means that human life exists on two planes of dependence and interdependence, in two spheres of relationship. They may be described as vertical and horizontal so long as the vertical relationship is delineated with God both above us (because he is lord and author of the life of his children) and beneath us (because he is the loving Father who lifts us up and cuddles us to himself in Christ). The horizontal relationship has bound us to the rest of creation as people who are held accountible for exercising God-given responsibilities in an adult manner toward other creatures, human but also animal, mineral, and vegetable. God's human creatures are right—really human—in their vertical relationship because their faith embraces the God who loves them through Jesus Christ with the reckless trust of total dependence and reliance on him which constitutes their identity. They are right—really human—in their horizontal relationship with God's other creatures when they live a life which is active in reflecting his love through the deeds that deliver his care and concern. Two spheres and kinds of relationship demand two different ways of being right or righteous.

The Righteousness of Identity
and the Righteousness of Performance

Thus, Luther's theology found its orientation in this distinction between the identity which God as creator gives to his creatures and the performance or activities with which that identity expresses itself within the relationships God has fashioned for human life. Luther compared the righteousness of our identity to the earth as it receives the blessing of rain.

> As the earth itself does not produce rain and is unable to acquire it by its own strength, worship, and power but receives it only by a heavenly gift from above, so this heavenly righteousness is given to us by God without our work or merit. As much as the dry earth of itself is able to accomplish and obtain the right and blessed rain, that much can we human creatures accomplish by our own strength and works to obtain that divine, heavenly, and eternal righteousness. Thus we can obtain it only through the free imputation and indescribable gift of God.[9]

That leads the Christian conscience to say,

> I do not seek active righteousness. I ought to have and perform it; but I declare that even if I did have and perform it, I cannot trust in it or stand up before the judgment of God on the basis of it. Thus I put myself beyond all active righteousness, all righteousness of my own or of the divine law, and I embrace only the passive righteousness which is the righteousness of grace, mercy, and the forgiveness of sins.[10]

A simple theological parable may clarify the point. Although by the definition of his own theology Thomas Aquinas had sufficient merit to proceed directly to heaven, without having to work off temporal punishment in purgatory, the Dominican saint dallied along the way, visiting old friends and doing research among those who still had purgatorial satisfactions to discharge there. He arrived at Saint Peter's gate some 272 years after his death, on February 18, 1546. After ascertaining his name, Saint Peter asked Thomas, "Why should I let you into my heaven?" "Because of the grace of God," Thomas answered, ready to explain the concept of prevenient grace should it be necessary. Peter asked instead, "How do I know you have God's grace?" Thomas, who had brought a sack of his good deeds with him, was ready with the proof. "Here are the good works of a lifetime," he explained. "I could have done none of them without God's grace, but in my worship and observation of monastic rules, in my obedience to parents, governors, and superiors, in my concern for the physical well-being and property of others, in my chastity and continence, you can see my righteousness—grace-assisted as it may be." Since a line was forming behind Thomas, Peter waved him in, certain that Thomas would soon receive a clearer understanding of his own righteousness. The next person in line stepped up. "Name?" "Martin Luther." "Why should I let you into my heaven?" "Because of the grace of God." Peter was in a playful mood, so he went on, "How do I know you have God's grace? Thomas had his works to prove his righteousness, but I don't see that you have brought any proof along that you are righteous." "Works?" Luther exclaimed. "Works? I didn't know I was supposed to bring my works with me! I thought they belonged on earth, with my neighbors. I left them down there." "Well," said Gatekeeper Peter, "how then am I supposed to know that you really have God's grace?" Luther pulled a little, well-worn, oft-read scrap of paper out of his pocket and showed it to Peter. On it were the words, "Martin Luther, baptized, November 11, in the year of our Lord 1483." "You check with Jesus," Luther said. "He will tell you that he has given me the gift of righteousness through his own blood and his own resurrection."

Martin Luther knew *how* he was righteous *where;* he knew *where* he was truly human *in what manner.* That is, he recognized that being human in God's sight means receiving the unconditional love of God. It means child-like dependence, expressed in the absolute trust of complete love. Furthermore, Luther recognized that being human in relationship to the creatures of God meant the exercise of adult responsibility as God designed it for human creatures, expressed in the care and concern of deeds of complete love for others.

Two Kinds of Righteousness: Inseparable but Distinct

Luther did see these two kinds of righteousness as inseparable. Human life is of one piece, not divided into separate or separable spheres of sacred and profane. Human life is cruciform—eyes lifted to focus on God, feet firmly planted on his earth, arms stretched out in mutual support of those God has placed around us. Having the focus of our lives directed toward Christ inevitably extends our arms to our neighbors. Human beings are truly human, that is, right or functioning properly (according to the design for human righteousness that God made) when their identity does express itself in the activities that flow from that identity. Luther gave his students a critical word of caution:

> The weak, who are not malicious or slanderous but good, are offended when they hear that the law and good works do not have to be done for justification. One must go to their aid and explain to them how it is that works do not justify, how works should be done, and how they should not be done. They should be done as fruits of righteousness, not in order to bring righteousness into being. Having been made righteous, we must do them; but it is not the other way around: that when we are unrighteous, we become righteous by doing them. The tree produces fruit; the fruit does not produce the tree.[11]

For, as Luther never tried of pointing out, our identity determines the validity of the activities it produces.

> The righteousness of the law is earthly and deals with earthly things; by it we perform good works. But as the earth does not bring forth fruit unless it has been first watered and made fruitful from above—for the earth cannot judge, renew, and rule the heavens, but the heavens judge, renew, rule, and fortify the earth, so that it may do what the earth has commanded—so also by the righteousness of the law we do nothing even when we do much; we do not fulfill the law even when we fulfill it. Without any merit or any work of our own, we must first become righteous by Christian righteousness, which has nothing to do with the righteousness of the law or with earthly and active righteousness. This righteousness is heavenly and passive. We do not have it of ourselves; we receive it from heaven. We do not perform it; we accept it by faith through which we ascend beyond all laws and works. . . for this righteousness means to do nothing, to share nothing, and to

know nothing about the law or about works but to know and believe only this: that Christ has gone to the Father and is now invisible; . . . that he is our high priest, interceding for us and reigning over us and in us through grace.[12]

Shortly after he presented such ideas in lectures before his students in 1531, Luther proclaimed them to the congregation in Wittenberg. In treating John 6:37 from the pulpit of the town church in 1532, he reminded his hearers that

In order to retain the purity of the doctrine of justification by faith it is necessary to distinguish clearly between justification by faith and justification by good works. The performance of good works is not forbidden here. If I live according to the law, do good works, keep the commandments of the second table of the Ten Commandments, honor my government, abstain from theft, murder, and adultery, I am conducting myself properly; and such works are not condemned here. It is work-righteousness, however, when the papists propose to do good works before acknowledging the Lord Christ and believing in him. They lay claim to their salvation by virtue of their good works, and they abandon the article of faith in Christ. But those who come to faith and know that Christ is not a taskmaster, and then begin to lead a good life and do acceptable and upright works, do not call these works, performed either before or after accepting Christ, holy or righteous, as is the wont of the papists. Only faith in Christ is our righteousness. . . [13]

In the end this more fundamental righteousness grasped by faith, God's gift of our identity as his children, reveals itself as that upon which human existence depends:

When this life ends and death is at hand, the rules of earthly justice [righteousness] also expire. Christ declares here: This earth's justice does not apply here; it does not endure. You must rise above what you have done and come before God with a different righteousness; you must despair of your own works and rely on, and believe in, Christ's words: "Truly, truly, your food is indeed my flesh given for you and my blood shed for you" [John 6:55]. Then you hear that your sins and mine cannot be atoned and paid for by you or by me, but solely by him who shed his blood for me.[14]

The Roots of the Distinction

Luther's insight into the distinct dimensions of what it means to be human was an idea that was born in the struggle for his evangelical breakthrough in 1518 and 1519. After having composed a tract on three kinds of righteousness in 1518,[15] he went on to preach a sermon at the end of that year or early in 1519 on two kinds of righteousness. "There are two kinds of Christian righteousness, just as human sin is of two kinds. The first is alien righteousness, that is the righteousness of another, instilled from without. This is the righteousness of Christ by which he justifies through faith."[16] This alien righteousness [from the Latin, "belonging to another"], which is bestowed from outside the human creature, belongs to the Christian "through faith in Christ; therefore, Christ's righteousness becomes our righteousness and all that he has becomes ours. . . this righteousness is primary; it is the basis, the cause, the source of all our own actual righteousness. For this is the righteousness given in place of the original righteousness lost in Adam. It accomplishes the same as that original righteousness would accomplish; rather it accomplishes more."[17]

Although Luther would continue to refine his definition of this alien righteousness, already in 1519 its basic elements were in place. This alien righteousness "instilled in us without our works by grace alone—while the Father, to be sure, inwardly draws us to Christ—is set opposite original sin, likewise alien, which we acquire without our works by birth alone." Luther went on to describe the active righteousness or "proper" [from the Latin "one's own"] righteousness as "the product of the righteousness of the first type, actually it is fruit and consequence." Luther continued, "Therefore through the first righteousness arises the voice of the bridegroom who says to the soul 'I am yours,' but through the second comes the voice of the bride who answers, 'I am yours.' " God gives us the identity as his bride by choosing us and bringing us to himself. The active righteousness of response takes form in the things we do which respond to his goodness.[18]

That Luther employed a double focus on human righteousness can be seen in his understanding that the righteousness which God gives "is not instilled all at once, but it begins, makes progress, and is finally perfected at the end through death."[19] This "partly righteous, partly sinful" view of the believer remained a part of Luther's discussion of the struggle of the Christian life for at least another decade. It describes the progress (or lack of it) experienced in the practice of actual righteousness, in the performance of God's will within the horizontal sphere of life. However, the logic of the distinction between the two kinds of righteousness, combined with his belief that God's Word creates reality, had already led him to define the situation of believers in another, clearer fashion. He recognized that God's children are also completely righteous and completely sinful at the same time. His mature understanding of the righteousness of God's chosen children, reflected in the later Galatians commentary, could label them righteous "in fact"—in God's sight—in spite of their experience of sinfulness because they had been re-created in Christ through faith by the power of the Word. For the Word has worked the forgiveness—the abolition—of sin by bringing the benefits of Christ's death and resurrection to believers. God removes the sinners from their sin.

For believers in Christ are not sinners and are not sentenced to death but are altogether holy and righteous, lords over sin and death who live eternally. Only faith can discern that, but the trust believers place in Christ diverts their eyes and ears away from their own sins. According to the theology of Paul, there is no more sin, no more death, and no more curse in the world, but only in Christ, who is the Lamb of God that takes away the sins of the world and who became a curse in order to set us free from the curse. . . . True theology teaches that there is no more sin in the world, because Christ, on whom, according to Isaiah 53:6, the Father has laid the sins of the entire world, has conquered, destroyed and killed it in his own body. Having died to sin once, he has truly been raised from the dead and will not die any more (Rom. 6:9). Therefore wherever there is faith in Christ, there sin has in fact been abolished, put to death, and buried.[20]

Luther's ontology recognized that reality springs from and rests upon what God says. This ontology of the Word convinced him that when

God declares, "forgiven," he restores the original humanity of his chosen children.

Original Righteousness and Original Sin

The Word of forgiveness and life—fashioned through Christ's death and resurrection—has restored the original relationship between God and the human creature. In lecturing on Genesis 2 Luther revealed his presupposition that human creatures are totally dependent upon their Creator, products of his hand and breath, given their human identity purely out of his sovereign grace and favor.

Adam and Eve had no time of probation in which to perform deeds which would make them eligible for and worthy of their humanity. They were created truly human.

> We are vessels of God, formed by God himself, and he himself is our potter, but we his clay, as Isaiah 64 [:8] says. And this holds good not only for our origin but throughout our whole life; until our death and in the grave we remain the clay of this potter. . . in a state of merely passive potentiality, not active potentiality. For there we do not choose, we do not do anything; but we are chosen, we are equipped, we are born again, we accept, as Isaiah says: "Thou art the potter, we thy clay."[21]

The Wittenberg professor rejected the scholastic traditions which interpreted the original righteousness of Adam and Eve as a quality implanted in them. God had created them as his children, made them "righteous, truthful, and upright not only in body but especially in soul." They knew God and obeyed him with the utmost joy and understood the works of God even without prompting. The peace of Eden was God's gift to his human creatures. "It is part of this original righteousness that Adam loved God and his works with an outstanding and very pure attachment, that he lived among the creatures of God in peace, without fear of death and without any fear of sickness, and that he had a very obedient body, without evil inclinations and the hideous lust which we now experience."[22] The gift of human life had established Adam's and Eve's existence and identity. The activities which flowed from that identity expressed who they were. At the center of their beings was their knowledge and trust of their Creator.

Luther formulated the negative side of this definition of the original human righteousness by defining original sin:

> . . . human nature has completely fallen; . . . the intellect has become darkened, so that we no longer know God and his will and no longer perceive the works of God; furthermore, the will is extraordinarily depraved, so that we do not trust the mercy of God and do not fear God but are unconcerned, disregard the Word and will of God, and follow the desire and the impulses of the flesh, likewise, our conscience is no longer quiet but, when it thinks of God's judgment despairs and adopts illicit defenses and remedies. . . . the knowledge of God has been lost; we do not everywhere and always give thanks to him; we do not delight in his works and deeds; we do not trust him; when he inflicts deserved punishments, we begin to hate God and blaspheme him.

From the broken relationship with God come broken relationships with others. Luther continued his definition of sinfulness with a focus on the actual sins that flow from original sin, the doubt and defiance of God: "when we must deal with our neighbor we yield to our desires and are robbers, thieves, adulterers, murderers, cruel, inhuman, merciless, etc. The passion of lust is indeed some part of original sin. But greater are the defects of the soul: unbelief, ignorance of God, despair, hate, blasphemy."[23] The root of sin is this doubt of the Word of God which created and shaped the relationship of love and trust between God and his human creatures. Breaking the contact, going deaf on God, destroyed the relationship that stood at the heart of what it meant to be human.

Righteousness in and through Christ

Luther knew that his definition of righteousness deviated from the commonly understood meaning of the word. In preaching on

John 16:10 in 1537 he observed to his hearers that the righteousness which Christ bestows upon believers, "the righteousness which abolishes sin and unrighteousness and makes human creatures righteous and acceptable before God," is "completely concealed, not only from the world but also from the saints. It is not a thought, a word, or a work in ourselves, as the scholastics fantasized about grace when they said that it is something poured into our hearts. No, it is entirely outside and above us; it is Christ's going to the Father, that is, his suffering, resurrection, and ascension."[24] Luther further commented,

> This is a peculiar righteousness; it is strange indeed that we are to be called righteous or to possess a righteousness which is really no work, no thought, in short, nothing whatever in us but is entirely outside us in Christ and yet becomes truly ours by reason of his grace and gift, and becomes our very own, as though we ourselves had achieved and earned it. Reason, of course, cannot comprehend this way of speaking, which says that our righteousness is something which involves nothing active or passive on our part, yes, something in which I do not participate with my thoughts, perception, and senses; that nothing at all in me makes me so pleasing to God and saves me; but that I leave myself and all human thoughts and ability out of account and cling to Christ. . . .[25]

Luther could not speak of restored human righteousness in God's sight apart from Christ. For sin had indeed destroyed that righteousness which consisted in trust in the Creator. Christ took sin into himself and substituted himself for sinners before the law's tribunal. Christ took the punishment for sin, its wage of death, into himself and satisfied the law's condemnation of human creatures who fail to be and behave like the creatures they were designed to be. No cheap atonement was possible from Luther's point of view. The Lamb had to die. Luther employed the Pauline baptismal model of dying and rising in Romans 6:3—11 and Colossians 2:11–15 to speak not only of God's saving action in baptism but also of his action of justifying.[26] The sinner's sin kills Christ. Christ buries the sinner's sin. Christ raises the sinner to new life—to a new identity and a new way of practicing that identity.

Therefore Luther can state quite simply, "The work of Christ, properly speaking, is this: to embrace the one whom the law has made a sinner and pronounced guilty, and to absolve that person from his sins if he believes the gospel. 'For Christ is the end of the law, that everyone who has faith may be justified' (Rom. 10:4); he is 'the Lamb of God, who takes away the sin of the world' (John 1:29)."[27]

> We cannot deny that Christ died for our sins in order that we might be justified. For he did not die to make the righteous righteous; he died to make sinners into righteous people, the friends and children of God, and heirs of all heavenly gifts. Therefore since I feel and confess that I am a sinner on account of the transgression of Adam, why should I not say that I am righteous on account of the righteousness of Christ, especially when I hear that he loved me and gave himself for me?[28]

Luther followed the apostolic dictum regarding the source of that new life in righteousness, as Paul expressed it in Romans 4:25. Paul "refers to the resurrection of Christ, who rose again for our justification. His victory is a victory over the law, sin, our flesh, the world, the devil, death, hell, and all evils; and this victory of his life he has given to us. Even though these tyrants, our enemies, accuse us and terrify us, they cannot drive us into despair or condemn us. For Christ, whom God the Father raised from the dead, is the Victor over them, and he is our righteousness."[29]

> We must turn our eyes completely to that bronze serpent Christ nailed to the cross (John 3:14). With our gaze fastened firmly to him, we must declare with assurance that he is our righteousness and life and care nothing about the threats and terrors of the law, sin, death, wrath, and the judgment of God. For the Christ on whom our gaze is fixed, in whom we exist, and who also lives in us, is the Victor and the Lord over the law, sin, death, and every evil. In him a sure comfort has been set forth for us, and the victory has been granted.[30]

For "he alone makes us paupers rich with his superabundance, expunges our sins with his righteousness, devours our death with his life, and transforms us from children of wrath, tainted with in, hypocrisy, lies, and deceit, into children of grace and truth."[31]

Christ is our righteousness not in his obedience to the law but rather in his obedience to the Father, not merely in his death or solely in his resurrection. What makes Christ the righteousness given to sinners which makes them human once again? "It is Christ's going to the Father, that is, his suffering, resurrection, and ascension."[32]

Adam and Eve, Luther believed, had also possessed only this passive righteousness. They were human in God's sight not because they had proved their humanity through specific activities which had won God's favor. Instead, they had been created by his breath and hand because he wanted them as his children. His love and mercy expressed themselves by forming his creatures as right and righteous in his sight. He formed them with the expectation that they would perform as his children in relationship to the rest of his creation as they trusted in him and showed him their love.

"Faith" or "trust" is the operative word. Trust defines the new creature's identity as child of God. Passive righteousness is the trust which embraces the loving Father and throws itself upon him. Just as that was true in the Garden, until doubt broke in and broke down the relationship of trust in God, so it becomes true as Christ's word of love draws trust back to God in the human creatures that word re-creates.

For fallen sinners the gift of this passive righteousness, which expresses itself first of all in trust toward the loving Father, comes through Christ's obedience to the Father as he took the sinfulness of fallen creatures into death with himself and as he reclaimed life for them in his resurrection. Christ promises forgiveness and life through his death and resurrection, and thus he elicits trust from those sinners whom the Holy Spirit has turned back to himself. That trust, directed toward the Crucified and Risen God, is the righteousness of Eden, restored and revivified, ready to advertise its identity in the performance of activities suitable for God's children.

Conclusion

The concept of the two kinds of human righteousness had sprung upon Luther as he was engaged in the study of the biblical text. In his exegetical studies, as he ran through the passages of Scripture, he found this concept to be a true and accurate description of what it means to be human. The concept also rang true in the midst of his own struggles against doubt about his own identity in God's sight and as he helped others with the pastoral care he was called to give them. He believed that the biblical message was given to the church for pastoral purposes, and this connection of biblical confession and pastoral practice stands at the heart of the Lutheran enterprise.

In the midst of societies around the world, in which new technologies, new economic forces, new political constellations, and new social structures join with the age-old sinfulness of individuals to unsettle life and deprive human beings of their humanity, Lutheran churches need to witness to Christ using the distinction of identity and performance, the distinction of passive and active righteousness. This insight into humanity enriches our ability to make the gospel of Jesus Christ meet individual human needs as we draw those outside the faith into the company of Christ's people. It also is one of the chief gifts Lutherans have to offer within the ecumenical conversation about how best to express the biblical message. For the distinction of the two dimensions in which we relate to God and his world, the two aspects which constitute our humanity, is "our theology," and it is impossible to understand the Lutheran tradition without recognizing and employing it.

Notes

1. *Dr. Martin Luthers Werke* (Weimar: Bohlau, 1883–) [henceforth WA] 40,1:45.24–27; *Luther's Works* (Saint Louis and Philadelphia: Concordia and Fortress, 1958–1986) [henceforth LW] 26:7. For a summary of Luther's definition of "righteousness," and bibliography, see Bengt Hagglund, "Gerechtigkeit. VI. Reformations- und Neuzeit," *Theologische Realenzyklopadie* XII (Berlin: de Gruyter, 1984): 432–434, 440. See also the December 1998 Beiheft issue of *Zeitschriftur Theologie und Kirche* 95, on Luther's understanding of righteousness and justification, particularly as it pertains to the "Joint Declaration on the Doctrine of Justification" (which ignores Luther's distinction of the two kinds of righteousness); see especially in that issue Reinhard Schwartz, "Luthers Rechtfertigungslehre als Eckstein der christlichen Theologie und Kirche," pp. 15–46.

2. On nominalist covenant conceptions of the relationship between God and the human creature, see Alister E. McGrath, *Luther's Theology of the Cross:*

Martin Luther's Theological Breakthrough (Oxford: Basil Blackwell, 1985), 100–113.

3. Comments on Psalm 130:7, 1525 (1517), WA 18:520.27–30; LW 14:193–194.

4. Comments on Psalm 51:14, 1525 (1517), WA 18:505.28–30; LW 14:173.

5. Comments on Psalm 51:14, 1532 WA 40, II:444.36–445.29; LW 12:392.

6. "Preface to the Complete Edition of Luther's Latin Writings," 1545, WA 54:186.3–16; LW 34:337.

7. WA 40,1:40.16–27; LW 26:4.

8. WA 40,1:41.15–26; LW 26:4–5.

9. WA 40,1:43.18–25; LW 26:6.

10. WA 40,1:42,26–43,15; LW 26:6.

11. WA 40,1:287.17–23; LW 26:169.

12. WA 40,1:46,20–47,21; LW 26:8.

13. On John 6:37, WA 33:85.23–86,17; LW 23:58.

14. WA 33:281.13–15; LW 23:178. Cf. his comments on John 6:54, WA 33:219.13220.15; LW 23:140–141.

15. WA 2:41.43–47.

16. WA 2:145.7–10; LW 31:297.

17. WA 2:146.12–19; LW 31:298–299.

18. WA 2:147.7–18; LW 31:300.

19. WA 2:146.32–35; LW 31:299.

20. WA 40,I:444.34–445.33; LW 26:285–286.

21. WA 42:64.22–26; LW 1:84.

22. WA 42:86.11–16; LW 1:113.

23. WA 42:86.17–41; LW 1:114.

24. WA 46:44.23–28; LW 24:346–347.

25. WA 46:44.34–45,3; LW 24:347.

26. See Robert Kolb, "God Kills to Make Alive: Romans 6 and Luther's Understanding of Justification (1535)," *Lutheran Quarterly* 12 (1998): 33–56, on the use of the baptismal enactment of the death of the sinner and the resurrection of the believer in Christ, as Luther developed the idea in the Galatians commentary of 1535.

27. WA 40,I:250.10–13; LW 26:143.

28. WA 40,I:300.15–22; LW 26:179.

29. WA 40,1:65.10–17; LW 26:21–22.

30. WA 40,I:282.35–283.17; LW 26:166–167.

31. WA 46:649.36–650.2; LW 22:131.

32. WA 46:44.26–27; LW 24:347.

3

Two Kinds of Righteousness as a Framework for Law and Gospel in the Apology

By Charles P. Arand

IN THE APOLOGY OF THE AUGSBURG CONFESSION, Melanchthon gave the Western church one of its most thorough and sustained treatises on the gospel to be found among all Reformation writings. This observation applies not only to Article IV on justification (even though it is nearly one half of the Apology). Each and every article of the Apology ultimately centers on the confession of the gospel. Equally important, this confession of the gospel arises within a specific matrix or framework for thinking about the gospel in a way that serves to preserve and promote it. Thus the Apology not only makes an important contribution to the articulation of the gospel itself, but it also provides Lutherans with an invaluable conceptual framework for thinking about the gospel in the twenty-first century by laying out the theological presuppositions necessary for its proclamation.

Most often, students of the Lutheran confessions have identified the Apology's theological framework as the distinction of law and gospel.[1] The distinction of law and gospel works especially well for Articles IV and XII of the Apology. And yet, when defined in terms of God's activity of killing and making alive, the distinction of law and gospel does not adequately take into account all of the articles, particularly, Articles XXII-XXVIII. Part of the reason that this distinction of law and gospel does not characterize the entire Apology is because the way in which law and gospel are often construed turns the distinction into an antithesis. At that point, the distinction between law and gospel turns into an opposition in which the gospel triumphs over the law itself, and not only the wrath of God. Any talk about good works is automatically understood to be talk about works righteousness. Furthermore, when this distinction is treated as a conceptual framework within which the coherence of the Christian faith is thought out, then whatever does not fit under the category of gospel is regarded as part of the law. Even the doctrine of creation becomes law for no other reason than that it is not gospel. This does not allow the theological space needed to speak positively about the Christian life within a world where the Judeo-Christian ethic—that could once be taken for granted—is crumbling.

The distinction between two kinds of human righteousness provides a more comprehensive theological framework than the distinction between law and gospel for understanding the coherence of the Apology's confession of the gospel.[2] More specifically, it offers a more comprehensive framework to speak positively about life in this world while not undermining the doctrine of justification. It enables us to better appreciate the arguments in Articles XXII-XXVIII (articles that are often ignored). The distinction between two kinds of righteousness brings out the unity of faith and practice, thereby allowing us to distinguish between faith and works while affirming the value of each. It thus brings into clearer focus the claim of the *Augustana* as paraphrased by Wengert: "Our teaching is orthodox and catholic; we have changed some practices to match that teaching."[3]

The Apology's Theme and Central Framework

Melanchthon's distinction between the two kinds of righteousness moves to the foreground as the conceptual framework of the Apology when one considers the rhetorical character of the entire Apology. The document falls squarely within the rhetorical form of discourse known as the *genus iudicale*, for it involves an ecclesiastical dispute. The purpose of the judicial genre is to plead a case in order to win a favorable judgment.[4] In the Apology Melanchthon appeals the emperor's decision to accept the Roman *Confutation* and refuse the

Lutheran *apologia*.[5] Melanchthon must persuade the emperor not to follow through on his threatened use of force, which the papal legate Cardinal Cajetan had urged and which was implicit in the Recess of the Diet of Augsburg.[6] At the same time he must prepare the adherents of the Lutheran cause for possible resistance and martyrdom should war ensue as a result of Lutheran non-compliance with the demand to accept the *Confutation*.[7]

Nothing is more important in the judicial genre than to identify the *status* of the case. The *status* deals with "the chief subject of inquiry, the proposition that contains the gist of the matter toward which all arguments are aimed, in other words, the main conclusion."[8] Melanchthon used the *status* in order to bring coherence to the argument of individual articles in the Apology like Articles IV (Justification) and XII (Repentance).[9] But does it apply to the Apology as a whole with its many topics? When we compare the point at issue in the disputed articles between the *Confutation* and the Augsburg Confession, when we consider the rhetorical markers for the status such as *propositio* and *krinomenon*, and when we examine the transitional statements at turning points of Melanchthon's arguments, a common *status* emerges that can be set forth in terms of the question: What constitutes our righteousness before God?[10]

An important clue is found in Apology VII:34, 37. There Melanchthon writes, "But we are not now discussing the question whether or not it is beneficial to observe them [human traditions] for the sake of tranquillity or bodily usefulness. Another issue is involved. The question is whether or not the observance of human traditions is necessary for righteousness before God. This is the point at issue." Again, in paragraph 37 he states, "Moreover, the point to be decided in this controversy must be raised a little later below, namely, whether human traditions are necessary acts of worship for righteousness before God." In both cases, he uses the technical rhetorical term *krinomenon*, which refers to the central question or issue in a dispute. In his *Elements of Rhetoric*, Melanchthon defines *krinomemon*: "Of these the one about which there is controversy and by which when confirmed the true conclusion is made evident, is called the *krinomemon*, the point to be decided upon."[11]

The *status* can be addressed from two vantage points, which Melanchthon calls the two chief topics of Christian teaching (*loci praecipui*, Ap IV:5). The first deals with a righteousness of works that we achieve based on reason's comprehension of the law. Melanchthon variously describes this as the righteousness of reason (*iustitia rationis*),[12] the righteousness of the law (*iustitia legis*),[13] civil righteousness (*iustitia civilis*),[14] one's own righteousness (*iustitia propria*),[15] carnal righteousness (*iustitia carnis*),[16] righteousness of works (*iustitia operum*)[17] and philosophical righteousness. The second is a Christian righteousness that we receive by faith's apprehension of the promise of Christ. Melanchthon variously expresses this as spiritual righteousness (*iustitia spiritualis*),[18] inner righteousness, eternal righteousness (*iustitia aeterna*),[19] the righteousness of faith (*iustitia fidei*),[20] the righteousness of the gospel (*iustitia evangelit*);[21] Christian righteousness (*iustitia Christiana*);[22] righteousness of God (*iustitia Dei*),[23] and the righteousness of the heart (*iustitia cordis*).[24]

These two topics supply Melanchthon with the material for formulating his chief propositions, both of which appear throughout the Apology in various forms. His first proposition charges that the opponents combine the two kinds of righteousness into a single righteousness by making the righteousness achieved in the eyes of the world to constitute our righteousness before God as well. The second and main proposition is that we must distinguish between the two kinds of righteousness so that before God we seek a different kind of righteousness than we seek in the eyes of society. It does not mean that the righteousness of works is not important or useful. To the contrary, by distinguishing them, both kinds of righteousness find their proper role and place within theology and life. In particular, it shows that the Lutherans have not abolished the importance of a righteousness of works.

The Two Dimensions of Human Life

What is meant by two kinds of human righteousness? Theologically, to be righteous is to be human as God envisioned in creation, and again in redemption. One might modify the Athanasian *dictum* to say, "God became fully human that we might become fully human." The distinction between two *kinds* of righteousness rests upon the observation that there are two dimensions to being a human creature.

One dimension involves our life with God, especially in the matters of death and salvation. The other dimension involves our life with God's creatures and our activity in this world. In the former we receive righteousness before God through faith on account of Christ. In the latter, we achieve righteousness in the eyes of the world by works when we carry out our God-given responsibilities. Kolb has suggested that we refer to the former as the righteousness of identity; the latter as the righteousness of performance[25] or character.

We can compare the righteousness of works and the righteousness of faith as Melanchthon develops them in the Apology by examining several characteristics of each. First, the righteousness of works is a righteousness that we achieve by human ability; the righteousness of faith is a righteousness that we receive from God. Second, the anthropology that underlies righteousness of works is the human as creature. The anthropology underlying righteousness of faith is the human as sinner. Third, the standard by which human righteousness is measured is the law in its various forms including the structure of life. The standard by which Christian righteousness is determined is the promise of Christ. Fourth, the purpose of a righteousness of works is the welfare of this world. The purpose of a righteousness of faith is restoration of our identity as children of God and thus a restoration of shalom with God.

As a rule, Melanchthon identified a righteousness of reason or works with the principle expounded in Aristotle's *Nichomachean Ethics* that by doing virtuous things one becomes virtuous. Melanchthon defines it this way: "Virtue is a habit of the will which inclines me to obey the judgment of right reason."[26] Three elements are involved in this definition. First, human excellence or righteousness is found in the right and able exercise of a person's rational powers. A person must choose certain actions that are deemed moral over actions that are not. This in turn requires instruction and information so that one knows what is moral. Second, it requires that one fulfill the chosen task in a superlative manner. For example, one becomes a shoemaker by practicing the craft of shoes *well*, that is, according to the highest standards of the craft. The aim of ethics, of human behavior, is to act in a way that is judged to be moral or virtuous. Finally, Melanchthon's definition highlights the need for constant habit. To achieve this righteousness requires a lifetime. Excellence is not an act, but a habit. One act of bravery does not make a brave man. It is the entire life that is judged to be righteous or not.

Behind Melanchthon's definition with its reference to reasoned choice and willful obedience lies an anthropology that Melanchthon inherited from the early church and the Middle Ages. It distinguishes between the "higher powers" (intellect and will) and "lower powers" (sensual appetites and the emotions) of the human person. It is the higher powers or faculties that were seen to constitute the image of God and make us distinctively human. Working with these categories throughout the Apology (articles II, IV, XVI, XVIII), Melanchthon notes that for his opponents, "it is necessary for righteousness to reside in the will," (Ap IV:283 +)[27] since it is the will that elicits acts of righteousness.[28] Through the use of these creaturely powers human beings can strive to live on a high moral plane. Aristotle was looked upon as the philosopher who had come the furthest with respect to ethical questions (Ap IV:14).

Melanchthon himself expresses a high regard for human rational powers when it comes to life in this world. He affirms that much of this life comes under our rational control, or to use biblical language, under our dominion (Ap XVIII:4). In Apology XVIII Melanchthon shows what reason is capable of doing in terms of the Ten Commandments. "It can talk about God and offer God acts of worship with external works; it can obey rulers and parents. By choosing an external work it can keep back the hand from murder, adultery, and theft" (Ap XVIII:4).[29] In as much as these are external actions, we can accomplish these works apart from the Holy Spirit (Ap XVIII:4).

Human righteousness is pursued through the selection and development of certain habits in accord with an approved standard. Melanchthon observes, "Obedience to a superior, approved by that superior, is called righteousness" (Ap IV:283 +).[30] The righteousness of reason is achieved in accordance with obedience to the law (Ap IV:283 +).[31] Melanchthon most often ties this righteousness to the requirements of the Decalogue, which in turn is tied back to natural law and the structures of creation. It reflects observations about how the world works. In that connection the law can be conceived "more like a general standard of measurement than a norm which predicts the will of God in all individual cases."[32] This would include not only the Ten Commandments, but advice for daily living as found in the wisdom literature of Scripture, and humanly established standards found in various fields of endeavor.

This conception of the law as a "general standard of measurement" applies to a variety of spheres in life. In the case of civil righteousness, there may be different laws governing society from one country to the next, but one set of laws is not more "right" than the other. In whichever country one finds oneself one is bound to obey its laws as if given by God himself—whether they were formulated by pagans or Christians (Ap XVI:3). The same applies to vocations. Melanchthon distinguishes between personal callings (which are individual) and obedience (which is universal). People are called to different walks of life and therein each person is bound to obey God (Ap XXVII:49). Yet the precise character of that obedience will vary from vocation to vocation. It will mean one thing for a parent and another thing for a child. In the case of ceremonial righteousness, there may also be different ways of ordering the church, structuring its calendar, and conducting its liturgy. Celebrating Easter on one day or another is not more "correct" than the other although Christian love may oblige one to accept one day instead of the other (Ap XV:50).

So we are to help our neighbor within these different spheres of life, but how? When it comes to virtues and social ethics, Melanchthon suggests that we can turn to Aristotle, who, he praises, "has written so eruditely about social ethics that nothing further needs to be added" (Ap IV:14). Aristotle described the obedience that is virtuous as the mean or the middle (often referred to as the "golden mean"). Virtue as the mean is that which avoids excess and hence would be considered a vice. Thus when it comes to the emotions, which often impel us to action, Melanchthon cautions that "too much fear, and too much daring, too much anger, and too much joy etc. injure people."[33]

Yet the "golden mean" is not the same for everyone. It is relative to a person's character. Melanchthon concludes his 1531 "Disputation on Faith and Love,"[34] by stating, "Aristotle rightly and wisely said that moderation in virtue is to be determined geometrically, not arithmetically." In practice this means that one cannot establish a fixed standard (one size fits all) of virtue for everyone. "Temperance is not the same mean in a strong man and a weak man."[35] While we can highlight temperance as a mean, what constitutes temperance will differ from one person to another. With regard to liberality, we cannot establish a single sum that constitutes liberality for all people. It will be proportionate in such a way that when a prince gives liberally and a pauper gives liberally, it will constitute the same mean for both people.

Melanchthon stresses that this righteousness of works is highly praised by God who even honors it with material rewards (Ap IV:24).[36] Civil ordinances are good creations of God. They have his command and approval. In this connection Melanchthon approves Aristotle's statement that "neither the evening star nor the morning star is more beautiful than righteousness" (Ap IV:24). The righteousness of works in all its forms contributes to the preservation and promotion of life in this world. Philosophical righteousness deals not only with the study of metaphysics, but with what today we call the liberal arts. Medicine serves health, meteorology serves navigation, civic virtues serve public tranquillity.[37] Ethics assists statecraft and the construction of laws.[38] Rhetoric assists writing and oratory. Civil righteousness serves the welfare of society (Ap IV:18) by enabling people to live together for the common good. Even the observance of ceremonial traditions (ceremonial righteousness) serve to discipline the body to bow the head or bend the knee. The saints used obedience, poverty, and celibacy as non-obligatory forms of discipline in order to have more leisure for teaching and other pious duties (Ap XXVII:21).

While righteousness in society is based upon the level of our performance, Melanchthon stresses that God considers us on a different basis than do human courts in at least two ways. First, God judges the believer according to mercy. "God does not regard a person as righteous in the way that a court or philosophy does (that is, because of the righteousness of one's own works, which is rightly placed in the will). Instead, he regards a person as righteous through mercy because of Christ, when anyone clings to him by faith" (Ap IV:283 +).[39] Second, "In human courts and judgments, the law and what is owed are certain while mercy is uncertain. But before God it is a different matter. Here mercy has the clear mandate of God. For the gospel itself is the mandate that commands us to believe that God wants to forgive and save on account of Christ" (Ap IV:283 +).[40] In brief, the righteousness of faith is not a righteousness that we achieve; it is a righteousness that we receive.

For the sake of argument with his opponents (in the *confutatio* section of the Apology IV), Melanchthon willingly works with the same anthropology he had used in the discussion regarding the righteousness of works, namely, the distinction between a person's higher and lower powers. Thus as the righteousness of works was located in the obedience of the will to right reason (for purposes of comparison), so Melanchthon is willing to locate faith also in the will. "Faith resides in the will (since it is the desire for and the reception of the promise)" (Ap IV:283 +).[41] In part, this is to counter the objection raised by his opponents who conceived of faith merely as knowledge and thus located in the intellect.[42] "To avoid the suspicion that it is merely knowledge, we will add further that to have faith is to desire and to receive the offered promise of the forgiveness of sins and justification" (Ap IV:48). Yet in another sense, it really does not matter for Melanchthon where one locates faith within the human person. "Faith can be called righteousness because it is that which is reckoned as righteousness (as we say with Paul), regardless in which part of a person it may finally be located" (Ap IV:283 +).[43] From his standpoint, faith involves the whole person.[44]

Of greater importance for Melanchthon is the point that faith—as confidence in the divine mercy of God—lies far beyond the reach and power of the human person. While acknowledging that faith may be located in the will, Melanchthon insists that neither reason nor the will is capable of producing it. This is the point that he hammers home repeatedly in Article II (II–13, 26, 42), "On Original Sin." There he shows how sin affects the entire person rather than simply creating an imbalance in the relationship of the various faculties within the human being. In this article he never tires of reiterating that the *higher affections* lie beyond the control of human beings. Affections like grief and despair simply lie beyond our ability and control. When they have us in their grip, a divine word of consolation is needed to overcome our despair. This requires the Holy Spirit working through the promise of the gospel.

Continuing to work with the definition that righteousness is obedience to an approved standard, Melanchthon argues that faith is in fact our righteousness before God in as much as it is obedience to the gospel. "Now faith is obedience to the gospel, therefore faith is rightly called righteousness" (Ap IV:283 +).[45] How can Melanchthon regard faith as obedience to the gospel and thus as righteousness? By obedience he means that faith is the only right or proper response to the promise. One might say that faith "hearkens unto" the gospel. In other words, a promise cannot be received in any other way than by faith (Ap IV:252+).[46] This is the key argument in Ap IV:48–60. It is why the account of Abraham in Romans 4:3 is so important that Melanchthon inserts a lengthy paragraph about it into his revised Apology text (Ap IV:58 +).[47] Abraham illustrates the point that faith honors God by taking him at his word.

The promise appropriates another's (or alien) righteousness (Ap XII), namely, the benefits of Christ. Melanchthon builds upon the ancient Christology by bringing out its ramifications so that the honor of Christ is directly related to the *beneficia Christi*.[48] To speak of Christ as our righteousness is to speak of Christ as our mediator and propitiator. The atoning work of Christ provides the content and foundation for the righteousness of faith. For that reason, Melanchthon most often refers to Christ as our mediator and atoning sacrifice. Christ's work has the approval of God (Ap XXI). The promise is free on account of Christ. This is another way of saying that the benefits conveyed in the promise are not owed to us.

The righteousness of faith brings about a state of peace between God and human creature, which the Hebrews called shalom. Here it should be noted that Melanchthon draws upon a rich variety of images in order to describe our life with God. Next to justification, Melanchthon's most frequently used term is the forgiveness of sins. Beyond that, he uses reconciliation, conciliation, and peace with God.

Relating the Two Kinds of Righteousness

Melanchthon's distinction between the righteousness of reason and the righteousness of faith does not pit the two against each other as opposing alternatives. Instead, it affirms both, but without confusion. In the Apology Melanchthon contends that Christians seek both kinds of righteousness, but for different reasons and for different purposes. They come into conflict only when a righteousness of works becomes the basis for our righteousness before God or when the righteousness of faith is used to eliminate the need for good works.

Just because works do not justify before God does not mean that they are of no value here on earth. Kept in its proper place, human righteousness remains a very good thing for us and for the world. Similarly, just because faith does justify us before God does not excuse us from carrying out our God-given responsibilities here on earth.

Christ is the fulcrum on which the distinction of two kinds of human righteousness balances. A cursory glance at the frequent references to the glory of Christ and the comfort of sinners will bear this out. "In this controversy the main doctrine of Christianity is involved; when it is properly understood, it illumines and magnifies the honor of Christ and brings to pious consciences the abundant consolation that they need" (Ap IV:2–3, 21, 24, 157, 165, 213, 215, 257, 269, 285, 317; XX:4). While often used as a device to keep the attention of the reader (*attentio*), it must also be regarded as something of a *leitmotiv* for the entire Apology.[49] Conversely, Melanchthon will consistently charge that his opponents obscure the glory of Christ and rob Christians of their comfort because they combine the righteousness of works with the righteousness of faith into one kind of righteousness. Conversely, maintaining a proper distinction between the two kinds of righteousness restores the righteousness of reason to its proper place.

Throughout the Apology Melanchthon charged that the fundamental flaw in his opponent's position lay in their failure to distinguish between two kinds of human righteousness. Instead they championed only one kind of righteousness that availed both in the eyes of society and in the eyes of God. Put bluntly, they saw no difference between philosophical righteousness and Christian righteousness (Ap II:12, 43, and Ap IV:12—16, 43). According to Melanchthon's analysis, the fundamental principle by which his opponents operated had already been expounded by Aristotle in the *Nichomachean Ethics*. That is to say, a life-long practice of doing righteous works makes us righteous.[50] What we do determines who we are. Worthwhile activities makes our lives worthwhile. By practicing virtue, we become virtuous.

In Melanchthon's eyes the Christian theology of his day had constructed a Christian chassis for the Aristotelian engine that powered the system. It had taken over the Aristotelian pattern for obtaining righteousness, raised the bar, and incorporated Christ and the church's sacramental system into the process. Melanchthon felt that the opponents, by advocating one kind of righteousness, had come to view life as a single vertical continuum. His opponents thus conceived of life not in terms of two perpendicular axes (two different bases for two different kinds of righteousness), but as a single vertical continuum by which we ascend from this world to God. They had turned the horizontal axis onto its head and made it into a vertical ladder by which one ascended from earth to heaven. At the bottom of the continuum lay the profane or secular world. In this sphere human beings relate to other human beings and to the created world.[51] Toward the top of the continuum lay the world of the sacred. In this sphere the human relates directly to God and not to other humans.

This continuum of virtue thus erected a scale of value for our works and the walks of life within which we carry out those works. Where one located our various works on the continuum distinguished the works that brought one closer to God (and achieving righteousness before God) from those works that did not. Specific acts of piety toward God drew one close to God or appeased his wrath. A person's focus and energy became devoted to that which is "holy" or "religious," works of cult and ceremony (Ap IV: 10). It resulted in a distinction that moves from faith to love, from the Ten Commandments to evangelical counsels, from commands rooted in creation to churchly established works, from everyday works to works of supererogation, from secular life to a religious life (*vita angelica*). Fasting for God was deemed holier than cooking for family. Forsaking family to dedicate one's life to God as a monk was deemed holier than taking care of aged parents as a child. In the end this created a hierarchical distinction between ordinary Christians (*carnali*) and "super-Christians" (*perfecti*), who were regarded as closer to God.[52]

For Melanchthon, his opponents had also adopted the Aristotelian anthropology that accompanied a righteousness of reason in this world and utilized it in a Pelagian way so as to attain righteousness *coram deo*.[53] The body was subordinated to the soul, and the lower faculties (sensual appetites and emotions) to the higher faculties (reason and will). The higher faculties drew us toward God, the lower faculties drew us toward the world. In the state of perfection, reason guided the will to elicit acts of love toward God and to keep the lower faculties (which pulled us downward) under control. Both sin and virtue came to be defined in terms of acts elicited by the will (Ap II:43). Original sin resulted in a disordering of the parts of the soul (Ap II:27—30). Reason was darkened, the will weakened, and the ordering principle (*donum superadditum*) for the parts of the soul had been lost. As a result, human appetites and passions elicited acts from the will as much as did right reason.

In light of this anthropology and the church's standards for achieving righteousness, salvation in Melanchthon's eyes had come to be seen in terms of a two-stage process. The first stage involved the movement from a state of sin to a state of grace through the infusion of grace at baptism. This was variously called initial grace (*gratia prima*), or the disposition of grace (*habitus gratiae*), the disposition of love (*habitus dilectionis*), justifying grace or sanctifying grace. This initial grace constituted the act of justification. With its infusion the human person recovered the *donum superadditum* or ordering principle lost in the fall. The second stage involved the movement from a state of grace to the attainment of eternal life, also referred to as final beatification or acceptance.[54] This movement was accomplished through the life-long practice and exercise of love.[55] At the end, God awarded a person condign merit (*meritum de condigno*) as a righteousness he was obligated to give (*iustitia debita*). In other words, this love was performed in a state of grace as God intended it. In this state of grace, acts of love were transformed from being good in and of themselves (*bonitas*) to being carried out according to God's intention (*dignitas*).

Melanchthon did not confine his critique to the authors of the *Confutation* of the Augsburg Confession. He diagnosed the same flaw in any number of theologians throughout the Middle Ages. In fact, he may seem unfair in the way that he lumped them all together and presented a composite picture of their theology. This is because regardless of their differences, the fundamental pattern established by Aristotle for how one became righteous remained the same for the *via antiqua*, the *via moderna*, and for that matter, even the humanism of Erasmus. The pattern was that one becomes righteous by doing righteous acts. All agreed that to be judged righteous one had to do one's best—and that required a lifetime of cultivating the habits of righteousness. In every case, the key came down to doing one's best. Their differences lay in questions of how Christ and grace assisted us in the development of that *habitus* leading to righteousness. The *via antiqua* insisted that the initial grace was given gratuitously. The *via moderna* stressed that we can even merit (*meritum de congruo*) that initial grace or *habitus* by doing the best we can (*facere quod in se est*).

The church's hierarchy and sacramental system assisted the Christian up the ladder, thereby creating a dependence upon both. The hierarchy established the acts of piety by which the believer could achieve righteousness (Ap XXVIII). When these were found to be too burdensome, they would mitigate them somewhat (Ap XI, XII). Of the sacraments, Melanchthon devotes more space to Penance (Ap XII) than any other (whereas in the Smalcald Articles II:ii Luther identified the mass as the brood of all vermin). For Melanchthon, *poenitentia* was the context and setting of justification. Here is where it occurred. It was also over this that the Reformation broke out in the first place.

In contrast to his opponents, Melanchthon affirmed that what made us genuinely human in God's sight had to be *distinguished* from what made us genuinely human in the eyes of the world. What constitutes righteousness in one realm does not constitute righteousness in the other.[56] The proper recognition of Christ required the distinction. One must "distinguish the promises from the law in order to recognize the benefits of Christ" (Ap IV:184). At the same time, Melanchthon had to address the legitimate concerns of his opponents. In doing so, he faced a twofold task of raising his objections to his opponents' position while addressing their concerns about his theology. On the one hand, it means that one must teach the righteousness of works without abolishing the righteousness of faith (Ap IV:188, 269). On the other hand, this means that we must teach the righteousness of faith so as not to abolish the righteousness of reason and good works (especially obedience of civil ordinances). Therein lies one of the most important contributions of the Lutheran Confessions.

Melanchthon accomplishes the task of teaching the righteousness of works without obscuring the righteousness of faith by stressing the purposes and limitations of law and works for the vertical dimension of life.

First, he stresses that just because something is commanded by God does not mean that it justifies. "Although medicine, ship navigation, and civil government were necessary and approved by God, taking medicine, studying storms, not bearing arms, or not wearing forbidden clothing, does not justify us—no more than God's command to eat justified us when we ate!"[57] He picks up the same line of argument in Ap XXIII:37–39 where he contends that virginity and marriage are not equal in value. "Just as one gift surpasses another, as prophecy surpasses eloquence, knowledge of military affairs surpasses agriculture, and eloquence surpasses architecture, so virginity is a more excellent gift than marriage." But he adds, "And yet, just as an orator is not more righteous before God on account of eloquence than an architect on account of building, so also a virgin does not merit justification by virginity any more than the married person merits it by conjugal duties. . ." (Ap XXIII:38–39).

So when God commands something, it may have purposes other than justification, such as promoting life in this world—as Melanchthon's examples from medicine and meteorology show. Similarly, good works serve our neighbor in this life. At the same time, they may well provide the context and setting within which the Spirit can accomplish his work through the gospel. Developing the habit of going to church places one in a position where the Word can break through. Learning biblical languages prepares one for inner apprehension of the word. Cultivating a discipline of daily prayer likewise provides a way of keeping the heart turned to God throughout the day. Human traditions and ceremonies provide a structured order for the whole counsel of God to be proclaimed. And similarly, virginity is praised because it provides time for learning or teaching the gospel (Ap XXIII:40).

Perhaps most importantly, the righteousness of works and righteousness of reason provide the context for the righteousness of faith in a negative way, that is, by showing human beings the limitations of their human powers in this world and beyond. In other words, the law will inevitably accuse. Melanchthon stresses this from the vantage points of our horizontal and vertical dimensions of life.

First, the pursuit of righteousness in the horizontal realm is difficult at best. External righteousness can be attained only in a limited way. In Apology XVIII Melanchthon argues that even though the Ten Commandments can be kept to some extent without Christ and the Holy Spirit, we are shackled by concupiscence and the devil.[58] For these reasons, "even civil righteousness is rare among human beings." Despite his praise for Aristotle, Melanchthon notes that "not even

the philosophers, who seemed to have aspired after this righteousness, attained it" (Ap XVIII:5). Second, while reason can achieve civil
righteousness to some extent (Ap XVIII:7, 9), reason cannot grasp
the real demands of the law, namely, the requirements of the First
Commandment. Reason deals with the senses and external actions,
not the inner heart (Ap IV:134).[59] "We concede to free will the freedom and power to perform external works of the law; nevertheless
we do not ascribe to free will those spiritual capacities, namely, true
fear of God, true faith in God, the conviction and knowledge that
God cares for us, hears us, and forgives us, etc." These are works
which "the human heart cannot produce without the Holy Spirit"
(Ap XVIII:7). Finally, both of these are highlighted in the life of the
Christian whose inchoate obedience is impure, scanty, and imperfect.
"Although the renewal has begun, nevertheless the remnants of sin
still cling to this nature and always accuse us unless by faith in Christ
we take hold of the forgiveness of sins" (Ap IV: 159 +).[60]

Melanchthon's analysis of his opponents' position can be
summed up in a simple rule that he introduces at the point he takes
up their specific arguments. They quote passages about law but not
about promise (which is why they speak of only one kind of righteousness). Thus, first, "To all their statements about the law we can
give one reply: the law cannot be kept [coram Deo] without Christ and
the Holy Spirit" (Ap IV: 142). "And if any civil works are done without Christ, they do not conciliate God" (Ap IV:183). A little further,
he continues, "The rule I have just stated interprets all the passages
they quote on law and works" (Ap IV:185).[61] Second, "therefore when
works are commended, we must add that faith is required—that they
are commended on account of faith, because they are the fruits and
testimonies of faith" (Ap IV:183).

The Righteousness of Faith Serves Good Works

Having rejected the righteousness of reason (horizontal dimension) as a basis for the righteousness of faith (vertical dimension),
Melanchthon seeks the latter's proper place in the horizontal dimension of life. While stressing that righteousness of works cannot serve
as a basis for righteousness before God, Melanchthon also addresses

the issue whether or not the righteousness of faith absolves people from pursuing a righteousness of works. This is why Melanchthon fashions the important section of Apology IV, "Love and the Fulfilling of the Law (§121–183). Having argued for *sola fide* in the matter of justification, Melanchthon stresses that such faith does not abolish good works. To the contrary, he stresses that the Lutherans teach good works, show how they can be done, and why they are pleasing to God.

In an important way the distinction of two kinds of righteousness restores the law of God and the structures of life to their original place of importance. It may sound odd to say that the gospel resulted in a recovery of the law of God. But many humanly instituted laws had arisen in order to obtain righteousness before God and had obscured God's law by taking precedence over it. The recovery of the gospel within the context of two kinds of righteousness rendered these humanly achieved works as irrelevant and unnecessary for salvation. They were rendered further obsolete when compared to the Ten Commandments. Luther stresses this point very strongly in the Large Catechism. Hence one frequently finds the insistence to do such good works *as God has commanded* (see CA VI, XX:27). No such command can be found for humanly instituted works and traditions.

The demotion of humanly contrived works also led to a demotion of humanly established walks of life as spheres within which a person could pursue perfection. Neither justification nor sanctification is tied to the particular walk of life that one chooses (Ap XXVII:8). In the place of church vocations, the structures of life wherein people carry out our responsibilities reemerged as the places in which God has called them to serve and seek perfection or sanctification. And so Melanchthon stresses that the life of a farmer or artisan "are states for acquiring perfection" (Ap XXVII:37), that is, growing "in the fear of God, in trust in the mercy promised in Christ, and in dedication to one's calling" (Ap XXVII:27).[62]

Melanchthon pays special attention to the works required by civil authorities. In part this is because the Lutherans were accused of undermining civil authority by undermining ecclesiastical authority.[63] To the contrary, Melanchthon argues that civil authorities have God's authority to construct binding laws upon their subjects. These laws, established *iure humano*, should be obeyed as if God himself had instituted them. Churchly established ceremonies, religious practices, and devotional disciplines, by contrast, are merely human traditions that lack the authority of God. They may be used for the purpose of bodily discipline. Ceremonies in worship—lessons, chants, and the like—can be tolerated "if they were used as exercises, the way lessons are in school, that is, for the purpose of teaching the listeners and, in the process of teaching, to move some of them to fear or faith" (Ap XXVII:55).

Since faith sends the Christian back into the world and recovers the value of God's law, it would suggest that some correspondence exists between the fruits of faith and creaturely virtues. For example, Melanchthon refers to the philosophical virtue of fairness on several occasions and connects it with 1 Peter 4:8 (love covers a multitude of sins), which Melanchthon sees taken from Proverbs 10:12. He comments that what the Apostle calls the responsibility of love the philosophers called "fairness" (*epieikeia* as used by Aristotle and some Stoic philosophers, Ap IV:243). Both mean that at times a person must overlook certain mistakes of friends. He cites the proverb, "know, but do not hate the conduct of a friend" and comments that this "virtue is necessary for preserving public harmony" (Ap IV:243). "Dissension," he says, "grows by means of hatred, as we often see that the greatest tragedies arise from the most trifling offenses. Certain minor disagreements arose between Julius Caesar and Pompey, in which if one had yielded to the other just a little, civil war would not have broken out" (Ap IV:241). The same also happens in the church. Melanchthon describes this in AC XXVI:14 as the search for a "fair and gentle solution" so as not to entangle consciences in ceremonies.

Yet despite the similarities in externals, there were at least two significant differences. First, when it came to externals, a righteousness of works or virtuous habits could shape the conduct of a person, but not change the heart. Here Jeremiah 31 emerged as an important text for Melanchthon. There it was pointed out that people had kept the works externally but were unable to keep them according to the heart. Jeremiah looks forward to the day when people would be equipped to do so. It is a time when the Spirit, rather than Satan, stands in control and produces the new life. Second, while a righteousness of works can be achieved in the eyes of the world, these works please God only on account of faith. Faith must be regarded as the presupposition for good works. When one deals with passages that speak of good works, one must remember that they require faith, as in the case of the woman whose love Christ praises after she touches him in faith (Luke 7:47; Ap IV:152).

Conclusion

The distinction between two kinds of righteousness offers an important framework for reexamining and broadening our thinking regarding the distinction of law and gospel. First, it affirms that there are two kinds of righteousness and both are God-pleasing, but for different reasons and different purposes. Where the distinction between law and gospel runs the risk of affirming only a passive righteousness while ignoring our active righteousness, recognizing the two kinds of righteousness carves out more room to speak in a positive way about the law, orders, and structures of life, according to the first article of the creed. Second, recognizing the two kinds of righteousness enables us to see a true dialectical relationship between creaturely and Christian righteousness. On the one hand, while affirming the value of creaturely righteousness, it still lays the foundation for the law's accusation whenever creaturely righteousness becomes the basis for Christian righteousness. On the other hand, it enables us to see a Christian righteousness that contributes to our creaturely righteousness as our new identity leads to new ways of living.

Notes

1. Edmund Schlink and Holsten Fagerberg are two good examples of such an approach. Schlink devotes nearly one half of his book to an exposition of the distinction of law and gospel before proceeding to the other articles; see his *Theology of the Lutheran Confessions*, trans. Paul F. Koehneke and Herbert J. A. Bouman (Philadelphia: Muhlenberg, 1961). Fagerberg does a similar thing in *A New Look at the Lutheran Confessions* (1529–1537) (St. Louis: Concordia, 1972). There he treats the two kinds of righteousness as a subsection under treatment of law and gospel.

2. In some ways, they are treated as synonymous, especially when one finds the language, "righteousness of the law" and "righteousness of the gospel."

3. See Timothy J. Wengert, "Philip Melanchthon's Last Word to Cardinal Lorenzo Campeggio, Papal Legate at the 1530 Diet of Augsburg," *Dona Melanchthonia: Festgabe fur Heinz Scheible* (Stuttgart-Bad Cannstatt: fromann-holzboog, 2001) p. 466. Wengert's wording economically summarizes the relationship between the two parts of the Augsburg Confession.

4. *Elementorum rhetonces libri duo* in *Corpus Reformatorum*. 28 vols. Eds. C. G. Bret-schneider et al. (Brunsvigae and Halis Saxorum: C. A. Schwetschke et Filium, 1834–60), XIII:417458 [hereafter cited as CR]. For a translation, see, Sister Mary J. LaFontaine, *A Critical Translation of Philip Melanchthon's 'Elementorum Rhetorices Libri Duo,'* (Ph.D. dissertation, University of Michigan, 1968), 113 [hereafter cited as LaFontaine, *Critical Translation*].

5. See Christian Peters' work for an account of the various drafts of the Apology. *Apologia Confessionis Augustanae: Untersuchungen zur Textgeschichte einer lutherischen Bekenntnisschrift* (1530–1584) (Stuttgart: Calwer Verlag, 1997).

6. Melanchthon alludes to this threatened use of force in Ap XXI:44; Ap XII:122–129; and especially in Ap XX:6, 9, where he notes, "we see that a horrible decree has been drawn up against us." See also Wengert's "Melanchthon's Last Word." All translations, unless otherwise noted, are taken from *The Book of Concord: The Confessions of the Evangelical Lutheran Church*, ed. Robert Kolb and Timothy J. Wengert (Philadelphia: Fortress Press, 2000) [hereafter cited as BC]. This edition uses Melanchthon's revised Apology text, otherwise referred to as the octavo text, which adds significant material. See note 27 below for the particular form of citation used for the additional sections not in the Tappert edition.

7. Melanchthon urges his readers in Ap XX:9, "Therefore, the cause is a worthy one. Because of it we shrink from no danger. 'Do not yield to the wicked, but boldly go forward.'"

8. LaFontaine, *Critical Translation*, 115.

9. See Arand, "Melanchthon's Rhetorical Argument for *Sola Fide* in the Apology," *Lutheran Quarterly* 14 (2000): 281–308, and Wengert, "Melanchthon's Last Word."

10. For examples of where it appears in the various articles, see Ap XXIV:10; XXVII:9, 69; XXVIII:6; XVI:2; XVIII:8; II:12, 43; XI:8; IV:5–9, 39, 47, 121, 183; VII:43, 37; XII:85–86, 89, 120. 131; XV:22, 50.

11. LaFontaine, *Critical Translation*, 118; See Wengert, "Melanchthon's Last Word."

12. Ap IV:9, 22.

13. Ap IV:21, 39, 43, 47, 49, 106, p. 149, 238, 252; Ap VII:31, 21, 24.

14. Ap IV:34; Ap XII:142; Ap XVIII:4, 5, 9.

15. Ap IV:20, BC, 147–149, 165; Ap IV:283; Ap XII:79, 108; Ap XV:9; Ap XXIV:23.

16. Ap IV:179; Ap XVIII:4; Ap XXIII:4; cf. CR 15:453.

17. Ap XVIII:40.

18. Ap XVIII:2, 9; 7, 31.

19. Ap IV:132; Ap XVI:2, 8; Ap XVIII:10, 23.

20. CA XX:8; 27, 48; CA XXVIII:62; Ap IV:18. 20, 39, 43, 47, 155, 211, BC, 165; Ap IV:358, BC, 172–73; Ap VII:31, 45; Ap XII:10, 15, 16, 29; Ap XV:4, 10, 16, 22, 25, 32, 42, 43, 50: Ap XXIII:37; Ap XXIV:27, 43, 57, 60, 63, 77, 96, 97, 98; Ap XXVII:23, 54.

21. Ap IV:27, 47.

22. CA XX:8; 26. 29; Ap IV:12, 16.

23. CA XVIII:2; Ap IV:30, 32, 41.

24. Ap IV:92; Ap VII:13, 31, 32, 36.

25. Robert Kolb, "Luther on the Two Kinds of Righteousness: Reflections on His Two-Dimensional Definition of Humanity at the Heart of His Theology," *Lutheran Quarterly* 13 (1999): 453. See also Kolb, "God Calling, 'Take Care of My People'. Luther's Concept of Vocation in the Augsburg Confession and its Apology," *Concordia Journal* 8 (1982): 4–11.

26. LaFontaine, *Critical Translation*, 102.

27. The "+" indicates that this citation is from the second or octavo edition of the Apology and is found in an addition to the first edition in the text after the paragraph indicated in the first edition, here at p. 164 in *The Book of Concord*.

28. This will prove to be a most important distinction in as much as his opponents will locate faith only in the intellect (and hence cannot be righteousness) whereas Melanchthon will consistently place it also in the will (Ap IV:48; BC, 164–165). "Let us add the following scholastic argument: it is necessary for righteousness to reside in the will; therefore, since faith resides in the intellect, it does not justify" (Ap IV, 283 +, BC, 164). Note the citation there from Thomas Aquinas, n. 205: For intellect assents to those things, which are of the faith, by the command of the will." Melanchthon argues that faith resides not only in the intellect, but also in the will (since it is the desire for and the reception of the promise" (Ap IV:283 +, BC, 165).

29. It is interesting, however, that he does not speak of the ninth and tenth commandments which speak of coveting, a movement or impulse of the heart

30. BC, 164.

31. Ibid., 165.

32. Fagerberg, *New Look*, 104.

33. Cf. CR 16:211.

34. This is an important source for Ap IV. See *Sources and Contexts of the Book of Concord* (Minneapolis: Fortress Press, 2001). Also see Peters, *Apologia*, 351–374.

35. CR 16:212.

36. Cf. CR 15:500.

37. Timothy J. Wengert, *Human Freedom, Christian Righteousness Philip Melanchthon's Exegetical Dispute with Erasmus of Rotterdam*, (New York: Oxford University Press, 1998), 15 [hereafter cited as Wengert, *Human Freedom*].

38. Ibid., 93.

39. BC, 165.

40. Ibid., 167

41. Ibid., 164.

42. This also explains why the discussion of faith's location within the human person occurs in the section where he responds to the concerns of the opponents.

43. Ibid., 165.

44. Note Wengert's discussion on "though faith" and "by faith," "Reflections on Confessing the Faith in the New English Translation of *The Book of Concord,*" *Lutheran Quarterly* 14 (2000): 3–4.

45. BC, 164.

46. Ibid., 160.

47. Ibid., 129.

48. Already in CA III Melanchthon used the very wording and framework of the Apostles' Creed and then brought out the soteriological ramifications of those statements with the words "in order to.." In the Apology, a corollary of the glory of Christ centers on the exclusivity of Christ's role as mediator (IV.157, 213, 317, 324; XXI: 14–31). Other corollaries would include the *sola fide* emphasis found throughout (IV:1–3; 73–108; 287300).

49. Cf. Arand, "The Apology as Polemical Commentary," in *Philip Melanchthon (1497–1569) and the Commentary*, ed. Timothy J. Wengert and M. Patrick Graham (Sheffield: Sheffield Academic Press, 1997), 171–193.

50. "We acquire [virtues] by first having put them into action [. . .], becom[ing] builders by building houses, and harpists by playing the harp. Similarly, we become just by the practice of just actions [. . .]." *Nichomachean Ethics*, trans. Martin Ostwald (Indianapolis: Bobbs-Merrill, 1962), 34.

51. Robert Kolb, "God Calling," 4

52. We have the same problem today. Evangelicals often turn the Christian life into a two tiered existence when they stress, "now that you have accepted Jesus as your savior, make him the Lord of your life." Pentecostals work with a similar view with their distinction between water baptism for justification and Spirit baptism for sanctification.

53. See Steven Ozment's analysis of Luther's Disputation against the Scholastics in *The Age of Reform, 1250–1550: An Intellectual and Religious History of Late Medieval and Reformation Europe* (New Haven: Yale University Press, 1980), 235–236.

54. Ap IV: 17: "They first urge us to earn this disposition [*habitus*] though preceding merits; then they urge us to earn an increase of this disposition

[*habitus*] and eternal life by the works of the law." This two-stage process is evident in Roman Catholic literature throughout the sixteenth century.

55. Steven Ozment (*The Age of Reform*, p. 32; see note 53 above) uses the analogy of a tennis player to illustrate this process. While all people can play tennis, not all are tennis players. Two things are needed to become a tennis player. First, an infusion of instruction. Second, the practice of playing tennis in order to develop the muscle memory that results in one becoming a tennis player. The infusion of grace represents the first part, the exercise of love the second part.

56. "Whereas Erasmus was ever the moral philosopher who, with his *philosophia Christi* and his love for good Latin, sought ethical and philological standards and held to a fundamental continuity in God's work, Melanchthon demanded a theological core that put language and morals in one distinct, God-given sphere and the gospel in another." Wengert, *Human Freedom*, 110.

57. Ibid., 86.

58. "This also may be seen in the philosophers, who, though they tried to live honestly, were still not able to do so but were defiled by many obvious crimes. Such is the weakness of human begins when they govern themselves by human powers alone without faith or the Holy Spirit" (CA XX: 33–34).

59. Here one might postulate that when Melanchthon refers to the righteousness of the law throughout the Apology, he uses it as shorthand to mean the righteousness of reason, that is, reason's apprehension or understanding of the law.

60. BC, 145.

61. A little later on he enunciates the principle, "wherever good works are praised and the law preached," we must hold fast to the principle, "that the law is not kept without Christ—as he himself has said, "Apart from me you can do nothing" (Ap IV:269).

62. Note Melanchthon's use of Rom 14:7 and especially 2 Cor 3:18.

63. See Wengert, *Human Freedom*, 140.

4

Civic Participation by Churches and Pastors: An Essay on Two Kinds of Righteousness

William W. Schumacher

Since September 2001, much ink has been spilled and swords have been drawn (metaphorically) in The Luthran Church—Missouri Synod over a cluster of theological problems which include the one to be addressed in this essay: civic participation by churches and pastors. Yet even a cursory glance should tell us that "civic participation" per se does not pose any theological problems, at least for Lutherans. After all, the reformers of the sixteenth century reclaimed the sphere of secular government as a legitimate and proper scope for Christian living and vocation. Augsburg Confession XVI deals with precisely this issue, arguing against the medieval ideal of the so-called "religious" life. There it is asserted plainly:

> . . .that all political authority, orderly government, laws, and good order in the world are created and instituted by God and that Christians may without sin exercise political authority; be princes and judges; pass sentences and administer justice according to imperial and other existing laws; punish evildoers with the sword; wage just wars; serve as soldiers; buy and sell; take required oaths; possess property; be married; etc. . . . . The gospel does not overthrow secular government, public order, and marriage but instead intends that a person keep all this as a true order of God and demonstrate in these

walks of life Christian love and true good works according to each person's calling.[1]

Secular life—including civic, political, and economic life—is thus staked out as the arena in which Christians are expected to exercise or live out the new reality which God has given them in Christ and which they have received by faith. The Christian's good works are not self-devised displays of conspicuous piety, but are the ordinary duties of human life in the world, including such activities as active civic involvement, military service, and marriage. This positive evaluation of civic, political, secular life is a corollary of the fundamental Reformation insight about two kinds of righteousness. The passive righteousness of faith depends entirely on the person and work of Christ; this alone establishes and determines our identity and righteousness before God. On the other hand, and at the same time, our righteousness in the world (*coram hominibus*) is active, not passive; it depends on the activities by which we fulfill our vocation and serve our neighbor.

These two different kinds of righteousness are not alternatives between which we must choose, but rather two simultaneous dimensions of genuine human identity. They serve different purposes and must, therefore, be kept distinct. Luther's recovery of a right understanding of justification involved the insight that our own activity and works have no place in deciding our standing before God. Similarly, the preaching of the Gospel does not govern nations, feed children, build houses, punish criminals, etc. Both kinds of righteousness are God's will, and both kinds are necessary for us to live in the world as fully human creatures restored in Christ.

The distinction between—and affirmation of—the two kinds of righteousness certainly contributed to Luther's clarification of the Gospel in all its glory. But it also led to a new appreciation of secular life as good for its own sake. As Gerhard Ebeling puts it, it is only the recovery of a proper understanding of justification which "truly lets creation be creation and redemption be redemption."[2] Once our works no longer have to carry the unbearable freight of our own salvation—that load Christ has taken on Himself—they are free to be put to good use to help our neighbor. Once I no longer have to evaluate my activities based on some supposed religious value or merit which I need, the only needs that matter are those defined by the vocation(s) in which my Creator has placed me. The distinction between the two kinds of righteousness lets us get all our works out of the Second Article of the Creed (where they can only distract us from Christ) and locate them in the First Article where they belong. For that is where our Creator gives, protects, nurtures, and preserves life for us through others—and for others through us.

The Creator created originally and ex nihilo, but He also continues His creative work perpetually and through means in the created world. Speaking of the Creator's work, Luther says in the Large Catechism: "He makes all creation help provide the benefits and necessities of life—sun, moon, and stars in the heavens; day and night; air, fire, water, the earth and all that it yields and brings forth; birds, fish, animals, grain, and all sorts of produce."[3] To this cosmic picture Luther then adds one more dimension of the Creator's loving work which brings us back to our topic: "Moreover, he gives all physical and temporal blessings—good government, peace, security." Secular, civic, political life is good because through these structures and relationships the Creator is at work to provide what is needed for life, and to protect life in a sin-twisted world. And since our Father works through such things, we Christians embrace secular, civic, economic, and political life as the proper sphere of our lives of Christian love and service.

Religion in American Public Life

If our involvement in civic events and public life were really as simple as that, we could end this essay here. But, of course, it is not really as simple as that. In a host of ways we are challenged as confessional Lutheran Christians by questions regarding civic participation, not because the civil, public realm is too secular—secular things are no problem for us, thanks to Augsburg Confession XVI and the Large Catechism—but because it is too religious. In other words, the trouble comes when various kinds of "civic events" in the world are laden with elements which are not merely civic, but incorporate religious actions, vocabulary, and themes. Many events which take place in the civic realm are rich with religious imagery or overtones. Pull some money out of your pocket and you are immediately confronted with an overtly religious motto:

"In God we trust." The Bible and some invocation of God are routinely used for public oaths, whether swearing in witnesses in court or installing public officials up to and including the President of the United States. The Declaration of Independence, of course, grounds its claim of legitimacy in explicitly religious terms by asserting natural equality of rights endowed by the Creator to all His human creatures. Many of the greatest examples of political speech and thought in American history are rich in religious language and themes. In a famous passage from George Washington's farewell of 1796, the connection between religious faith and honorable public service is accented:

> Of all the dispositions and habits which lead to political prosperity, religion and morality are indispensable supports. In vain would that man claim the tribute of patriotism, who should labor to subvert these great pillars of human happiness, these firmest props of the duties of men and citizens. The mere politician, equally with the pious man, ought to respect and to cherish them. A volume could not trace all their connections with private and public felicity. Let it simply be asked: Where is the security for property, for reputation, for life, if the sense of religious obligation desert the oaths which are the instruments of investigation in courts of justice? And let us with caution indulge the supposition that morality can be maintained without religion. Whatever may be conceded to the influence of refined education on minds of peculiar structure, reason and experience both forbid us to expect that national morality can prevail in exclusion of religious principle.[4]

Abraham Lincoln grappled with the agony of the American Civil War in his second inaugural address of 1865:

> Neither party expected for the war the magnitude or the duration which it has already attained. Neither anticipated that the cause of the conflict might cease with or even before the conflict itself should cease. Each looked for an easier triumph, and a result less fundamental and astounding. Both read the same Bible and pray to the same God, and each invokes His aid against the other. It may seem strange that any men should dare to ask a just God's assistance in wringing their bread from the sweat of other men's faces, but let us judge not, that we be not judged. The prayers of both could not be answered. That of neither

has been answered fully. The Almighty has His own purposes. "Woe unto the world because of offenses; for it must needs be that offenses come, but woe to that man by whom the offense cometh." If we shall suppose that American slavery is one of those offenses which, in the providence of God, must needs come, but which, having continued through His appointed time, He now wills to remove, and that He gives to both North and South this terrible war as the woe due to those by whom the offense came, shall we discern therein any departure from those divine attributes which the believers in a living God always ascribe to Him? Fondly do we hope, fervently do we pray, that this mighty scourge of war may speedily pass away. Yet, if God wills that it continue until all the wealth piled by the bondsman's two hundred and fifty years of unrequited toil shall be sunk, and until every drop of blood drawn with the lash shall be paid by another drawn with the sword, as was said three thousand years ago, so still it must be said "the judgments of the Lord are true and righteous altogether."[5]

Neither Washington nor Lincoln conceived of American society or the American political system as a theocracy, but both appreciated how important it was to govern with the awareness that human beings are accountable to their Creator. To be sure, the First Amendment of the U.S. Constitution both guarantees the free exercise of religion and forbids the legislature from establishing anything like a "state church." Legal scholar Stephen L. Carter and others correctly argue that whatever "separation" is built into that constitutional limitation originally had the intention of protecting religious people and religious groups from pressure or interference by political authorities.[6] But in more recent times, and especially since the mid-twentieth century, it has become common to talk of a "wall of separation" between church and state as a protection against religious meddling in politics and government.[7] Be that as it may, while church and state may be judicially separated in America, it is clear in many ways that religion and politics are not; nor are they likely to be any time soon.

Is that a problem? More specifically, in light of our topic, does the interplay of religious life and political or civic life pose a problem for Christians (or at least for confessional Lutheran Christians)? How you answer that question, whether in general or in specific cases that arise, will depend on how you understand the sphere of civic, political, secular life, and also on how you understand the place of the church and the religious life of Christians in the world. The following paragraphs will briefly sketch some ways in which we might be led in divergent directions as we look to various sources for help.

In recent years, there have been many voices calling for a renewed appreciation for the wisdom of the early church. Part of the motivation for such a call is the sense that we may be moving (or have already moved) into a "post-Constantinian" age in which the rough, uneven alliance between the church and the culture—more specifically, the state—is coming unglued and falling apart. If one reads the contemporary culture as a place where Christianity has lost its predominant role in determining public values, then one is drawn to the earliest centuries of Christian thought, when those who confessed the lordship of Christ lived (and often died) as exiles even in their home countries. Conversion to the faith involved a change of citizenship, albeit a peaceful change which did not aim at subverting the existing political order. An example of this sense of alienation from one's own culture is captured in the second century Epistle to Diognetus:

> The Christians are distinguished from other men neither by country, nor language, nor the customs which they observe. For they neither inhabit cities of their own, nor employ a peculiar form of speech, nor lead a life which is marked by any singularity. . . . But, inhabiting Greek as well as barbarian cities, according as the lot of each of them has been determined, and following the customs of the natives in respect to clothing, food, and the rest of their ordinary conduct, they display to us their wonderful and confessedly striking [paradoxical] method of life. They dwell in their own countries, but simply as sojourners. As citizens, they share in all things with others, and yet endure all things as if foreigners. Every foreign country is to them as their native land, and every land of their birth as a land of strangers. . . . They pass their days on earth, but they are citizens of heaven.[8]

The external situation of Christians in society changed dramatically after the conversion of the Emperor Constantine. Once Christians were no longer a relatively small minority, the sense of exile and alienation was to some extent moderated by the awareness that Christians "had a stake in the rule of law, in stability, in order, in civic concord, in peace with those peoples who lived outside the Roman Empire."[9] This is why a sense not of exile but of dual citizenship is one theme of Augustine's *City of God*. But the participation of Christians in the earthly city envisioned by Augustine ultimately turns out to be of a different kind than the Lutheran reformers' conception of two kinds of righteousness serving different purposes. For Augustine, Platonist that he was, there is but one Good, one righteousness, and therefore the earthly city must be fashioned into a community of justice that is oriented toward faith in and love for the true God. The church, which is the city of God and the people of God, has a temporary, but real, stake in the earthly city because temporal order and law may serve the ultimate goal of the city of God. One might even say that Augustine's argument in the *City of God* inverts the image of Christians as exiles and strangers in a foreign country, and pictures the people of God almost as benevolent occupiers (and ultimate conquerors) of the wayward earthly city.

We see, then, that listening to the early church does not lead us in a single direction. Rather, which voices of the early church resonate in our ears will depend very much on how we regard our contemporary situation vis-à-vis our own culture and society. If we are still in a society that is more or less Christian in its orientation, then the church has a responsibility to help shape and direct the society toward the worship of the true God (since, according to Augustine, that is the real purpose of society). Part of that responsibility will also involve the struggle against non-Christian or anti-Christian influences, also in the realm of politics and law. The world needs the church, in this view, because the world must be Christianized. If, on the other hand, we judge that we have already slipped from a Constantinian to a post-Constantinian age, then the earlier paradigm of strangers and exiles will seem more compatible with our situation.[10] Like the Christians described in the letter to Diognetus, we may desire to live our lives as exiles and "resident aliens" rather than as full citizens (let alone conquering occupiers!) of the earthly city. The early church fathers that inform such a posture toward the world will teach us a spirit of witness, even of martyrdom, by which the church shall learn again and again the blessings of suffering for the Name. But the pre-Constantinian fathers will not teach us how to participate in the governance of earthly communities, since their hope is one of escape at the end of their exile.

The contrast between these two stances toward the culture is especially clear when we consider "civic" events which include religious elements. Strangers and aliens cannot participate even in token formalities of the cult of Caesar. In a Constantinian world, church and state each have a stake in the other—Constantine himself presided at the Council of Nicea.

If we shift from the ancient church to our American context, we see that since colonial times, American religious life has included both the impulse to build the kingdom of God on earth (starting in America, of course) as well as the instinct to withdraw from the world and focus exclusively on an eschatological hope of heaven. Thus, the theological movement labeled American Evangelicalism exhibits some of the same tensions and alternatives we have pointed to in the theology of the early church. Today's evangelicals are influenced both by groups such as the Christian Coalition (motto: "Giving Christians a voice in government again") and by the writing of theologians like Stanley Hauerwas who envision Christians and the church as much more distinct from, and therefore less engaged with, the surrounding culture. That is to say, evangelicals seem pulled between the notion that America is (or was, or at least ought to be) a Christian nation, and the sense of radical discontinuity between the kingdom of God and the kingdom of this world.[11]

Thus, American Christians wrestle with the old alternatives of conquest or exile, in slightly altered form. If we reach back to the Lutheran distinction between the two kinds of righteousness, we might say that the first of the twin temptations of evangelicalism is to forget that there are two kinds and imagine instead that Christian righteousness and active (or civic) righteousness are one and the same. Ideally, in this view, the country should be governed according to the Bible. Personal faith becomes perhaps the single most important criterion by which to evaluate candidates for public office. The flip side of this is the temptation to regard the two kinds of righteousness as alternatives between which we should choose. The Christian's active righteousness is then understood as something quite different from ordinary civic duty and responsibility. An extreme version of this view results in the production of a Christian Yellow Pages, as if it were important to know that the plumber who fixes your sink is a fellow-believer, rather than simply that he knows how to do plumbing. The different streams of American evangelicalism also take different stands toward American civil religion, ranging from quietism and separatism to the President's prayer breakfast.

Missouri Synod Approaches

I said at the beginning that "civic participation" per se does not pose any difficulties for Lutheran Christians. Problems arise much more when some events and activities in civic life are too religious than when they are too secular. This seems perhaps paradoxical. Does this mean, for example, that Lutherans favor a rigorously secular state and society, what Richard John Neuhaus calls a "naked public square" in which religion is scrupulously excluded from public (and especially from political) discourse? We may be tempted to think that such clear boundaries and distinctions would simplify life. We might even suppose that a Lutheran understanding of the two kingdoms would lead us in that direction.

As a matter of fact, there is a strong stream in our Missouri Synod tradition which seems to favor a sharp and unambiguous distinction between religious life and civic life. Such a clear demarcation would allow us to follow equally clear and unambiguous principles or rules to guide our decisions regarding participation in all kinds of events. In his widely used and influential *Pastoral Theology* (1932), J. H. C. Fritz argued that civic events which included religious elements were inherently unionistic:

> [A]ny religious exercises (prayer, religious address or sermon, religious hymns) in connection with school commencements, so-called baccalaureate services and the like, or religious exercises of any kind in connection with political meetings, or other meetings of civic bodies, whenever members of different denominations take part, is unionism. In these particular instances such is also the result of a failure to understand the doctrine of the separation of Church and State, not keeping each within its own proper sphere.[12]

Fritz is talking about events or occasions in public, civic, or even political life, and he is concerned about two different dangers. The first is a mingling or confusion of confessions, which he regards as necessarily implied by any and all "religious exercises" which involve members of different denominations. To be precise, Fritz is here extending the definition of unionism beyond what was described in the Missouri Synod's constitution, which located "unionism" in the context of the regular worship and sacramental rites of a local church which made room for multiple confessions. For Fritz, the same principle applies to any and all religious expressions, in whatever context, where members of different denominations take part. It is important to remember that Fritz was assuming that denominational membership could be taken as reliable shorthand for a person's confessional position, an assumption which could be made more confidently in his day than in ours. Note also that Fritz's definition is comprehensive enough to exclude any and all joint prayer between Christians of different denominations, a position which today more closely reflects the practice of the Wisconsin Synod than that of the Missouri Synod.

The second danger on Fritz's mind is a perceived threat to what he calls "the doctrine of separation of Church and State." This is a very remarkable phrase, since it seems to attribute the status of doctrine to what is really a tradition of American jurisprudence and constitutional interpretation. The separation of church and state is part of the ongoing American political experiment,[13] not part of the dogma of Christianity. A distinction between God's two ways of reigning in the world is an important part of the Lutheran theological tradition; it is a corollary of the idea of two kinds of righteousness, and echoes a distinction between Law and Gospel. But the doctrine of the two kingdoms is by no means identical with what American courts mean by separation of church and state. The kind of strict separation of church and state envisioned by Fritz has almost never been the condition under which Lutheran churches have lived, or have sought to live. If we do equate these two ideas, as Fritz seems to urge us to do, we would be pushed toward a position generally associated with the ACLU and the Americans United for the Separation of Church and State. In other words, a strict and consistent separation of church and state, pursued as a doctrinal principle, results in a naked public square, where any and all religious language, arguments, and expressions are simply ruled out of order in public discourse.

Such a position, though clear and consistent, leads in a hazardous direction for a number of reasons. For one thing, when "public" equals "government," then everything that isn't government (including religion) is "private"—and thus can be easily dismissed as "merely private." But the privatization of religion is one of the trends in American culture that the church needs to resist and speak against. Of course, Christian faith necessarily involves the dimension of personal, individual conviction and commitment, but it distorts the Gospel to pretend that the church and its mission in the world is a purely private matter. As long as conscientious Lutheran Christians mistakenly identify the "public square" (or civic life) exclusively with the arena of state and government, we let Christianity be confined to a private religious ghetto and mute the voice of our theology in discussions of many important public questions.[14]

Fritz, as others before him in the Missouri Synod's history, reacted against the threats they saw embodied in the hated Prussian Union. That forced fusion of Lutheran and Reformed churches in Prussia, decreed by King Friedrich Wilhelm III in 1817, epitomized both of the dangers Fritz cautions against. That is, the Prussian Union was at the same time both a mingling and confusion of differing confessions, and also a blatant intrusion of political power into the life and theology of the church. The First Amendment, it was hoped, would be protection against the threat of government meddling, but the American scene presented a host of confusing, sectarian variations on the theme of mingled confessions. While the European context posed the challenge of forced combination of confessions, the American scene has been characterized by new situations where "religious people" may not be aware that their "confession" (i.e., what they believe, and say that they believe) is playing a role in public life at all.

Life in Two Realms

Part of our confusion, of course, arises from the fact that "religious" life and "civic" life are not really airtight, mutually exclusive categories. If it were really as easy as simply deciding which one of two distinct boxes a given event should be filed in, it is hard to see how there could be any disagreement. Those who would argue in favor of such a clear or obvious distinction between "civic" and "religious" events may want to follow Fritz and maintain that the inclusion of any religious element whatsoever means that we must consider the event to be religious in nature.

But civic events do include religious themes for a variety of reasons (some good and some bad), and they do not thereby automatically become "religious" events in the normal sense of the word. In fact, religious language is fundamental to the American system because an acknowledgment of God by government or civic leaders serves as a crucial and meaningful reminder of the penultimate nature of the authority of the state. This is the case with the inclusion of the motto "In God we trust" on the coins and currency of the United States. Such a motto is religiously generic and unspecified, and thus theologically inadequate. But the usefulness of such an acknowledgment does not depend on a theologically precise definition of the referent (God). Rather, such references are extremely important because they express a fundamental self-limitation of government, and the recognition that there is a transcendent divine power to which citizens, and even the sovereign state itself, are subject and accountable. The religious elements which are generally included in such contexts as courtrooms and presidential inaugurations can be seen in the same light. In each case, individuals are reminded that they are responsible to divine, omniscient justice for their trustworthiness and integrity. So, too, we can endorse the observance of a day of thanksgiving as proclaimed by the President. Similarly, government could well encourage religious practice generally for the sake of public order and morality, and thus might urge its citizens to worship in the church, synagogue, or mosque of their choice. Such generalized encouragement of religion is theologically deficient because it does not confess saving faith in the true, triune God revealed in Jesus Christ. But it seems to be a sound expression of "religion" as an element of active righteousness in the civic realm. Does not this pose some challenges for us as Lutheran Christians, and especially as Lutheran pastors as "public religious figures"? The 1850 convention of the Missouri Synod referred to "a certain religious interest of the government." If we accept that, then we are accepting a religious dimension in the realm of active righteousness, not as the basis of our standing before God, but for the sake of public decency and order, for the building and maintenance of strong communities.

On the other hand, it is also possible (indeed, much more than possible, for it happens very frequently) that a civic event is draped with religious themes and language in an attempt to legitimate some merely political agenda or bolster civic or patriotic feeling with the help of religious emotion. In this way, religion becomes co-opted by the civic realm, and is made instrumental to the ends and goals of the political sphere. It is, I suggest, very hard to distinguish in practice between these two different kinds of events. On the one hand, there are events or occasions which express in a proper, humble way the penultimate, conditional character of the civic/political sphere by means of religious elements. We need not be embarrassed or theologically distressed by the overtly religious language of the Declaration of Independence, or by the motto on our money. On the other hand, there are events or occasions which misuse religion as a tool to serve merely political or jingoistic ends. The shameful history of Hitler's "Deutsche Christen" and the servile stance of much of Russian orthodoxy during the Soviet era illustrate this risk. In view of the deplorable history of the twenthieth century, the threat of political powers claiming ultimacy and subverting everything else to merely political ends (in a form of totalitarian ideology) may be as great as the risk of purely privatized religion.

While civic or political events may frequently (and even appropriately) acknowledge and use religious elements, nearly all religious events are to some extent "public" and consequently include a dimension of civic responsibility. This is simply another way of saying that religion is never merely private, never strictly personal. This need not be as blatantly political as a church endorsing a political candidate or distributing voting lists (although that sort of thing happens, too, of course). It simply means that churches, like other public institutions, participate in public, civic life in the world in a variety of ways. This is probably easier to see in the local community than at a national level. Churches participate in the economy, paying their utility bills and wages for their staff. They may engage in "political" activities such as discussions with the city council or zoning board about public works projects or changes in public services (police and fire protection come to mind). A church school is also a prime location of such an interface between the "religious" and the "civic," since church schools aim at preparing their students to be good citizens as well as trying to form them as Christians. If it is inappropriate for the civic or political realm to indulge in religious speech, it is presumably just as wrong for institutions of the church to involve themselves in merely civic matters. But in that case why do church schools teach mathematics, or American history, or geography? The answer is that church schools (and other religious institutions to one degree or another) live in both realms, the "religious" and the "secular." They have a proper interest in the active righteousness of good citizenship, moral decency, and good social behavior. Knowing the difference between Thailand and Taiwan, or the capitals of all fifty states, clearly has nothing to do with our standing before God, but it is good for people in our society (including Christians) to know such things.

Churches and other religious institutions participate necessarily and properly in the life of their communities and societies. And this implies that pastors function not only as religious leaders of congregations, but also sometimes in civic roles as well. Such civic functions of pastors are never to replace or overshadow their distinctive proprium as "called and ordained servants of the Word." In America, at least, much of the civil side of public ministry is carried out informally and ad hoc. But more formal arrangements are not uncommon. Pastors exercise legal power to perform weddings. Both federal and state legislatures commonly open their sessions with prayer by religious chaplains. Governments at local, state, and national levels recognize the civic, societal benefits of religion by granting religious professionals special tax privileges. As discussed above, such arrangements can serve an important civil function by acknowledging a transcendent dimension of accountability and the self-limitation of government which was a presupposition for modern liberal democratic political systems. Pastors who serve in such public capacities contribute to the active civil righteousness of their communities. Of course, in so doing they will want to remember and guard against the very real risk of being simply co-opted for merely political ends and muting the voice of the Gospel itself.

It is dangerously simplistic to restrict the church and its pastors solely and unambiguously to the service of the passive righteousness of faith and to pretend that they function exclusively in the right-hand kingdom of grace. Such an attempt hands everything which is not directly related to the Gospel over to "the world" or to government, or to people acting strictly as individuals. The church is an institution in society, whether we like it or not. Acknowledging that fact will not answer all our questions in hard cases—in fact, it plunges us into all the complexities of radical religious pluralism. But a Lutheran appreciation of the two kinds of righteousness can help us reclaim what Robert Benne has called the "paradoxical vision"[15] of public theology in and for the society in which we live. It may mean that our stance toward American "civil religion" will not be a simple choice between optimistic acceptance or flat rejection. We need to approach the distinction between the two kingdoms with the help of another classic Lutheran distinction, namely in terms of the two kinds of righteousness. Civic participation (and even, perhaps, participation in some civic events which include religion) would then reveal another dimension as part and parcel of the Christian's (and the church's) active righteousness which neither replaces nor is replaced by the preaching of the Gospel.

Notes

1. Robert Kolb and Timothy J. Wengert, eds. *The Book of Concord* (Minneapolis: Fortress, 2000), 48 & 50.

2. Gerhard Ebeling, "Das Problem des Natürlichen bei Luther" in Lutherstudien, vol. I (Tübingen: J. C. B. Mohr [Paul Siebeck], 1971), 278f.

3. LC II, 14. Kolb-Wengert, 432.

4. Quoted in Mark A. Noll, *America's God: From Jonathan Edwards to Abraham Lincoln* (Oxford & New York: Oxford University Press, 2002), 203–204.

5. The entire text of Lincoln's address is quoted in James M. McPherson, gen. ed., and David Rubel, ed., *"To the Best of My Ability": The American Presidents* (New York: Dorling Kindersley, 200), 367.

6. Stephen L. Carter, *The Culture of Disbelief: How American Law and Politics Trivialize Religious Devotion* (New York: Basic Books, 1993), 115–120.

7. Philip Hamburger, *Separation of Church and State* (Cambridge, MA: Harvard, 2002).

8. Alexander Roberts and James Donaldson, eds. *Ante-Nicene Fathers*, vol. 1 (Peabody, MA: Hendrickson, 1994), 26f.

9. Robert L. Wilken, "Augustine's City of God Today," in *The Two Cities of God: The Church's Responsibility for the Earthly City*. Ed. Carl E. Braaten and Robert W. Jenson. (Grand Rapids: Eerdmans, 1997), 35.

10. See George Weigel, "The Church's Political Hopes for the World; or, Diognetus Revisited," in *The Two Cities of God*, 59–77.

11. On this tension between church and society as it developed in early nineteenth-century America, see Mark Y. Hanley, *Beyond a Christian Commonwealth: The Protestant Quarrel with the American Republic, 1830-1860* (Chapel Hill, NC: University of North Carolina Press, 1994).

12. Quoted in Carl S. Meyer, ed., *Moving Frontiers: Readings in the History of The Lutheran Church—Missouri Synod* (St. Louis: Concordia, 1964), 379. Fritz explains his position in a note: "It is at variance with the principle of separation of Church and State when a pastor conducts a so-called public-school baccalaureate service in his own church, even if given full charge of the service. This does not go to say that a pastor must, where it has been customary to hold baccalaureate services in conjunction with public-school graduations, under all circumstances forbid his members for conscience' sake to attend; but they should do so under protest, thus safeguarding the principle."

13. The strict enforcement of a "wall of separation" is also of fairly recent origin even in American political life. Cf. Hamburger, *Separation of Church and State*, and A. James Reichley, *Religion in American Public Life* (Washington, D.C.: The Brookings Institution, 1985).

14. Conceding the entirety of public life to the state is also a dangerous move toward unlimited government and even weakens the argument against totalitarianism, but that is a separate concern.

15. Robert Benne, *The Paradoxical Vision: A Public Theology for the Twenty-First Century* (Minneapolis: Fortress, 1995).

5

"The Chief Controversy between the Papalists and Us"

Grace, Faith, and Human Righteousness in Sixteenth-Century Ecumenical Exchange

Robert Kolb

Martin Luther's teaching on how the sinner becomes righteous in God's sight introduced a paradigm shift in Western Christian thought. This is true not only in regard to the entire constellation of the body of biblical teaching and its formulation for the use of the congregation of God's people. It is true above all to the way in which the topic of salvation was conceived and proclaimed. By framing the definition of salvation in terms of justification—rather than, for instance, Scotus' "acceptation" or the mystics' "divinization" but instead the restoration of righteousness or humanity—Luther created one of the most controversial questions in the history of theology. For him the way in which God restored his chosen human creatures to the fullness of their humanity was the central, guiding point of orientation for the entire biblical message.

Similarities and Differences

In his comprehensive study of the Lutheran doctrine of justification, Gottfried Martens has summarized the results of sixteenth century exchanges between Lutheran and Roman Catholic theologians on the topic. Martens notes that when the lines hardened on both sides, in the decrees of the Council of Trent and Martin Chemnitz's examination of them, three fundamental points of agreement on justification between Rome and Wittenberg were clear. First, both sides agreed on the biblical basis of the doctrine and the necessity of expressing it through the proclamation of God's Word. Secondly, both sides agreed that justification takes place as the gracious action of the Triune God, and both taught that sinners under God's wrath because of their sin, unable to free themselves from Satan and the forces of darkness, are saved from condemnation by the reconciling work of Christ, performed because of the mercy of God and conveyed through what Lutherans call the means of grace. Thirdly, both sides agreed that justification effects a change; it creates a new reality in the life of the sinner.[1]

However, Martens notes two significant points of difference between Lutheran and Roman Catholic teaching on justification. The first is that Lutherans teach justification within the context of the proper distinction of Law and Gospel, with the affirmation that the forgiveness actually effects the death of the sinner and the bestowal of a fully righteous life in God's sight; Roman Catholics view justification as part of a gradual healing process. Second, the two theological programs operate with different understandings of reality. The Lutheran confession of the faith presumes that the new reality in the sinner's life, which God's grace speaks into existence through the forgiveness of sins, is in no way dependent on the sinner's performance of God's Law, produced by divine grace. Reality is defined by God's gracious Word of forgiveness that creates new life in Christ. Believers' reaction to that grace, in both trust and deeds of love, according to the Lutheran understanding, is the product of the new reality, the sainthood bestowed by God's act of new creation through his Word. Roman Catholic focus falls instead upon the sinner and insists that justification, the creation of a reborn child of God, is complete only when human actions are taken into account. The reality of the new person living in grace is measured in terms of human performance, behavior, actions. Even if these actions are produced only with the assistance of God's grace, which is the case according to Thomas Aquinas and many other Roman Catholic theologians, the Lutherans viewed any such focus upon human performance as a denial or compromise of the biblical doctrine of justification.[2]

Martin Chemnitz anticipated Martens' assessment in his *Examination of the Council of Trent*, but he expressed the key disagreement between himself and the theologians of the Council with slightly different terminology.

> For it is regarding the good works of the regenerate, or the new obedience, that there is now the chief controversy between the papalists and us, namely, whether the regenerate are justified by that newness which the Holy Spirit works in them and by the good works which follow from that renewal; that is, whether the newness, the virtues, or good works of the regenerate are the things by which they can stand in the judgment of God that they may not be condemned, on account of which they have a gracious and propitiated God, to which they should look, on which they should rely, in which they should trust when they are dealing with that difficult question, how we may be children of God and be accepted to eternal life.[3]

When Chemnitz addressed the teaching on justification propagated by the Council of Trent, he recognized that official Roman Catholic theology honored and emphasized God's grace in the salvation of sinners and that it did not deny an essential role to faith. It must be observed that the working definitions of those two terms in Chemnitz's writings and in the decrees of Trent differed significantly. Scholastic understanding of these words was based upon an Aristotelian conceptual framework, and Luther had returned to biblical presuppositions in defining grace as God's favor toward his human creatures and faith as trust and reliance upon God, who loves fallen sinners in Christ. But these definitions were not the point at which Chemnitz perceived a critical difference between the soteriology of the followers of Martin Luther and the leading theologians faithful to Rome. That crucial difference lay in the understanding of what renders believers righteous in God's sight, of what the believer's righteousness before God consists.

Luther's Two Kinds of Righteousness

In fact, a series of disputes between the Wittenberg reformer and his Roman opponents revealed a profound difference in the understanding of justification: for instance, the indulgence controversy over the nature of repentance, and the controversy with Erasmus over the bondage or freedom of human choice. But Chemnitz focused on the definition of the righteousness of the sanctified human creature. It cut to the heart of Luther's critique of medieval doctrines of salvation and to his fundamental paradigm shift in Western Christian teaching on the relationship between the creator and His human creatures. Luther had called the distinction of the two kinds of righteousness "our theology" in 1535, and his appraisal of what it means to be human in terms of the distinction between passive and active righteousness shaped Chemnitz's assessment of the decrees of Trent regarding justification.

Luther first formulated his distinction between two ways of being righteous as a human being in 1518 with the publication of his sermons on three kinds of righteousness and then on two kinds of righteousness.[4] He developed the concept further in subsequent writings, particularly in his Galatians lectures of 1531, published in commentary form in 1535.

> This is our theology, by which we teach a precise distinction between these two kinds of righteousness, the active and the passive, so that morality and faith, works and grace, secular society and religion may not be confused. Both are necessary, but both must be kept within their limits.[5]

Luther's distinction between two kinds of righteousness—two ways in which we are human creatures—parallels Jesus' distinction between two ways of fulfilling the Law: loving God with all our heart, soul, and mind, and loving our neighbors as our selves (Mt 22:37, 39). Righteousness, Luther observed, has many meanings. It can refer to political righteousness, ceremonial righteousness, the moral righteousness of the decalogue; all are genuine forms of righteousness. "Over and above there is the righteousness of faith."[6] Luther defined "this most excellent righteousness, the righteousness of faith, which God imputes to us through Christ without works" as a "merely passive righteousness."

> For here we work nothing, render nothing to God; we only receive and permit someone else to work in us, namely, God. Therefore it is

appropriate to call the righteousness of faith or Christian righteousness "passive." This is the righteousness hidden in a mystery, which the world does not understand. In fact, Christians themselves do not adequately understand it or grasp it in the midst of their temptations.[7]

Although Luther did not use the analogy of the relationship of child to parents and siblings to one another to explain his concept of two kinds of righteousness, this analogy is a helpful basis of comparison. The relationship between creator and creatures is essentially different from relationships among the creatures. Parents establish the fundamental, core identity of their children; parents bear responsibility for their children in ways that no sibling or other caretaker—by definition—can. Parents bestow life. They program their children's genetic identity, and they mold the understanding and behavior of their offspring through loving care in unique ways. Siblings, friends, and acquaintances relate to each other in quite different ways than the ways in which human beings relate to parents. Siblings live with each other in interdependence, shaped by mutual obligations of service and love appropriate to their age, abilities, and other factors. These two different spheres of relationship issue from—and express themselves in—God's design for our humanity. God is creator of his human creatures and alone is responsible for their identity. From that identity as his creatures and children proceeds the performance of activities which reflect that identity. Human creatures identify themselves as God's creatures when they live according to that identity which God has given them.

Luther taught that human life exists on two planes of dependence and interdependence, in two spheres of relationship: vertical—God both above us (because He is lord and author of the life of His children) and beneath us (because He is the loving Father who lifts us up and cuddles us to Himself in Christ)—and horizontal. The horizontal sphere binds us to other creatures through the God-given responsibilities of daily life. In the vertical relationship, according to God's design, we are children: trusting, dependent children. In the horizontal relationships, God has made us to act in an adult manner. God's human creatures are right—really human—in their vertical relationship because their faith clutches the God who loves them through Jesus Christ with the confident trust and total dependence and reliance on Him who defines their identity. They are right—really human—in their horizontal relationship with God's other creatures when they live a life which is active in reflecting His love through the deeds that deliver His care and concern. Two spheres and kinds of relationship demand two different ways of being right or righteous.

Thus, Luther proposed a radically new framework for thinking about what it means to be human to the discussion of late medieval theology. Revolutionary was his distinction between the identity which God as creator gives to His creatures and the performance or activities with which that identity expresses itself within the relationships God has fashioned for human life. Luther compared the righteousness of our identity to the earth as it receives the blessing of rain.

> As the earth itself does not produce rain and is unable to acquire it by its own strength, worship, and power but receives it only by a heavenly gift from above, so this heavenly righteousness is given to us by God without our work or merit. As much as the dry earth of itself is able to accomplish and obtain the right and blessed rain, that much can we human creatures accomplish by our own strength and works to obtain that divine, heavenly, and eternal righteousness. Thus we can obtain it only through the free imputation and indescribable gift of God.[8]

That leads the Christian conscience to say,

> I do not seek active righteousness. I ought to have and perform it; but I declare that even if I did have and perform it, I cannot trust in it or stand up before the judgment of God on the basis of it. Thus I put myself beyond all active righteousness, all righteousness of my own or of the divine law, and I embrace only the passive righteousness which is the righteousness of grace, mercy, and the forgiveness of sins.[9]

Luther taught the righteousness of human works. God created human creatures to love one another and to exhibit their humanity in the good works He has ordained. But this righteousness does not define their core identity. It does not make them righteous in God's sight. In His presence they are righteous only because of His favor, His mercy, His love, which elicits the human response of trust in Him alone.

Defining Human Righteousness in Augsburg, 1530

It was this understanding of justification that Melanchthon presented to Emperor Charles V in Augsburg in 1530. Melanchthon confessed quite simply, in article four of his confession, "We cannot obtain forgiveness of sins and righteousness before God through our merit, work, or satisfactions . . . we receive forgiveness of sins and become righteous before God out of grace for Christ's sake through faith."[10] Luther's colleague reiterated this position in article twenty of the Augsburg Confession: "our works cannot reconcile us with God or obtain grace." "Good works should and must be done, not that a person relies on them to earn grace, but for God's sake and to God's praise."[11]

Charles and his theological advisors could not understand. Charles himself was educated under the tutelage of Adrian Dedel, later Pope Adrian VI, a proponent of an Erasmian reform program, who imbued his young charge with a concern for the improvement of ecclesiastical life.[12] But Charles' concept of reform did not grow beyond the concern for institutional and moral renewal of the church; he never came to understand Luther's call for the reformation of teaching. He could not grasp the shift of paradigm which Luther brought to Western Christian understanding of Scripture. Throughout his reign the coterie of religious advisors in his employ included a number of Erasmian reformers, although the number of more ardent papal loyalists (who tended to favor a stricter adherence to medieval standards) among his ecclesiastical advisors rose again in the 1540s.[13] Nonetheless, regardless of differences in details, the teaching formulated by Charles' theologians from 1530 through his retirement in 1555 followed a fairly consistent line of thinking in defining grace, faith, and human righteousness.

For all those in Charles' company the chief questions of theology circled around the issue of authority in the church and thus around ecclesiology. Luther's paradigm shift placed the question of the identity of the sinner in God's sight at the heart of the theological enterprise. Luther's proclamation of a new human identity based alone on God's grace and his assertion that only God's grace bestows merit and worthiness in His sight—through faith apart from any and every performance of God's plan for human obedience—demanded a response from the imperial-papal establishment. It not only seemed to threaten public order. It challenged a basic premise of all medieval theological systems: that human identity in God's sight is based upon human performance of God's commands.

All medieval theologians agreed that sinners needed the help of grace to produce the works that completed what God enables through His gift of grace, but all also presumed that there is only one kind of human righteousness. Thus, they fashioned a definition of grace that did not undercut the only kind of righteousness they understood: keeping the law—the righteousness of human performance. They defined the grace that effects salvation as an entity understandable within an Aristotelian concept of reality, a *habitus* that God places within us. Luther's and Melanchthon's opponents clearly wanted to reject any complete denial of God's grace, every attempt to place human confidence upon works alone with no reference to grace. They probably recognized that this was indeed a problem in popular piety, even though Luther's criticism had made it difficult for them to admit it.

The committee which Charles appointed to the task of refuting the errors of the Augsburg Confession had to try several times before its members produced a confutation of the Augsburg Confession sufficiently conciliatory to find the emperor's acceptance, yet precise enough in regard to justification to defend the presupposition that human works performed on the basis of grace do have merit in God's sight. Charles' religious policy sought reconciliation with his Evangelical subjects on the basis of a refined and reformed version of medieval dogma and practice.[14] That is what the Confutation of the Augsburg Confession finally presented. It responded to Melanchthon's view of justification in part as follows:

> In the fourth article [of the Augsburg Confession] the Pelagians are condemned. They judged that human beings could merit eternal life by their own powers and without the grace of God. This condemnation is in accord with the catholic faith and is consistent with the early councils. It is also clearly in agreement with Holy Scripture. John the Baptist says: "No one is able to receive anything except what has been given from heaven," John 3 (:27).

Further biblical evidence is cited from Jas 1:17, 2 Cor 3:5, Jn 6:44, and 1 Cor 4:7.[15] The Confutation continues, however, with the critical discussion of human merit:

> However, to reject human merit, which is acquired through the assistance of divine grace, is to agree with the Manicheans and not the catholic church. St. Paul says: "I have fought the good fight, I have finished the race, I have kept the faith. From now on there is reserved for me the crown of righteousness, which the Lord, the righteous judge, will give me on that day," 2 Timothy 4 (:7–8).

Further support was marshaled from 2 Cor 5:10, Gn 15:1, Is 40:10, Is 58:7–8, Gn 4:7, Mt 20:8, and 1 Cor 3:8. The Confutation continued, "All Catholics admit that our works of themselves have no merit but God's grace makes them worthy to earn eternal life."[16] The worth of these works, produced by grace, justifies penitent sinners by producing the performance of the only kind of human righteousness medieval theologians could conceive: human fulfillment of the Law. They knew of no other proof that they were God's children than their good behavior. That the Father could love His chosen children for no good reason apart from His mercy and could take delight simply in their trust, undermined the entire medieval understanding of what humanity is.

In his Apology, Melanchthon devoted thirty percent of his pages to the doctrine of justification. He presumed Luther's distinction between active and passive righteousness, and he countered claims that human worthiness before God rests upon, or rises from, human performance in any way, whether it was wrought by grace or not. "Because faith, which freely receives the forgiveness of sins, sets against the wrath of God Christ as the mediator and propitiator, it does not offer up our merits or our love."[17] Melanchthon used the example of Abraham, who also after he was reborn knew that he was God's chosen child only because of the favor of the Lord.

> He realized that God keeps a promise on account of his faithfulness and not on account of our works or merits. Terrified hearts are unable to find rest if they are supposed to think that they please God

on account of their own works or their own love or the fulfilling of the law, because sin clings to the flesh and always accuses us. However, hearts only find rest when in these terrors they are convinced that we please God because he has promised, and that God keeps his promise on account of his faithfulness, and not on account of our worthiness.[18]

Thus, "Faith brings this peace not because it is a worthwhile work in and of itself, but only because it receives the promise that is offered and does not look upon its own worthiness."[19] This is true, Melanchthon insisted, not only when believers first come to faith. "Christ does not stop being our mediator after we are reborn. They err who imagine that he has merited only a first infusion of grace and that afterward we please God and merit eternal life by our fulfillment of the law. Christ remains the mediator, and we must always affirm that because of him we have a gracious God, even though we are unworthy."[20] Pastoral concerns coincided with biblical truth in Melanchthon's mind in this case, for "if we had to believe that after our renewal we must become acceptable not by faith on account of Christ but on account of our keeping of the law, our conscience would never find rest. Instead, it would be driven to despair."[21]

Defining Righteousness in Leipzig, 1539

Melanchthon's argument did not persuade his opponents. The debate continued, raged, in the 1530s, and the emperor's impatience grew. He pressed for a settlement of the religious differences within his German domains. He was not alone. Duke George of Saxony was particularly concerned to secure the obedience of the churches in his lands to Rome as he grew older and as his elder son Johann died, leaving George's Lutheran brother Heinrich the heir apparent to his throne. In secret negotiations in Leipzig in January 1539, with Georg Witzel representing the Roman church and Martin Bucer and Philip Melanchthon the Evangelical, an attempt was made to bridge the gap between the two sides. A former Wittenberg student who had once attached himself to Luther's movement, Witzel represented an Erasmian interpretation of medieval catholic teaching and sought reform along Erasmian lines. In the statement that Bucer composed for Duke George's consideration, the topic of justification was, of course, treated.

> When the Lord, moved alone by His mercy, sends His human crea-
> tures His holy Word and gives it to them so that they may trust in it;
> that is, when they recognize and feel on the basis of the Law their sin
> and corruption, and have true remorse and heartfelt regret, and on the
> basis of the Gospel recognize and believe that God has pardoned all
> their sins by His grace, through the merit of His Son, our Lord Jesus,
> and will give them eternal life; then they are made righteous in God's
> sight, a child of God and heir of everlasting salvation, through this
> faith, without any human contribution.[22]

But inevitably, comments about works had to follow. In this statement they are not formulated in a way that clearly distinguishes between two kinds of righteousness. "Because such people live in Christ the Lord and Christ in them, in their lives follow necessarily good works as good fruit comes from a good, healthy tree . . . for the good works [done] in true faith and love are necessary for salvation." Grace and the merit of works come together as the article on justification comes to an end with the words:

> That God accepts the good works of believers and so graciously and
> richly rewards them is not due to the worth of the works in themselves,
> as said above, but rests on the grace and merit of Christ, through
> which God accepts the persons who believe in His fatherly love and
> favor; therefore, their works and activity please Him.[23]

This statement could be understood evangelically but also preserves the possibility of defining righteousness as human performance.

Defining Righteousness in Regensburg, 1541

The Leipzig conference did not produce immediate results, and the emperor pressed on. He inaugurated his grandest attempt at reconciliation of the Lutheran and Roman Catholic estates of his empire at a series of meetings that began in Hagenau in summer 1540,

continued at Worms, and climaxed the following year in negotiations held during the imperial diet at Regensburg. Melanchthon and
Bucer led the Evangelical team; Johann Eck and the reform-minded
cardinal Gasparo Contarini were the leading minds who engaged
them. Although this religious dialogue finally failed because of the
unbridgeable differences on the Lord's Supper (that is, the mass and
transubstantiation) and on ecclesiology (particularly papal authority), a common confession on justification was reached. Indeed, its
authors were not completely satisfied with it, but it does reveal the
extent of agreement between reform-minded adherents of Rome and
some of the most influential theologians of the Evangelical churches.
In part its text reads as follows:

> No human being can be reconciled to God, be liberated from slavery
> to sin, except through the one mediator between God and human
> creatures, Christ, through whose grace, as the apostle says to the
> Romans, we are not only reconciled to God but also freed from slav-
> ery to sin—and also made partakers of the divine nature and children
> of God. Likewise, it is clear that adults do not obtain these benefits of
> Christ without the prevenient movement of the Holy Spirit, by whom
> their minds and hearts are moved to detest sin. For it is impossible,
> as Augustine says, to begin the new life without prior penitence. . . .
> For the human mind is moved by the Holy Spirit toward God by
> Christ. And this movement takes place through faith, through which
> the human mind, believing with certainty all those things which were
> handed down by God, most certainly and without doubt assents to
> the promises given to us by God. . . . [Faith] takes form in trust,
> on account of the promise of God, by which the remission of sins
> is promised by grace and adoption as sons to those who believe in
> Christ, those who repent of prior vice, and who by this faith are
> lifted up to God by the Holy Spirit and receive the Holy Spirit, the
> remission of sins, the imputation of righteousness, and countless
> other gifts.

However, the justification of the sinner only begins with this
faith and the imputation of righteousness. Because Contarini, Eck,
and the other Roman Catholic representatives could think of human
righteousness only in terms of keeping the Law, they had to build in

a second stage of justification to meet the demand for human performance as well. The terminology "duplex iustitia" which expresses
this concept was used by Luther to designate two realms or kinds of
righteousness: in relationship to God and in relationship to other
human beings. The Roman Catholic party at Regensburg used this
term instead to designate two stages of becoming righteous in God's
sight. The text of the Regensburg Book continues:

> That nevertheless happens to no one apart from, at the same time,
> cleansing love be infused into the will so that a cleansed will, as
> St. Augustine said, begins to fulfill the Law. A faith that is living
> is that which receives the mercy of God in Christ and believes
> the righteousness which is in Christ is imputed to him by grace,
> and at the same time accepts the promise of the Holy Spirit and
> love. Thus, faith that justifies is that faith which is at work through
> love. . . . Indeed, although the inheritance of eternal life is owed to
> the reborn because of the promise, and they are first of all reborn in
> Christ, nonetheless, God rewards their good works, not according
> to the substance of their works or according to that which is from
> us, but insofar as they are done in faith and are from the Holy Spirit
> who dwells in us, running with our free choice doing its own part.[24]

God's grace is primary, but for the critical test of righteousness the
focus finally falls on human works. Produced by grace though they
may be, they are still what defines human righteousness in God's
sight. Even those Evangelical theologians who had composed the
statement were troubled by this denial of the sovereign creative activity of God's Word of death for sinners and their life-bestowing restoration to being children of God. The opposition in Rome, however,
was even greater to any such settlement with the German schismatics
and heretics.

Regensburg indeed tried to find common language upon which
to build a common confession regarding salvation. It did so without
clarifying positive teaching through explicit rejections of those ideas
that undermine the truth. Therefore, the definition of what constitutes humanity, or human righteousness, in God's sight was not made
clear, and grace and faith were not placed within the context of a
biblical understanding of the creative and re-creative Word of God,

the unconditional and unconditioned favor and mercy of the creator and re-creator. "The result is a theology of mediation that is shaped by Roman-Catholic, Thomistic concerns."[25]

Defining Righteousness in Augsburg, 1548

With the collapse of his plans at Regensburg, Charles slowly shifted his religious policy. One last show of openness to a negotiated settlement, at the next diet held at Regensburg in 1546, where the emperor also sponsored a dialogue between Evangelical and Roman Catholic theologians, was only a political ploy. Imperial plans for war against the leading Lutheran princes, Johann Friedrich of Saxony and Philip of Hesse, were well advanced by the time the colloquy began in January 1546. In fact, Charles' leading spokesman, Pedro de Malvenda, did not build on the consensus of 1541 but repeated a doctrine of salvation with more emphasis on human works and merit than the previous Regensburg document contains.

Within six months the emperor initiated hostilities. Johann Friedrich and Philip went down to defeat and to prison. The emperor held the power to dictate a religious settlement, and he did so, laying down its foundations in a document popularly dubbed "the Augsburg Interim." Its authors, following the lead of the Erasmian humanist reformer Johannes Gropper, led by two like-minded Roman Catholic leaders also inclined toward reform, Julius Pflug and Michael Helding, treated the topic of justification in some detail:

> Those who are redeemed by the precious blood of Christ and to whom the merit of Christ's passion is applied, are justified immediately, that is, they find forgiveness of their sins, are absolved from the guilt of eternal damnation and renewed through the Holy Spirit. In this manner the unrighteous are made righteous.

But for Gropper, Pflug, and Helding justification was a two-step process. They did not distinguish between two kinds of righteousness but rather between two stages of righteousness or justification in God's sight. The Augsburg Interim continues:

For when God justifies, he does not act only in a human way with people, by merely ignoring their sin, forgiving them the sin, and absolving them from guilt, but he also makes them better, something that human beings are not accustomed to granting and cannot grant. For God shares with them the Holy Spirit, who purifies the heart and rouses it through the love poured out in the same heart, so that they desire what is good and just and with good works pursue what God desires.

That is the true kind of inherent righteousness [the righteousness of human performance] that David desired when he delivered these words: "Create in me a clean heart, O God, and put a new and right spirit within me" [Psalm 51:10]. . . .

Therefore, since as long they live here on earth, people cannot attain the full perfection of inherent righteousness, Christ . . . most graciously hastens to help us also in this situation. Since, just as through sharing his righteousness he produces inherent righteousness in the one with whom he shares it, so also he increases it, so that it is renewed from day to day, until that person is fully perfected in the eternal fatherland. And through the merit of his precious blood and righteousness, which is perfect, he procures indulgence for people, so that what they cannot perform adequately because of their infirmity is obtained and granted through the perfection of Christ himself. . . .

Thus, Christ's merits and inherent righteousness come together, and we are renewed in them by the gift of love. They are inherent, so that we may thereby live "self-controlled, upright, and godly lives in this world, while we are waiting for our blessed hope, the manifestation of the glory of our great God and Savior" [Titus 2:12–13]. But Christ's merit is involved, so that it may be a cause of our inherent righteousness and so that in the same merit and precious blood of Christ we may recover and find that by it we are able to be strengthened in the hope of eternal life most firmly since we stumble and fall in many matters, and because of our weakness and imperfection many things happen that disturb our hearts and are able to tempt us to despair.[26]

The Interim dedicated a separate article to the topic, "On the Manner by Which the Human Creature Receives Justification." In it occurs the only passage repeated by the electoral Saxon theologians as they composed the so-called "Leipzig Interim":

Since God does not justify human beings on the basis of the works of righteousness that they do, but gratuitously, that is, without his merit, if they want to glory, let them glory in Christ alone, by whose merit alone they are redeemed from sin and justified. Yet the merciful God does not deal with such people as with a dead block of wood, but draws them through acts of will, if they are of the age of reason. For such people do not receive those benefits of Christ, unless his mind and will are moved by the prevenient grace of God to detest sin.[27]

After establishing the necessity of the faith created by prevenient grace, the Interim continues:

And those who rest through such faith on the mercy of God and the merit of Christ and entrust themselves to his mercy and merit receive the promise of the Holy Spirit, and so they are justified through faith in God according to the Scriptures. Not only is their sin remitted, but they are also sanctified and renewed through the Holy Spirit. For this faith obtains the gift of the Holy Spirit, through which the love of God is poured out into our hearts. To the extent that love is added to faith and hope, to that extent we are truly justified by inherent righteousness. For this righteousness is made up of faith, hope, and love, so that if you would subtract any of these from their righteousness from it, you would clearly leave it incomplete.[28]

Melanchthon's harsh critique of the Augsburg Interim was published in July, little more than a month after its promulgation by Charles V, and it was followed by a number of other sharp rejections of this document, not only but certainly in large part because its teaching on justification. Although his treatment of the articles on justification in the Interim was much longer, it can be summarized with his first words on them: "the book clearly holds that righteousness consists in love."[29] To rely on God's grace and to praise the role of faith was not enough to appease the Lutheran confessors in the years after Luther's death. They insisted that justification supply a righteousness beyond the righteousness of human performance.

Defining Righteousness in Trent, 1545

By the time the Augsburg Interim was composed, the Council of Trent had already formulated its doctrine of justification. Appeasing Lutherans was not the intention of those theologians assembled in Trent in the months immediately preceding the Smalcald War, in early 1546. Their decree on justification was wrought in the midst of intense maneuvering between two camps of theologians loyal to Rome, who had a longer history of disagreement over the role of human merit in attaining God's acceptance. The one school of thought, represented by the Dominicans who were engaged in the revival of Thomism, and Augustinians who were reading more of Augustine than had been read for centuries, stressed the prevenient nature of grace.[30] Nothing happens in the sinner's mind and will apart from God's grace coming first to effect change. On the other hand, Franciscans who were continuing to teach elements of Scotist and Ockhamist theology placed human performance and merit in a more central role in the sinner's salvation. It was the desire of all these fathers at the council to reject Luther's heresy on salvation by grace through faith alone, not because they did not believe that God's grace and the response of faith were vitally important for salvation but because Luther had rejected any role for human merit, even that produced by grace, in establishing human righteousness in God's sight. Therefore, they taught:

> People are disposed for that justice when, roused and helped by divine grace and attaining the faith that comes from hearing, they are moved freely towards God and believe to be true what has been divinely revealed and promised, and in particular that the wicked are justified by God by his grace through the redemption which is in Christ Jesus. At the same time, acknowledging that they are sinners, they turn from fear of divine justice, which profitably strikes them, to thoughts of God's mercy; they rise to hope, with confidence that God will be favorable to them for Christ's sake; and they begin to love him as the fount of all righteousness.[31]
>
> This disposition and preparation [in Baptism or in coming to faith as an adult] precede the actual justification, which consists not only in the forgiveness of sins but also in the sanctification and renewal

of the inward being by a willing acceptance of the grace and gifts whereby someone from being unjust becomes just, from being an enemy becomes a friend, so that he is an heir in hope of eternal life. . . . Consequently, in that process of justification, together with the forgiveness of sins, a person receives, through Jesus Christ into whom he is grafted, all these infused at the same time: faith, hope and charity. For faith, unless hope is added to it, and charity, too, neither unites him perfectly with Christ nor makes him a living member of His body.[32]

Recognizing that terminological clarity is important, the fathers at Trent then defined "how it should be understood that the ungodly is justified by faith and grace":

We are said to be justified by faith because faith is the first stage of human salvation, the foundation and root of all justification, without which it is impossible to please God and to come to the fellowship of his children. And we are said to receive justification as a free gift because nothing that precedes justification, neither faith or works, would merit the grace of justification.[33]

It must be noted that the word for "merit" in this last citation points to a finely crafted compromise within the council itself, which bridged the gap between Thomists and Ockhamists, between the more Augustinian and the less Augustinian wings of the church of Rome. Late medieval usage of two verbs, "mereri" and "promereri," establishes a significant difference for theological definition between the two. "Mereri" means simply "to merit," in any way. "Promereri" means "to merit fully," "to merit completely," or "truly." The drafters of the Tridentine decree used "promereri," a word which made the sentence acceptable to those who defended the place of human merit and human performance in the process of salvation.[34] Thus, the council left room for those who taught with Luther's *bete noir*, Gabriel Biel, that doing your best is necessary to attain the initial grace that makes works truly meritorious.[35]

For Martin Chemnitz, whether his opponents taught that prevenient grace produces all works of any worth in God's sight, or instead that works without inherent worth win grace for the production of truly worthy works, made little difference. Any human performance, any human merit, conceived of in any way, has no place in justification, Chemnitz argued. Having identified the difference between the Roman party and the Lutheran confession of the faith as the question of what constitutes human righteousness in God's sight after rebirth, as a believing child of God, Chemnitz contended that Paul's "excluding phrases," the *particulae exclusivae*—such as "without the works of the Law" and "by grace alone"—required defining the trust that God creates as the response to His love for the human creature as that which makes believers righteous in God's sight. Abraham was his example. Paul talked about him in Romans 4 both before and after his conversion from idolatry.

> But when he had obeyed God in faith for a number of years from the very beginning of his call, from Genesis chapters eleven through fifteen, then he was certainly renewed in the spirit of his mind and adorned with many outstanding works and fruits of the Spirit, according to Hebrews 11:8–10. In the very middle of the course of the good works of Abraham, Moses in the Old Testament and Paul in the New Testament put the question: "What then was the justification of Abraham before God for the inheritance of life eternal?" It is to this already regenerate Abraham, adorned with spiritual newness and with many good works, that Paul applies these statements: "To one who does not work but trusts Him who justifies the ungodly, his faith is reckoned as righteousness." To this Abraham he applies also this statement: "David pronounces a blessing upon the man to whom God reckons righteousness apart from works." But that at that time the already regenerate Abraham was certainly not without good works but had performed many truly good works through faith, the Epistle to the Hebrews testifies in chapter eleven. And yet the Holy Spirit through Paul clearly removes and takes away from the operation and works of the renewed Abraham the praise and glory of justification before God to life eternal.[36]

The same could be said of Paul himself, according to Chemnitz.

> The apostle Paul says of his works which he performed while he was a Pharisee, before his conversion, Philippians 3:4–7: "If any other man thinks he has reason for confidence in the flesh, I have more; . . . as

to righteousness under the Law blameless. But whatever gain I had, I counted as loss for the sake of Christ." However, of the works which he did after his renewal, when he had labored more than the others, what, I say, does he say concerning them with respect to the article of justification? Let the reader examine the passage, and he will find that Paul not only uses the past tense of hJgou'mai ("I count") for the works that preceded his conversion but that he also by means of the particle ajlla; menou'n ("indeed") moves forward and uses the present tense hJgou'mai to show that also after his renewal he does not attribute to his works his justification before God to life eternal. On the contrary, when trust in righteousness before God to life eternal is patched on these works, he declares them to be refuse and loss. And he shows at the same time what was his righteousness before God to life eternal at the time when he wrote this epistle from prison, yes, what will be his righteousness, when he attains to the resurrection of the dead.

That righteousness Chemnitz defined as "that which is through faith in Christ, the righteousness from God which depends on faith."[37] Chemnitz knew but one source and cause for the righteousness which human creatures bring before God: God's favor, His unconditional and undeserved mercy.

Martin Chemnitz had begun to speak out in the public discussion of biblical teaching, as a young librarian in Königsberg, when Andreas Osiander set forth his interpretation of Luther's doctrine of justification. It did not rest upon an Aristotelian conceptual framework, but rather on Platonic conceptions. Osiander did not share Luther's understanding of the power of God's Word, and so he rejected what he understood as a forensic doctrine of justification that involved God in lying about sinners, calling them righteous when they were not. He did not understand that Luther's nominalistic presuppositions, derived from the Old Testament, defined reality as that which God says exists. Instead, he placed the divine nature in the human creature to give it righteousness because only the divine could give the sinner the corrective to the weakness that sin induced. Chemnitz recognized that God's love and favor, expressed in His forgiving Word, based upon Christ's obedience to the Father in dying and rising for sinners, establishes the new reality of His new creation, the believer.

Righteousness before God lies in the mercy of God, effected through Christ, apprehended by the human creature's trust in Him.

Thus, when Chemnitz encountered a different doctrine of grace, faith, and righteousness in the teaching of Trent, he returned to his critique of Osiander, and he reaffirmed what Melanchthon had confessed at Augsburg, that no human merit can make the sinner righteous in God's sight. Truly righteous human works are produced by those whom God has made righteous through His Word of recreation in Christ, on the basis of His mercy alone. He incorporated this position in the Formula of Concord. There he taught,

> In order that the troubled heart may have a reliable and certain comfort and that Christ's merit and God's grace may be given the honor due them, Scripture teaches that the righteousness of faith before God consists only in the gracious reconciliation or forgiveness of sins [Rom. 4:6–8; 2 Cor. 5:19–21]. This he bestowed upon us out of sheer grace solely because of the merits of Christ our mediator, and it is received only by faith in the promise of the gospel. Therefore, in the justification of the sinner before God, faith relies neither on contrition nor on love or other virtues, but only on Christ and (in him) on his perfect obedience, with which he fulfilled the law for us and which is reckoned to believers as righteousness. Thus, neither contrition nor love nor other virtues, but faith alone, is the sole means and instrument with which and through which we may receive and accept God's grace, the merit of Christ, and the forgiveness of sins, which are delivered to us in the promise of the gospel.[38]

* * *

The accord reached between the Lutheran World Federation and the Roman Catholic Church in the "Joint Declaration on the Doctrine of Justification" has opened a new chapter in the confession of Lutheran insights into the biblical teaching regarding the justification of fallen sinners. The purpose of ecumenical exchange was modeled in the confession at Augsburg. In that conversation among Christians, Melanchthon aimed to confess God's truth clearly for the sake of His people. The exposition of biblical teaching and pastoral care are inextricably linked in Lutheran confession of the faith throughout the sixteenth century. Both the concern for the pastoral care of terrified consciences and the clear enunciation of Luther's insight into the biblical way of thinking about the salvation of sinners are inadequately expressed in the common declaration on justification. At too many points where Luther's distinction of two ways of being human could have helped, no definition of righteousness is given, and the classical Roman Catholic definitions of grace, faith, and righteousness continue to function. Therefore, the task of Lutheran confessing at the beginning of the twenty-first century must assert again the best of what we have to offer our brothers and sisters in the whole household of faith. The assertion of Luther's understanding of the two dimensions of humanity, and God's action to restore our righteousness in His sight through Christ, remains our challenge and calling in the years ahead.

Notes

1. Gottfried Martens, *Die Rechtfertigung des Sünders—Rettungshandeln Gottes oder historisches Interpretament? Grundentscheidungen lutherischer Theologie und Kirche bei der Behandlung des Themas "Rechtfertigung" im ökumenischen Kontext* (Göttingen: Vandenhoeck & Ruprecht, 1992), 112–14.

2. Ibid., 114–17.

3. Martin Chemnitz, *Examen concilii Tridentini*, ed. Eduard Preus (1861; Darmstadt: Wissenschaftliche Buchgesellschaft, 1972), 153. English translation: *Examination of the Council of Trent, Part I*, trans. Fred Kramer (Saint Louis: Concordia, 1971), 481–82.

4. WA 2: 145–52; AE 31:297–306.

5. WA 40^I:45.24–27; AE 26:7. For a summary of Luther's definition of "righteousness," and bibliography, see Bengt Hägglund, "Gerechtigkeit. VI. Reformations- und Neuzeit," *Theologische Realenzyklopädie* XII (Berlin: de Gruyter, 1984): 432–34, 440. See also the December 1998 Beiheft issue of *Zeitschrift für Theologie und Kirche* 95, on Luther's understanding of righteousness and justification, particularly as it pertains to the "Joint Declaration on the Doctrine of Justification" (which ignores Luther's distinction of the two kinds of righteousness); see especially Reinhard Schwarz, "Luthers Rechtfertigungslehre als Eckstein der christlichen Theologie und Kirche," pp. 15–46; and Robert Kolb, "Luther on the Two Kinds of Righteousness. Reflections on His Two-Dimensional Definition of Humanity at the Heart of His Theology," *Lutheran Quarterly* 13 (1999): 449–66.

6. WA 40^I:40.16–27; AE 26:4.

7. WA 40^I:41.15–26; AE 26:4–5.

8. WA 40^I:43.18–25; AE 26:6.

9. WA 40^I:42.26–43,15; AE 26:6.

10. K-W, 38–41; BKS, 56.

11. AC XX.9, 27; BKS, 76–77, 80; K-W, 54, 56.

12. See Ingetraut Ludolphy, *Die Voraussetzungen der Religionspolitik Karls V.* (Stuttgart: Calwer, 1965).

13. Horst Rabe, *Reichsbund und Interim, Die Verfassungs- und Religionspolitik Karls V. und der Reichstag von Augsburg 1547/1548* (Cologne/Vienna: Böhlau, 1971), 104–17.

14. See Gunther Wenz, *Theologie der Bekenntnisschriften der evangelisch-lutherischen Kirche, Band 1* (Berlin/New York: de Gruyter, 1996), 399–409.

15. *Die Confutatio der Confessio Augustana vom 3. August 1530,* ed. Hermann Immenkötter (Corpus Catholicorum 33, ed. 2; Münster: Aschendorff, 1979), 84/85. English translation in *Sources and Contexts of the Book of Concord,* ed. Robert Kolb and James A. Nestingen (Minneapolis: Fortress, 2001), 108.

16. *Confutatio,* 84–87; *Sources and Contexts,* 109.

17. Ap. IV.46, BKS, 169; K-W, 127.

18. Ap. IV.58, from the September 1531 revision of the text, here cited from the Latin Book of Concord of 1580 *Concordia . . .* (Leipzig, 1580), 72; K-W, 129.

19. Ap. IV.179, from the September 1531 revision of the text, *Concordia,* 92; K-W, 146.

20. Ap. IV.179, from the September 1531 revision of the text, *Concordia,* 93; K-W, 147.

21. Ap. IV.179, from the September 1531 revision of the text, *Concordia,* 94; K-W, 148.

22. *Martin Bucers Deutsche Schriften, Bd. 9/1, Religionsgespräche (1539–1541),* ed. Cornelis Augustijn (Gütersloh: Gütersloher Verlagshaus, 1995), 24–25.

23. *Bucers Deutsche Schriften,* 9/1: 24 and 25.

24. *Bucers Deutsche Schriften,* 9/1: 399 and 401.

25. Martens, *Die Rechtfertigung des Sünders,* 67.

26. *Das Augsburger Interim von 1548,* ed. Joachim Mehlhausen (ed. 2; Neukirchen: Neukirchener Verlag, 1996), 42–47; English translation in *Sources and Contexts,* 150–51.

27. *Das Augsburger Interim,* 4a8/49, *Sources and Contexts,* 152; cf. the text of the Leipzig Interim, *Corpus Reformatorum, Philippi Melanthonis Opera quae supersunt omnia,* ed. C. G. Bretschneider and H. E. Bindweil (Halle and Braunschweig: Schwetschke, 1834–60, henceforth CR), 7:51, *Sources and Contexts,* 185–89.

28. *Das Augsburger Interim,* 50/51, *Sources and Contexts,* 152.

29. CR 6:924–42, esp. 927.

30. See Hubert Jedin, *Girolamo Seripando, Sein Leben und Denken im Geisteskampf des 16. Jahrhunderts* (1937, Würzburg: Augustinus Verlag, 1984); and idem, *Papal Legate at the Council of Trent, Cardinal Seripando*, trans. Frederick C. Eckhoff (Saint Louis: Herder, 1947).

31. *Decrees of the Ecumenical Councils. Volume Two: Trent to Vatican II*, ed. Norman P. Tanner, S.J. (London: Sheed and Ward, and Washington: Georgetown University Press, 1990), 672–73 §6.

32. Ibid. §7.

33. Ibid., 674 §8.

34. Heiko A. Oberman, "Duns Scotus, Nominalism, and the Council of Trent," in *The Dawn of the Reformation: Essays in Late Medieval and Early Reformation Thought* (Edinburgh: T. & T. Clark, 1992), 217–18.

35. Heiko A. Oberman, *The Harvest of Medieval Theology: Gabriel Biel and Late Medieval Nominalism* (1963; Durham: Labyrinth, 1983), 131–84, esp. 132–34.

36. *Examen*, 154; *Examination*, 1:483.

37. *Examen*, 155; *Examination*, 1:486.

38. SD III.30–31: BKS, 924; K-W, 567.

6

Why the Two Kinds of Righteousness?

Charles P. Arand and Joel Biermann

Lutherans have long struggled with issues related to the distinction between justification and sanctification. They have affirmed justification as the teaching by which the church stands and falls. But when it comes to issues related to sanctification or Christian living, the question has been raised, "Do Lutherans shout justification but whisper sanctification?"[1] Do Lutherans turn to Lutheran theology for justification, but to the books and broadcasting of Evangelical "experts" in Christian living for guidance on the Christian life? The questions of justification and sanctification within the Christian community are not unrelated to questions raised by the wider human community, namely, what does it mean to be a human being? Who am I? What is the purpose and design of human life? Who is a human being? What is a person? What is it to be a human community? Since ancient times, these questions typically have been relegated to the purview of ethics. Ultimately, though, these are theological questions, questions that bring to the foreground the interrelationship between the divine works of creation and redemption.

Lutherans have resources for addressing the particular redemptive anthropological questions of justification and sanctification, as well as the wider anthropological issues related to our creational life. In the sixteenth century they accomplished this task by means of a theological matrix known as the two kinds of [human] righteousness.

This distinction is one of those elements that can be described as the "nervous system" running through the body of Christian teaching. With it they accomplished two tasks. On the one hand, they stressed the dignity of the human person given by God's Word of creation and again through His Word of justification on account of Christ, a Word received by faith alone. On the other hand, they recovered the value of ordinary activities (and with it the proper role of human ability) of daily life within our vocation as the sphere within which we try to live as God intended.

So important was this framework that Luther refers to the two kinds of righteousness as "our theology" in his famous *Galatians Commentary* [1535]. This work, regarded by Luther as his "apology" of the Augsburg Confession, represents the culmination of his thinking on the two kinds of righteousness. Luther had first hinted at it in the *Heidelberg Disputation* and then developed it in his *Sermon on Three Kinds of Righteousness* (1518),[2] his sermon on the *Two Kinds of Righteousness* (1519),[3] his *Sermon on Monastic Vows*,[4] and his Genesis sermons (1523/1527).[5] Similarly, Melanchthon identified the two kinds of righteousness as lying at the heart of the issue between him and his opponents in such a way that it shaped the entire theological argument in his masterwork, the *Apology of the Augsburg Confession;* although he had also been working with the presuppositions, it provided from as early as 1524.[6]

At Concordia Seminary a number of us believe that the distinction of the two kinds of righteousness has been neglected in recent Lutheran thought to the impoverishment of our lives as Lutherans today.[7] Thus faculty members have begun exploring the possibilities offered by the distinction to address a variety of issues today, from maintaining the Lutheran emphasis on justification, to providing us with ways of thinking about Christian living, to thinking about church and ministry. Robert Kolb has led the way with several writings on Luther's thought. These include "Luther on the Two Kinds of Righteousness: Reflections on His Two-Dimensional Definition of Humanity at the Heart of His Theology,"[8] "God Calling, 'Take Care of My People': Luther's Concept of Vocation in the Augsburg Confession and Its Apology,"[9] and "Mensch-Sein in Zwei Dimensionen, die Zweierlei Gerechtigkeit, und Luthers *De votis monasticis ludicium*" (forthcoming). Charles Arand has focused on Melanchthon with "Two Kinds of Righteousness as a Framework for

Law and Gospel in the Apology"[10] and has explored it more exten-
sively and systematically in "*Our Theology": Luther's Definition of the
Human Creature through "Two Kinds of Righteousness.*"[11] William
W. Schumacher has expounded its value for our understanding of the
two kingdoms in "Civic Participation by Churches and Pastors: An
Essay in Two Kinds of Righteousness."[12] Joel Biermann has brought
it into conversation with contemporary ethics in his dissertation,
"Virtue Ethics and the Place of Character Formation within Lutheran
Theology."[13] Several dissertations are exploring the use of the two
kinds of righteousness in different areas of Lutheran thought.[14] This
essay sketches in broad strokes the basic ideas of the two kinds of
righteousness and how they relate to the distinction of Law and
Gospel and the teaching of the two realms (more popularly known
as the two kindoms).

The Contours of the Two Kinds of Righteousness

Before describing the two kinds of righteousness, a word must be
said about the definition of righteousness. Righteousness has to do
with meeting God's "design specifications" for being a human creature and fulfilling the purpose for which God created us.[15] It has to
do with being fully human, that is, as God intended us to be when
He created us. Integral to His design, God created us as relational
beings; and human relationships take place within two fundamental
realms or arenas: we live before God (*coram Deo*), and before the
world (*coram mundo*). These realms are inhabited simultaneously;
we live in God's presence and at the same time in community with
one another where we have responsibility for fellow creatures. As
Luther put it, we inhabit two worlds "as it were, one of them heavenly
and the other earthly." These two worlds of human existence can be
plotted on two axes: a vertical axis for life with God and a horizontal
axis for life with our fellow human creatures and the non-human
creation. Righteousness, or being in a "right relationship," within
either realm is determined by the nature of the two respective relationships in which we find ourselves. Another way to put it is to say
that God designed these relationships to function in fundamentally
different ways. "Into these [two worlds] we place these two kinds of

righteousness, which are distinct and separated from each other."[16] And so in these two relationships we encounter a twofold definition of what it means to be the person God made us to be—hence two kinds of righteousness.[17]

On the one hand, human righteousness before God flows from God's activity toward us. Like human parents, God originally gave life to His creation apart from any contribution or participation from His creatures.[18] And so from the catechism, Lutheran believers have learned to confess that God has created us "out of sheer fatherly divine goodness and mercy, without any merit or worthiness in me." As His handiwork, we are by definition dependent and contingent beings who have been given life and who continue to live only from the reception of His gifts. We depend on the air we breathe, the food we eat, and the water we drink. Take these away, and we die. We are receivers in the presence of God. This receptive stance continues when God performs His work of redemption. When His human creatures lay dead in sin, God restored them to the fullness of their humanity through the self-sacrificial death and resurrection of His Son. He bestows the righteousness of Christ upon us as a gift, which alone consoles the troubled sinner. Being born anew, this also took place without any contribution or cooperative participation on our part. The Holy Spirit creates faith through the Gospel so that human beings can once again entrust all of life into God's care. In both instances, we can say that human beings "suffered" the work of God. In creation, God formed Adam from dust and breathed into him the breath of life. In redemption, the human creature lay on a slab in the morgue until God's miracle of revivification. Thus, before God (*coram Deo*) we are entirely passive, and so our righteousness is passive, not active.[19]

On the other hand, and at the same time, righteousness in the world with our fellow creatures (*coram mundo*) depends on our carrying out our God-entrusted tasks—tasks spelled out with sufficient specificity in the Law both revealed and written on human hearts—within our walks of life for the good of creation. God has created human beings as male and female to complement and complete one another. Together the first man and woman formed human community, and together they were given responsibility for tending God's creation. To guide them in their task, God hardwired His Law into the creation itself. At the same time, God has given human beings dominion in such a way that they have the freedom and responsibility to figure out how best to tailor that Law to the specific challenges and questions of daily life. Here God's gifts of human reason and imagination play critical roles in mediating the Law into our daily lives in such a way as to carry out God's ongoing work of preserving and promoting creaturely well-being. Human beings are created to carry out their God-given tasks for the well-being of both the human and non-human creation. Within the web of mutually constitutive human relationships, there exists a rich variety of ways to demonstrate and implement the human righteousness as designed by God. Within their relationships, humans stand accountable both to God and to their fellow creatures for how they carry out tasks for the well-being of life within the world. And so in the eyes of the world (*coram mundo*) our righteousness is ever active, never passive.[20]

Luther stressed that the two kinds of righteousness are not alternative forms of human existence. He did not see them as alternatives to one another, as if we could be fully human by possessing only one kind of righteousness, either the passive or the active. Luther did not compartmentalize the human being in such a way that one could be human by partly possessing passive righteousness and partly possessing active righteousness. To be a human being as God created us to be, a perfect human specimen, involves being totally passive—as a newborn child of God—and totally active—as a responsible neighbor to other people and to the whole of God's world. People need both kinds of righteousness in order to be completely and genuinely human. "We must be righteous before God and man. Without one or the other we find our humanity diminished."

The Relationship of the Two Kinds of Righteousness

The crux of the Lutheran Reformation rested on maintaining the distinction between the divine righteousness that is salvific before God and the human righteousness that is good for the world. In the Lutheran view, the medieval church failed to distinguish between these two kinds of righteousness. It had confused the two by giving human righteousness an ultimate significance before God that it does not and cannot possess. It disparaged faith as insufficient for salvation and for our relationship with God. But the corrective to medieval teaching was not to disparage good works. Luther insisted that to affirm both dimensions of human existence they must be kept distinct. "This is our theology, by which we teach a precise distinction between these two kinds of righteousness, the active and the passive, so that morality and faith, works and grace, secular society and religion may not be confused. Both are necessary, but both must be kept within their limits."[21] Only keeping each in its proper sphere, to use the words of Gerhard Ebeling, "truly lets creation be creation and redemption be redemption."[22]

The need to distinguish the two kind of righteousness necessitates that our active righteousness dare never become the basis for our righteousness *coram Deo*. For any attempt to bring works into the presence of God will lead to a rejection of the Creator-creature relationship whereby we receive our identity and life as children of God as a sheer gift. And so the Reformation teaching argued that standing before God in heaven, human beings must leave all works behind on earth and seek nothing but the righteousness of Christ that is received by faith. When terrors of conscience result from the recognition of one's inability to obtain salvation (Rome) or inability to find assurance of salvation (Pietism), it becomes dramatically obvious that active righteousness must remain on earth within the realm of our relationships with our fellow human creatures. Among Muslims the assurance of salvation is only found in martyrdom.

> But if it [the Law] wants to ascend into the conscience and exert its rule there, see to it that you are a good dialectician and make the correct distinction. Give no more to the law than it has coming, and say to it: "Law, you want to ascend into the realm of conscience and rule there. You want to denounce its sin and take away the joy of my heart, which I have through faith in Christ. You want to plunge me into despair, in order that I may perish. You are exceeding your jurisdiction. . . . You shall not touch my conscience. For I am baptized. . . ."[23]

By confusing the two kinds of righteousness, or by collapsing one into the other, the medieval church ultimately both undermined salvation and failed the neighbor. It failed the neighbor because it required that

I instrumentalize or objectify my neighbor by using him in order to obtain my salvation.[24] Unfortunately, this never works. When I wonder if I have done enough, the Law gives only one answer, "When in doubt, try harder!" Thus, striving to fulfill the Law as a means to righteousness before God, the focus is on us and not on Christ, and the neighbor is nothing more than a means to a self-serving end. Before God, one must ignore the Law and cling only to the Christ, who is delivered to us in the Word. Before God, the Law accomplishes its alien work and kills the sinner.

The danger posed by the Lutheran Reformation from the vantage point of its opponents' understanding of "faith alone" lay in a rejection of works that could undermine the social order and lead to anarchy. In fact, some placed responsibility for the Peasants' Revolt of 1525 squarely at the doorstep of Luther's Reformation with its emphasis on the freedom of the Christian person. In response, Luther argued that the righteousness of faith does not draw us out of the world or render life in the world as an inferior order of existence. Nor does it disparage the works of daily life as inadequate expressions of Christian living in favor of pursuing "spiritual" or so-called distinctively Christian forms of living. To the contrary, Luther stressed that the passive righteousness of faith does not remain relevant only for realities in heaven; it belongs also to earthly realities and contributes to the pursuit of active righteousness within the world. "When I have this [passive] righteousness within me, I descend from heaven like the rain that makes the earth fertile. That is, I come forth into another kingdom and I perform good works whenever the opportunity arises."[25] One could even say that as faith grows it revitalizes—and, indeed finally establishes—our life in this world so that others may for the first time see how God intended human beings to live for one another and in relation to the environment. Our relation to God empowers and provides the basis for our relation to creation. And so on earth, as we grow in faith we actively pursue a life of works and virtues in accordance with God's will for creation and His reclamation of creation in Christ.

Maintaining the distinction between the two kinds of righteousness allows us to affirm both dimensions of our humanity. The passive righteousness of faith brings about our salvation by restoring our creaturely relationship with God. The active righteousness of works serves the wellbeing of creation by looking after our neighbor and God's creation. This is not to say that a tension does not exist between affirming the Gospel of the forgiveness of sins along with the new identity that it brings as a child of God, while at the same time emphasizing the Creator's expectations for His restored creatures. This side of eternity, humans will always be tempted to think only in terms of one kind of righteousness, whereby humans lose what it means to be truly human. Maintaining a proper distinction between the two kinds of righteousness serves to preserve the proper relationship between them. Since there is nothing left to do *coram Deo*, the passive righteousness of faith means freedom to focus all attention on serving creation, leading us to appreciate earthly life as the sphere for our labors. The reception of passive righteousness leads us to embrace the world as the good creation of God.

Our Twofold Righteousness and Law-Gospel Distinction

The distinction between the two kinds of righteousness and the distinction between Law and Gospel arose about the same time in Luther's thought—around 1518-1519. It is, however, possible and quite helpful to see that these two foundational concepts approach the theological task from different perspectives. The distinction between Law and Gospel focuses on God's words and works, answering the question: "What does God say to me?" The distinction between the two kinds of righteousness focuses on the nature of the human being and the conformity of the human response to God's created (and re-created) design, answering the question: "What does it mean to be human?" The two kinds of righteousness makes explicit several, often unstated, assumptions upon which the proclamation of Law and Gospel depends. For example, it makes clear that the Gospel is completely and totally an unconditional gift. It also makes clear that the Law is a universal and objective design, one that is hardwired into creation. When the Law accuses, then, it is not like a bolt of lightning coming out of the clear, blue sky. In brief, the two kinds of righteousness address the nature and purpose of human life as the context within which the Lutheran Law-Gospel distinction carries out its work; Law and Gospel fit within the paradigm of the two kinds of righteousness.

The Law and Gospel distinction can be considered in two different ways: as *verba dei* and as *opera dei*. The former deals with the semantics (grammar) of Law and Gospel, while the other deals with the pragmatics (impact) of Law and Gospel.[26] Of these two ways (words and works) Lutherans have come to think of the Law-Gospel distinction primarily in terms of God's two works—for good reason. In the discussion of repentance (Ap XII, 53), Melanchthon stated, "These are the two chief works of God in human beings, to terrify and to justify the terrified or make them alive." God terrifies "in order to make room for consolation and vivification" (Ap XII, 51). For this reason, properly distinguishing between the pragmatics of Law and Gospel (their dual impact: crushing and comforting, killing and making alive, accusing and acquitting) becomes a vital factor in pastoral care. For C. F. W. Walther, the highest art of the pastoral ministry lay in knowing the spiritual condition of people to determine whether to apply the crushing work of the Law or the comforting work of the Gospel. Indeed, the distinction of Law and Gospel provides a framework for pastoral theology in such a way that nearly all the articles of faith can be experienced as Law or Gospel. Consider the omniscience of God. On the one hand, God knows about every skeleton hiding in the closets of our hearts. On the other hand, Christ knows our weaknesses and needs and provides for them. Or consider the omnipresence of God. Law: "You can run but you can't hide." Or Gospel: "I am with you always."

For much of their history, Lutherans practiced the distinction of Law and Gospel against the backdrop of various forms of legalism by which human beings used the Law in an attempt to attain justification *coram Deo*. Three moments in particular stand out. First, on the eve of the Reformation the medieval church worked with an Augustinian-Thomistic framework of salvation in which grace-assisted human activities provided the ultimate basis for a person's justification before God. The theology of Gabriel Biel went one step further when he maintained that even without the grace of God, a person could do his best and God would reward his effort with grace. Having merited grace, a person could now, with the assistance of that grace, perform further works that would be meritorious of final beatification or justification. Against this theology Luther contended that human beings are justified by faith apart from any works (whether produced with or without grace). Second, among Lutherans influenced by German and Scandinavian Pietism in the eighteenth century, the temptation arose to insist on certain forms of behavior as "evidence" of salvation. They tended to make the spiritual experience of those who had been "sanctified" into a new law "that is then expected of all believers in order to attest to the presence of true faith."[27] Such an emphasis resulted in an "unintended legalism." Against the backdrop of German Pietism, C. F. W. Walther delivered his influential lectures on Law and Gospel,[28] and against the backdrop of Swedish Pietism, Bishop Bo Giertz wrote his famous *Hammer of God*.[29] Similarly, many of Gerhard Forde's writings must be understood as a reaction against Norwegian Pietism. Third, following the publication of Karl Barth's *Gospel and Law* in 1935, Lutheran theologians in Europe and America protested against any attempts to make the Gospel subservient or secondary to the Law. Barth's treatment of the third use of the Law (its pedagogical function) implied that it superseded the Gospel. In response, Lutheran thinkers maintained that on this side of eternity the Law always accuses (*lex semper accusat*), because the Law always addresses human beings as sinners. Werner Elert, in particular, exercised much influence on Lutheran thought in developing a stark distinction between Law and Gospel in opposition to the perceived threat of Calvinism.[30]

Perhaps as an overreaction to Barth, a number of Lutheran theologians transformed the Lutheran dictum *lex semper accusat* into *lex sole accusat*. It was assumed and asserted that the Law cannot guide because it *only* accuses.[31] The distinction between Law and Gospel became an opposition in which the Gospel triumphs over not only the wrath of God but over the Law itself. It should be clear that in one's relatonship *coram Deo*, the Law can indeed do nothing else but crush and kill. It is when one fails to take into account the position of the Law/Gospel distinction, *within* the wider and more fundamental distinction between the two kinds of righteousness, that it is erroneously taught that the Law itself, in all of its applications and functions, is overcome and made irrelevant for the new man. When the law is removed from the life of believers (freed as they are not only from the guilt and condemnation of the Law, but also from the onerous burden of having to keep the Law), only the Gospel is left for the work of shaping Christian behavior. This is inevitably the destination at which one arrives once it is determined that the Law can only accuse. Theologians with such convictions, by necessity, then, came to speak of Gospel mandates, Gospel imperatives, Gospel invitations, and of a practical use of the Gospel (*usus practicus evangelii*).[32] In addition, the distinction between Law and Gospel was enlisted as a framework not only for pastoral theology but for systematic theology as well. Unfortunately, when the Law/Gospel distinction is treated as a conceptual framework within which the coherence of the Christian faith is understood and arranged, then whatever does not fit under the category of Gospel is necessarily regarded as part of the Law (which as God's alien work can only be considered as purely negative and oppressive inasmuch as we remain sinners). Even the doctrine of creation becomes Law for no other reason than that it is not Gospel, when in fact the doctrine of creation affirms the lordship of the Creator whose essence Luther defines as mercy.[33]

In some ways, Lutheran theologians in the twentieth century could urge a radical polarizing view of Law and Gospel in which the Gospel conquers and annuls the Law's claim on the creature because they still lived in a society in which the moral framework of a Judeo-Christian ethic could be taken for granted. The wider society provided the support structures for moral training. Television shows like "Leave It to Beaver" and "Fathers Knows Best" mirrored the moral behavior of how one acts within family and society in ways that were largely congruent with the Christian tradition. The Ten Commandments were often found posted in courtrooms and classrooms of the country. The church could count on the culture to take care of the need for training in morality—a task that was more than suspect anyway, tarred as it was by its close affiliation with the Law. In addition, the remnants of Pietism were still clinging to the life of the Lutheran church well into the twentieth century. By the century's end, however, those assumed structures in culture and church were rapidly crumbling. Shaped by a Darwinistic narrative, we have all but lost a sense of natural law (recall the Clarence Thomas hearings) or a universal common sense. People no longer know the larger creation-redemptive narrative of Scripture (as found in Psalm 136 and Nehemiah 9). And so it has become increasingly difficult to speak of objective universal standards for human behavior.[34]

Working within a Barthian understanding of revelation did not help the situation. Barth could not speak of a natural law and hence an objective basis for the Law that was universally acceptable. Instead, he maintained an impassable gulf between God and human beings that is overcome only when God chooses to step out and reveal Himself. Thus, for Barth, the proclamation of either Law or Gospel could be considered as good news inasmuch as God has chosen to reveal His will to us. In the twentieth century, Lutherans found Barth's neo-orthodox position attractive by allowing, as it did, for theology to be carried out apart from the prying eyes of naturalism. Yet it now became difficult, if not nearly impossible, to converse with the larger human community, or for the Law to enjoy any sort of positive role in the life of the believer. Establishing an antithesis between Law and Gospel with only a negative function for the Law had left the Law disconnected from creation and confined to the sphere of special revelation. Gustav Wingren was one of the first to see this and argued that theology had become myopically preoccupied with questions of epistemology. He contended that the first article came first in the creed for a reason. It (and with it the Law) was ontologically prior to redemption (Second Article) and prior to our epistemological rec-ognition of it (Third Article).[35]

Lutheranism in the twenty-first century finds itself in a unique situation. For the past five hundred years it has fought against con-ceiving of life only in terms of one kind of righteousness whereby human performance provided the basis for making the claim that God must accept us. But at times in the twentieth century, Lutheranism itself fell into its own form of one kind of righteousness whereby our passive righteousness before God became all we needed. And so active righteousness in conformity with the Law was left unstressed or was transformed into Gospel ways of talking.[36] One of the results of social Darwinism is that many define reality in such a way that they would now argue that there are *no kinds of righteousness*. There is no righ-teousness *coram Deo* (since there is no God) and no righteousness *coram mundo* (since there is no universal natural law). Instead we live by a principle that affirms the survival of the fittest or act in altruis-tic ways only to ensure the survival of one's gene pool, or because it provides momentary positive feelings or public acclaim. Humans are now left to construct their reality and the shape of their lives. And so anthropology has become a dominant topic of study. Christians must now deal not only with questions of "Christian identity," but of human identity. "Who are we?" "What does it mean to be a human person?" "What is the purpose for human life?"

In twenty-first-century post-modern America we thus find ourselves living in an antinomian society. "We can no longer depend on a society at least roughly Christian to socialize its members into anything approaching a Christian way of living."[37] The aftershocks of Kant have been felt by all. Standards became values that were then relegated to the private realm of the individual. Laws are nothing more than social constructions. Churches themselves have "pandered" to the trend of thinking about religious life as an individual idiosyncratic quest—one's "faith journey." Evangelical churches increasingly avoid speech about what is right or wrong, sin or not sin. When sin is addressed, it is considered in terms of vulnerabilities and weaknesses that have to do more with how sin affects the individual rather than how it harms the neighbor, let alone how it offends God. When the Law is no longer grounded in creation and is instead relegated to the realm of personal values that each person chose for himself or herself, the Law can no longer accuse (its authority comes from its congruence with creation). But because antinomianism is the only truly impossible heresy (that is, humans simply cannot function without some form or regulating Law), objective and universal standards for human life have been replaced with politically correct ways of acting—the only "binding" law in the twenty-first century.

The distinction of the two kinds of righteousness provides the context and basis for Law and Gospel to do their work *coram Deo* turning us away from sin and turning us to Christ. Because the two kinds of righteousness lay out what it means to be fully human as God created us, the paradigm provides the context for the Law to show how far we have fallen short of God's created design with respect to our human identity *coram Deo* and our human activities *coram mundo*. In the process, the two kinds of righteousness provide an expansive palette that takes into account the entire creedal story of creation and redemption.

First, it places our relationship to God as our redeemer into the larger context of our relationship to God as creator. The definition of our passive righteousness *coram Deo* makes clear the complete, unconditional character of our justification. In other words, it affirms the sovereignty of the Creator. The Creator is not dependent upon that which He creates, nor does He owe it to us to create us. God justifies Himself by "delivering and restoring us to the fullness of humanity through Christ's self-sacrifice on the cross."[38] Unlike Gnosticism, the Christian story of redemption does not destroy creation or draw us out of creation. As a corollary, it affirms that God created us as people who live from His gifts (that is, by faith), something that the contemporary human being is loathe to admit in his desire to be master of his life or escape the demands of life. The confession of a creator announces our limitations and inabilities. Yet the Creator-creature relationship is a relationship that the Gospel itself restores. This is the point that Luther stresses in the Large Catechism where he introduces the Apostles' Creed as that which "sets forth all that we must expect and receive from God. . .given in order to help us to do what the Ten Commandments require of us."[39] The Gospel (Creed) returns us to our responsibilities within creation where the Law (Ten Commandments) provides the needed specific direction.

Second, with reference to our human relationships, the two kinds of righteousness stress an active righteousness that gives Lutherans permission to speak positively about the Law within the Christian life without compromising or in any way threatening the doctrine of justification. It also expands our vision of Christian living in a way that includes all of our human activity in relationship to other human beings and the nonhuman creation.[40] *It provides warrant for human beings to use their reason and imagination in order to mediate the Law of creation into the specific contexts of our lives. Thus the definition of active righteousness provides the necessary theological space for reflection on the place of the social sciences, ethics, and moral theology for Christian living. It even creates space for Christians to actively consider and address such secular and mundane concerns as economics, environment, public policy, politics, and justice: thus affirming a common "worldliness" between Christians and non-Christians that is grounded in our creaturely existence. At the same time, it recognizes that the Gospel's work (coram Deo) will inform, empower, and even transform our creaturely activities in the world (coram mundo).*

Our Twofold Righteousness and the Two Realms

The two kinds of righteousness touch on countless facets of human living including everything from marriage, parenting, and vocation, to civil rights, higher education, and just war theory. The distinction, though, bears an especially close relationship to another important framework, namely, God's two forms of governance, or, as more popularly known, as the two kingdoms. A more detailed consideration of this particular application serves as a helpful illustration of the practical usefulness of the two kinds of righteousness.

In the left-hand realm God rules through the Law; whereas, in the right-hand realm He rules through the Gospel. Here we hear echoes of the distinction between Law and Gospel. But whereas the distinction between Law and Gospel was made for the sake of repentance (contrition and faith), the distinction of the two realms has in view something different. It stresses God's work through the Law primarily in its first use (as a curb) rather than in its theological use (as a mirror), that is, God uses the Law to maintain peace and justice in the world for the sake of preserving human life and furthering His creational intention. Following World War II, Lutheran interpretations of the two forms of God's governance have been criticized for rendering German Christians acquiescent to governing authorities and incapable of opposing governmental injustice.[41] The two kinds of righteousness provide ways to reappropriate the teaching on God's twofold governance within a democratic and post-Christian context.

For two hundred years the Enlightenment's distinction between public affairs and private life set the agenda for a Lutheran interpretation of God's twofold governance. Within this context, interpretations of God's twofold governance slid easily into a secular-sacred distinction that served (unintentionally) two different constituencies. Secularists argued for the autonomy of the state by confining (while claiming legitimacy for) faith and morals to the realm of the private and inner life of individuals. Confessional theologians thought that was well and good in as much as a concern for the distinction of Law and Gospel called for a separation between the two realms so that the Gospel was not transformed into an ideology of social action. But as confessional theologians emphasized the ultimate importance of salvation and righteousness before God, it had the effect of disparaging the left-hand rule of God since it was considered secular and, hence, profane.[42] The motto became, "Heaven is my home; I am but a stranger here." This means that the focus of our attention is on the spiritual, or the world to come, and implies that we have little interest in the old world that is passing away. In the meantime, Siemon-Netto commented, "we place our rears as comfortably as we can into our secular reality, leaving it to others to dirty their hands in political filth."[43]

The American distinction between church and state is related but not identical with the secular-sacred distinction that was fostered by the Enlightenment.[44] Originally, the American distinction was formulated in order to protect the church from interference by political authorities.[45] Throughout the nineteenth and twentieth centuries a close relationship existed between Christianity and American culture. But by the twentieth century legal scholars were speaking of a wall of separation between church and state whereby the church-state distinction became a protection "against religious meddling in politics and government."[46] In the first decade of twenty-first century America, the uneasy, unofficial alliance between church and culture (state) has come unglued and Christianity has begun to lose its predominant influence within the larger society. In other words, we are moving into a post-Constantinian age (really post-Theodosian age).[47] How shall Christians live in this transitional time?

Two options seem open to Christians: exile or conquest. Some have argued that Christians need to think of themselves as Christians did prior to the time of Constantine, namely, as exiles or "resident aliens." Here they pick up on the second-century epistle to Diognetus that said of Christians, "They pass their days on earth, but they are citizens of heaven."[48] We live in a foreign land, but do not participate. Stanley Hauerwas, for example, contends that Christians and the church need to be more distinct from, and therefore less engaged with, the surrounding culture.[49] Such an approach is not alien to LCMS tradition. J. T. Mueller argued that, ideally, Christians should create enclaves of Christian *diaconia* in the midst of a secular and condemned world. Christians, he contended, must establish their own institutions, both philanthropic and educational.[50] The other approach would be a form of conquest or transformation. Here one might appeal to Augustine. Although Augustine stressed a dual citizenship that at first glance may look like the two kinds of righteousness, for him "there is but one God, one righteousness, and therefore the earthly city must be fashioned into a community of justice that is oriented toward faith in and love for the true God."[51] In other words, the world needs the church's redemption, and the church should deliver this redemption by transforming the world into the kingdom of God. The point is to absorb or swallow the world into the church. Mark Noll has noted the predilection of American Christians to confuse "the history of the United States with the history of salvation." That is to say, Evangelicals seem pulled between the notion that America is (or was, or at least ought to be) a Christian nation and the sense of radical discontinuity between the kingdom of God and the kingdom of this world.[52] Either way, it is assumed that the world can only be good when it is subservient to (or at least supportive of) the church.

Considered within the two kinds of righteousness, the two realms cannot be seen as alternative forms of existence (with one being inferior to the other) in which we either live as citizens of this world or we live as citizens of heaven. "As long as conscientious Lutheran Christians mistakenly identify the 'public square' (or civic life) exclusively with the arena of state and government," they concede the Enlightenment claim that faith has nothing to say in the public realm and allow Christianity to be confined to a private religious ghetto with nothing to say on important public questions.[53] The Lutheran stress on active righteousness widens our vision regarding the left-hand realm and seeks to identify the common ground for moral reflection between Christians and non-Christians. Historically, when Christians were in league with the dominant culture they affirmed it even as they critiqued it. Such an approach is still needed; voluntary exile is not an option. Neither, however, is conquest. The conquest approach also confuses the two kinds of righteousness. In Augustine's Platonic world Christianity transforms the world, thus turning the two kinds of righteousness into one kind of righteousness. The same thing happens with groups like the Christian Coalition ("Giving Christians a voice in government again") that would see the United States as a Christian nation and thus fight for a distinctively Christian culture. Here we urge a distinction. Church *qua* institution lives in the left-hand realm—which is still God's realm—and is concerned for the extension of law and justice within that realm. A

"Lutheran appreciation of the two kinds of righteousness can help us reclaim what Robert Benne has called the 'paradoxical vision' of public theology in and for the society in which we live."[54]

A related consequence to the secular-sacred distinction has to do with how Christians live in the left-hand realm in relation to the governing authorities. When the French Revolution spilled over into Germany with its crusade for individual and human rights, the authority of the state became a central issue. What is the relationship between the sovereignty of the state and rights of individuals/citizens? What is the role of the state and its uses of political authority? What is the proper sphere of conduct of the individual, especially the believer, within the state? For many German thinkers in the nineteenth century, the state was a structure of creation for the purpose of maintaining order in the human community; whereas, revolution brought disorder. The Christian's calling to the political sphere, unless called to rule, was not one of active participation, but one of submission. German immigrants to America came with views shaped in a traditionally non-democratic society in which, as peasants, they had little role to play within society. In accord with Romans 13 and the Fourth Commandment, the Christian submits to the various authorities (fathers, priests, princes) under which he finds himself and renders the appropriate obedience due them. Thus the immigrants understood that their role over and against both the state and the institutional church could be described as "pray, pay, and obey." They were accustomed to thinking of themselves as subjects and not as citizens who participated in the shaping of government policies.[55]

And so Lutheran immigrants in the nineteenth century arrived on the shores of America with little understanding of or interest in their political responsibility under the new conditions of a democracy. The idea of active involvement in a participatory form of government—such as a democracy—required a fresh appropriation of Luther's thinking on the twofold rule of God—something that rarely took place. Instead, German immigrants lived within their own social enclaves and safely channeled their social concerns through the establishment of their own educational and charitable institutions. Pietism showed the way through the support of private charities. Scandinavian Lutherans were a little more active due to the influence of Haugean Pietism that gave laity an active role within church and society (with the resultant split from German Lutherans over issues involving slavery). In Scandinavian countries that were no longer major players on the world stage, the church worked closely with the state for the betterment of society; whereas, in Germany people worked for the maintenance of the state's place as a world power. And so during the past one hundred and fifty years, many Lutherans in America have quietly and contentedly raised families and contributed to the economy through their labor. But when it came to the matter of larger social and political matters (especially those requiring service within the government),[56] American Lutherans of German descent have often been invisible and their voice unheard by the larger community. To be sure, a certain quietism and minding of one's own affairs was reinforced during World War I when many German immigrants carefully kept their heads down and did their duty by buying war bonds.

When a separation of the two realms was combined with a view that subjects had to render unquestioning obedience (as long as it did not intrude upon their consciences) to their rulers, as in twentieth-century Germany, the consequences were predictably disastrous. In response to the Barmen Declaration that the one Word of God represents God's total demand upon our entire life, the Ansbach Proposal, under the leadership of Paul Althaus and Werner Elert, asserted otherwise. They argued for the separation of the two realms. Again, Nazi Germany did an especially effective job in separating the two realms with its insistence that the government has responsibility for the external life of its citizens, while the church is confined to looking after the spiritual welfare of its members. Thus, where was the church's voice during World War II in Germany aside from the Confessing Church? Nazi Germany infiltrated the state church with its German "Christians."[57]

A renewed appropriation of the two kinds of righteousness can revitalize our thinking on God's twofold rule so as to encourage Lutherans to be more active participants in the civil realm. We seek both kinds of righteousness as distinct but interrelated spheres of human existence! The distinction maintains that we do not simply relegate or relinquish the left-hand rule of God to impious non-Christians or to police forces. Christians do not seek and desire only the passive righteousness of Christ before God. They also seek active righteousness for the good of the human community. Indeed, since the passive righteousness of God frees Christians from needing to create or maintain a relationship with God, the believer's life may be completely devoted to the tasks of serving the rest of creation. Thus Christians find themselves within a variety of human communities in which they are called by God to cooperate and participate in His left-hand rule of the creation. In both realms, God works to accomplish His will for creation: the passive righteousness of faith as well as the active righteousness of human creatures by which He preserves the world. In other words, the distinction between the two realms reveals the distinct works of God within human life: God's providential/sustaining work through the Law and God's redemptive/restorative work through the Gospel. The first emphasizes God's care for the fallen world with His left hand through the rule of Law while the other emphasizes God's preservation of the church and consequent restoration of the whole creation (Rom. 8:18-23) with His right hand through the proclamation of the Gospel. Lutherans, then, to be faithful to God's intention and call, must learn to embrace and argue for natural law and not assume it a given. Far from quietism or indifference, they are urged into active and aggressive work within the civil realm—God's left-hand realm—and so need to be equipped for such activity. Undoubtedly, the most critical tool for such living is competence (which can be acquired and refined through careful training) in the art of moral reasoning.

Summary

Working within the matrix of the two kinds of righteousness, the reformers clarified the nature of the relationship between the Creator, who bestows "passive righteousness" upon His creatures (first in creation and then in redemption) through the creative and re-creative Word, and the human creature who responds in faith and trust. The distinction between the two kinds of righteousness allowed the reformers to extol the Gospel without qualification by removing human activity as a basis for justification before God. At the same time, it clarified the relationship of the human creature to the world in which God had placed it to live a life of "active righteousness" for the well-being of the human community and the preservation of the whole creation. The two kinds, however, are inseparable from one another—finding their nexus, as they do, in the life of each Christian person. The passive righteousness of faith provides and continually reaffirms the core identity of the believer, while the active righteousness of love flows from and through this justified child of God in service to the surrounding creation. This framework remains an indispensable tool for dealing with the perennial temptation to consider human existence one-dimensionally. Such occurs either when human works become the basis of justification before God, or when "faith alone" appears to render human activity irrelevant and unimportant to the Christian life. Over and against both tendencies, the two kinds of righteousness enable Lutherans to affirm fully and unreservedly two simultaneous, yet distinct and genuine dimensions of human existence without one compromising the other.

Notes

1. Carter Lindberg, "Do Lutherans Shout Justification but Whisper Sanctification?" *Lutheran Quarterly* 13 (1999): 1-20.

2. WA 2:41-47.

3. WA 2:145:9-146:35; LW 31:297-299.

4. WA 8:573-669.

5. WA 24:1-710.

6. Timothy J. Wengert, *Human Freedom, Christian Righteousness: Philip Melanchthon's Exegetical Dispute with Erasmus of Rotterdam* (New York: Oxford University Press, 1998).

7. Reasons for this neglect often stem from an attempt to use Law and Gospel as the guiding paradigm for all of Lutheran theology. In recent years, the consequences (and ultimate failure) of this effort has received increased attention by a variety of Lutheran scholars including David Yeago, Robert Benne, Gilbert Meilaender, and Reinhard Hütter.

8. *Lutheran Quarterly* 13 (1999): 453 (entire article 449-466).

9. *Concordia Journal* 8 (1982): 4-11. See also David A. Lumpp, "Luther's 'Two Kinds of Righteousness': A Brief Historical Introduction," *Concordia Journal* 23 (1993): 27-38.

10. *Lutheran Quarterly* 15 (2001): 417-439.

11. A book co-authored with Robert Kolb (forthcoming from Baker Books in January 2008).

12. *Concordia Journal* 30 (2004): 165-177.

13. Joel Biermann, "Virtue Ethics and the Place of Character Formation within Lutheran Theology" (Ph.D. diss., Concordia Seminary, 2002).

14. Makito Masaki, "Luther's Views on the Relationship between Clergy and Laity and Their Practice in the Early Postils." John Rhoads, "The Crux of *Communio*: Toward a Common Ecclesiology Beyond the Crisis of Reception." Guntis Kalme, "Words Written in Golden Letters: A Lutheran Anthropological Reading of the Ecumenical Creeds—'For Us' as the Constitutive Factor of What It Means to Be Human" (Ph.D. diss., Concordia Seminary, 2005).

15. It is attained by conforming to a standard or pattern of being and behaving that has been approved by a superior, someone whose judgment is vital to us and has an important impact upon our lives (Ap IV, Kolb and Timothy J. Wengert, eds., *The Book of Concord* (Minneapolis: Fortress, 2000), 164 [henceforth K-W]).

16. *Galatians Lectures*, 1531-1535, LW 26:8; WA 40:1:46:19-30.

17. For this reason, when the Lutheran Confessions speak about righteousness, they specify which relationship they are considering by speaking about righteousness "before God" (*coram Deo*) or righteousness "before the world" (*coram mundo / hominibus*). The reformers freely used a variety of specifying modifiers.

18. Robert Kolb, "God and His Human Creatures in Luther's Sermons on Genesis: The Reformer's Early Use of His Distinction of Two Kinds of Righteousness," in this issue.

19. "Heidelberg Disputation," 1518, LW 31:41; WA 1:354,29-30. Thesis 25. Melanchthon variously expresses this in the Apology as spiritual righteousness (*iustitia spiritualis*), inner righteousness, eternal righteousness, the righteousness of faith (*iustitia fidei*), the righteousness of the Gospel (*iustitia evangelii*); Christian righteousness (*iustitia christiana*); righteousness of God (*iustitia Dei*), and the righteousness of the heart.

20. Melanchthon variously describes this in the Apology as the righteousness of reason (*iustitia rationis*), the righteousness of the Law, civil righteousness (*iustitia civilis*), one's own righteousness (*iustitia propria*), carnal righteousness (*iustitia carnis*), righteousness of works (*iustitia operum*), and philosophical righteousness.

21. *Galatians Lectures*, 1531/1535, LW 26:7; WA 40:1:45, 24-27.

22. Gerhard Ebeling, "*Das Problem des Natürlichen bei Luther*" in *Lutherstudien*, vol. I (Tübingen: J. C. B. Mohr [Paul Siebeck], 1971), 278f.

23. *Galatians Lectures*, 1531-1535, LW 26:11; WA 40:1; 50:25-51:14.

24. A more common way of instrumentalizing our neighbor today is to help others (especially on mission trips) because it makes us feel good about ourselves. Gustaf Wingren insisted that as Christ is enthroned as Lord in our relationship with God, it is the neighbor who must be enthroned in our

relationships in this life. Gustaf Wingren, "Justification by Faith in Protestant Thought," *Scottish Journal of Theology*, 9 (December 1956): 374-383.

25. *Galatians Lectures*, 1531-1535, LW 26:11-12; WA 40:1; 51:21-31.

26. James W. Voelz, *What Does This Mean?: Principles of Biblical Interpretation* (St. Louis: Concordia, 1995).

27. Kolden, "Earthly Vocation," 286.

28. *Law and Gospel*, trans. Herbert J. A. Bouman (Saint Louis: Concordia, 1981).

29. Bo Giertz, *The Hammer of God*, 2 ed. (Minneapolis: Fortress, 2005).

30. *Law and Gospel*, trans. Edward H. Schroeder (Philadelphia: Fortress, 1967).

31. See Gerhard O. Forde, *The Law-Gospel Debate and Its Historical Development* (Minneapolis: Augsburg, 1969) for the nineteenth-century roots of the discussion regarding the place of the Law as well as the contribution of the Luther renaissance.

32. See Scott R. Murray, *Law, Life, and the Living God: The Third Use of the Law in Modern American Lutheranism* (St. Louis: Concordia, 2002), for an extensive overview of this period of history.

33. As such, even creation and its structures (male-female, etc.) must be transcended and overcome by the Gospel.

34. There is, though, some evidence that interest in natural law is on the rise. One noteworthy example is the work of J. Budziszewski, *What We Can't Not Know: A Guide* (Dallas: Spence, 2003) and *Written on the Heart: The Case for Natural Law* (Downers Grove: InterVarsity Press, 1997).

35. *Creation and Law*, trans. Ross Mackenzie (Edinburgh: Oliver & Boyd, 1961).

36. In a sense, antinomian tendencies have been a danger for Lutheranism reaching back into the sixteenth century. See Timothy J. Wengert, *Law and Gospel: Philip Melanchthon's Debate with John Agricola of Eisleben over Poenitentia* (Grand Rapids: Baker, 1997). The legacy of antinomianism has been helpfully explored by a number of contemporary scholars. See especially, Reinhard Hütter's "(Re-)Forming Freedom: Reflections '*after Veritatas splendor*' on Freedom's Fate in Modernity and Protestantism's Antinomian Captivity," *Modern Theology* 17 (April 2001): 117-161, and David Yeago, "Gnosticism, Antinomianism, and Reformation Theology: Reflections on the Costs of a Construal," *Pro Ecclesia* 2 (Winter 1993): 27-49.

37. Gilbert Meilaender, *Human Nature: Faith and Faithfulness* (Notre Dame: University of Notre Dame Press, 1991), 8.

38. Robert Kolb, "Confessing the Creator to Those Who Do Not Believe There Is One," *Missio Apostolica* 10 (May 2002): 35.

39. LC II, 1; *The Book of Concord*, ed. Robert Kolb and Timothy J. Wengert (Minneapolis: Fortress, 2000), 431.

40. See Gilbert Meilaender, *Human Nature: Faith and Faithfulness.*

41. See Uwe Siemon-Netto, *The Fabricated Luther: The Rise and Fall of the Shirer Myth* (St. Louis: Concordia, 1995).

42. Luther understood *weltliche* as temporal and civil, not as secular and profane.

43. Uwe Siemon-Netto, "Called to govern," Concordia Seminary Institute on Lay Vocation blogsite, December 2, 2005.

44. Mary Jane Haemig, "The Confessional Basis of Lutheran Thinking on Church-State Issues," in *Church and State: Lutheran Perspectives*, ed. John R. Stumme and Robert W. Tuttle (Philadelphia: Fortress, 2003), 16. The church-state distinction is not identical with Luther's two forms of governance. In the American conception, the church refers not to the hidden church (the one holy Christian church on earth) but to the church as an empirical or sociological reality, the church as an institution. Similarly, the state may be construed more narrowly as referring to the government alone and not to a wider realm that includes the family, economy, voluntary organizations, and charitable institutions. In Lutheran thought, both church (as an institution) and state belong in the left-hand realm. The church as *una sancta*, the assembly of believers, belongs in the right-hand realm.

45. Stephen J. Carter, *God's Name in Vain: The Wrongs and Rights of Religion in Politics* (New York: Basic Books, 2000).

46. Philip Hamburger, *Separation of Church and State*, (Cambridge: Harvard University Press, 2002).

47. It was Theodosius I who issued the edict in 380 that made acceptance of the Nicene Creed a precondition for citizenship within the empire. With that, heresy and treason became linked. To be a citizen of Rome one had to be a Christian.

48. *Ante-Nicene Fathers*, vol. 1 (Peabody, MA: Hendrickson, 1994), 26f.

49. See Joel Lehenbauer's disseration *The Christological and Ecclesial Pacifism of Stanley Hauerwas: A Lutheran Analysis and Appraisal* (St. Louis, Concordia Seminary, 2004).

50. See *What Lutherans Are Thinking: A Symposium on Lutheran Faith and Life*, ed. by E. C. Fendt (Columbus, Ohio: Wartburg Press, 1947) for a retrospective look after WWII.

51. William W. Schumacher, "Civic Participation by Churches and Pastors: An Essay on Two Kinds of Righteousness," *Concordia Journal* 30 (July 2004): 170.

52. On this tension between church and society as it developed in early nineteenth-century America, see Mark Y. Hanley, *Beyond a Christian Commonwealth: The Protestant Quarrel with the American Republic, 1830-1860* (Chapel Hill: University of North Carolina Press, 1994).

53. Schumacher, "Civic Participation," 174.

54. Robert Benne, *The Paradoxical Vision* (Philadelphia: Fortress, 1995).

55. William Sihler expounds the two realms with the church-state distinction in such a way that Christ's kingdom is not of this world and that subjects are to render obedience. To be sure, they should make certain such laws do not contradict that which God has written on our hearts. But there is "a God-pleasing antithesis between those who command and those who obey, between those who rule and those who are ruled." God is not concerned about specific forms of government. They can rule like patriarchs or absolute sovereigns. But "Christians acknowledge the governing authority even in its harshest form, that of unlimited absolute rule, as a beneficial order of God against the coarser outbursts of the corrupted human nature and against the increasing use of violence against the weak and the poor on the part of the godless rich and powerful." We subject ourselves even if they are tyrants. Only when the domain of the private is invaded or the conscience is at stake may the Christian say no. But then he must suffer the consequences. See Karl H. Hertz, ed., *Two Kingdoms and One World: A Sourcebook in Christian Ethics* (Minneapolis: Augsburg, 1976).

56. Uwe Siemon-Netto has noted that in the current 109th congress, the House of Representatives and Senate have only twenty Lutheran members and of those only three belong to the Missouri Synod. Even though the Missouri Synod is considerably larger than the Episcopal Church, there are forty-four Episcopalians from that rapidly shrinking branch of Anglicanism.

57. It should also be noted that soon after the Ansbach proposal, Althaus and Elert came out against Naziism. See Lowell Green, *Luther Against Hitler: The Untold Story* (St. Louis: Concordia, 2007).

7

God and His Human Creatures in Luther's Sermons on Genesis: The Reformer's Early Use of His Distinction of Two Kinds of Righteousness

Robert Kolb

In March 1523 Martin Luther began preaching on the book of Genesis in the town church in Wittenberg. Over the next year and a half he examined its text and applied it to his hearers' lives in the Sunday afternoon service. Some three years later, in 1527, the Wittenberg printer Georg Rhau published versions of these sermons in both Latin and German, based on notes taken by Luther's student, friend, and later official amanuensis, Georg Rorer, and edited by another former student, Caspar Cruciger, at the time a school rector in Magdeburg.[1] Often lost in the shadow of Luther's ten-year lectures on Genesis to his students in Wittenberg (1535-1545), these sermons offer a view of how the reformer was formulating his thought for a popular audience relatively early in the course of his call for public reform. This essay explores how these sermons put to use his recently formulated definition of humanness as two dimensional, totally passive in relationship to God and at the same time active in relationship to God's world. This distinction of "two kinds of righteousness" provided the anthropological framework for preaching about God and the human creature in his Genesis sermons.[2]

Luther's Sermons on Genesis

Preaching on biblical texts served as an important instrument in the fundamental task of the Reformation in the sixteenth century, the "recultivating" and "reforming" of the Christian faith among the common people.[3] This process intended to transform the religion of the faithful from a popular piety based on ritual observance to a practice of the faith which presumed that God engages His people in conversation through His Word. Luther aided the reconstruction of public preaching through his effective use of the printing press as well as his modeling of preaching from the pulpits of Wittenberg. Luther put the form of the "sermon" to use in several forms. Some of his earliest publications had claimed the title *homiliae* or *sermones*, even though they were never actually preached to a congregation and were topical rather than textual.[4] By 1522 Luther had begun to treat Biblical texts for homiletical use by pastors and lay people as he took up composing his first *postilla*, the medieval book of sermons generally containing expositions of the pericopal texts designated for each Sunday and festival of the church year. These served as a kind of continuing education program for parish priests who wanted to learn the new Wittenberg theology and who needed help in acquiring preaching skills.[5] They needed to understand the framework of the Wittenberg way of thinking, and they needed to know how to proceed from the presuppositions of that framework to interpret and apply Biblical texts for the benefit of their congregations. Soon after the publication of his first postil, the reformer began to preach "Bible study" sermons with a series of sermons on 2 Peter and Jude in 1523.[6] He had preached occasional sermons on Genesis in 1519-1521,[7] but in 1523 he undertook an exposition of the entire book over a longer period of time. Such series had little precedent in medieval preaching, which most often found its basis in the pericopes or the *Legenda aurea;* relatively few examples of series of sermons on a Biblical book have survived. Humanists indeed began the practice in the years preceding Luther's preaching on Genesis.[8] Like the postils, these Bible study sermons, such as those on Genesis, were subsequently published also for parish pastors to use as models and for families to read in devotional exercises. These sermons were designed to convey Biblical information and a method of reading

Scripture alongside their function as instruction in good preaching for these audiences.

Luther's Hermeneutical and Homiletical Method in the Genesis Sermons

In the Genesis sermons Luther operated with the framework his new insights into God's revelation in Scripture had created. To be sure, his "evangelical breakthrough" was a gradual process, and his theological development never ceased. Throughout his entire life the Wittenberg professor continued to conduct experiments in order to find the most effective ways of transmitting the Biblical message to hearers and readers. In these sermons on Genesis, he was displaying the hermeneutical and homiletical method that he and his Wittenberg colleagues were developing as one of the expressions of their new teaching and one of the vehicles for the translation of this teaching to the level of the congregation and the people. His sermons aimed to present the words of the text in their simplest, most straightforward meaning, and he wanted his hearers "to comprehend the words and the core of their meaning correctly and feel it in their hearts."[9]

The habits of humanistic rhetorical analysis helped hearers and readers recognize what was going on in the text. For example, the preacher identified the genre of chapter four as "narrative and example," a reflection of life on this earth.[10] Throughout these sermons the interpreter repeatedly had recourse to discussions of the original Hebrew, modeling the ideal of Wittenberg humanistic education.[11] In assessing what Luther proclaimed to the congregation in the town church, it must not be forgotten that he had before him students from the university as well as the permanent denizens of the town. Luther's philology and his theology were closely coordinated. The preacher also aided his readers with literary analysis when appropriate, observing that Moses employed *repetitio* as a rhetorical device (in Gen. 2:4-6).[12] Although the Wittenberg professor of Biblical studies had laid aside the "fourfold" method of allegorical interpretation as his guiding principle for his exegesis, he was not above an allegorical homiletical touch. He used them throughout the sermons, often under the explicit label *allegoria*. For instance, he compared the birth

of the church from the side of Christ asleep in death to God's drawing Eve from Adam's side (2:21-22).[13] His extensive allegorization of
Noah and the ark followed medieval patterns with evangelical theological applications.[14]

More importantly, his evangelical hermeneutic was functioning
as it delivered the power of God's Word into the lives of the congregation. He was working at putting the people's sinful identity to
death through the message of God's wrath and bringing them to life
as children of God through the message of Christ's death and resurrection. At several points the preacher mentioned explicitly what he
was consistently in fact practicing, distinguishing Law and Gospel.[15]
Already in 1523 Luther could explicitly employ his paraphrase of the
distinction of Law and Gospel, for example, by noting that the death
God imposed as judgment upon sin turned into an instrument of
God's grace, "indeed, the beginning of life."[16]

Luther's proclamation of God's Word intended to carry on the
re-creating conversation God wants to have with sinners. With the
publication of his Genesis sermons in 1527, and as he commented in
his preface, Luther hoped to use this first book of the Old Testament
to show readers "how the Scripture agrees at every point, and how
all the examples and stories, indeed the whole Scripture through
and through, lends itself to the goal that people know Christ."[17] For
Scripture can be read in two ways. The first, apart from faith, can
grasp its literal meaning with human reason and understanding, but
the second is taught by the Holy Spirit and practiced by those to
whom God gives "true understanding and experience in the heart,"
which lies beyond the grasp of reason alone.[18] The "most lofty article
of faith" was not, in Luther's view, the second article of the Creed,
as popular judgments about his theology often suggest. In preaching on Genesis, at least, Luther was beginning at the beginning. His
entire treatment of God's intervention in behalf of sinners through
the incarnation presumed the person of God as almighty Creator
and Lord. Therefore, the most lofty article of the faith, he told the
Wittenberg assembly, is "I believe in God, the Father almighty, creator of heaven and the earth." This was not an abstract axiom, the
preacher informed his hearers: whoever believes that God is Father
almighty and Creator "dies to everything else. . .and confesses from
the heart, that he has no capability on the basis of his own powers."[19]

Luther could not define God without reference to His relationship to His human creatures; the reformer could not define the human creature without reference to the Creator. Human life centers on and is founded upon trust in the Creator. God alone can bring it about that this kind of believer recognizes that "it is not at all in his hand but only in God's hand. For just as I believe that he created the entire world out of nothing, and that everything has come only from his word and command, so I have to confess, that I am a part of the word and his creation. Therefore, it must follow that in my power there is no ability to raise my hand, but God alone does and effects everything in me."[20] Everything depends on "his gracious will and fatherly love."[21] The Wittenberg exegete lay the foundation for his entire theology on the presumption that God is a person who is almighty, Creator, and Father. Corollary to this axiom is his definition of what it means to be human as, first of all, to trust in God and be completely dependent on him.

With that, Luther had begun to prepare readers of the sermons for a proper understanding of one dimension of their humanity. He went on in subsequent passages to examine the other, the horizontal dimension of being human. His examination of what it means to be human reflects his revolutionary redefinition of the human creature that arose from his own experience and his study of Scripture in the 1510s, as outlined in his treatises on two and three kinds of righteousness from 1518 to 1519. An investigation of how this new definition functioned as a presupposition reveals something of how Luther went about the task of reconstructing the public teaching of Biblical material. Even though he and his contemporaries did not explicate their system of thinking in detail, they did operate with a theory of how Biblical teaching is to function in the life of the church. Luther's application of his definition of humanity as two-dimensional illustrates this fact.

Two Kinds of Righteousness as a Nervous System of the Wittenberg Body of Doctrine

Luther's sermons on Genesis disclose how his method operated as it guided the proclamation of what the reformer found in the book, and they also unveil how his newly developed presuppositions shaped his treatment of fundamental questions regarding the person and nature of God and what it means to be human. Indeed, it is implicit in these sermons that for those subject to Biblical revelation these two topics cannot be explored independently of each other. For, Luther was certain, God does not reveal everything about His innermost being in Scripture. Some of the reaches of the depth of God's person belong to what he labeled in the Heidelberg Disputation of 1518 the "Hidden God" (*Deus absconditus*).[22] Scripture reveals instead how He relates to His human creatures, above all, in and through His incarnation, as Jesus Christ (*Deus revelatus*).[23] At the same time Luther's essential definition of what it means to be human, expressed in his distinction of the two dimensions of humanity—what he labeled two kinds of righteousness—centers on two persons. It posits, first, the personal, almighty Creator who bestows "passive righteousness" upon His human creature (in the very act of creation and in subsequent redemption from sin) through His creative and re-creative Word. Second, it posits the human creature, fashioned by the Creator in His own image to respond to His love in fear, love, and trust. God's gift of human identity as a child of God elicits and creates the trust that lies at the center of humanity. This "passive righteousness" is, however, inseparable from the "active righteousness" that meets God's expectation for human performance that properly expresses that core identity. Luther believed that human creatures are so fashioned in God's image that they are fully responsible for carrying out God's plan and will for human living in such performance, but at the same time God is completely responsible for everything in His creation as the almighty Creator. Other Christian theologians have also struggled with the question of the balance between God's power and human power, and many have tried to harmonize and homogenize these two Biblical claims of God's total responsibility and of human responsibility. Luther, in contrast, along with his Wittenberg colleagues and students, strove to hold the two responsibilities in creative tension. This tension produced presuppositions for his entire theological enterprise, such as the distinction of Law and Gospel, the distinction of the two dimensions of humanity, and the distinction of two realms of God's governance of His world.[24]

Luther would later, in 1535, dub the distinction of the two kinds of human righteousness "our theology."[25] By that time he had refined and enhanced the concept in its details, but even as he first gave utterance to this Biblical axiom some four years before preaching on Genesis, it was clear that he was laying down the foundation of his anthropology. His *Sermon on Three Kinds of Righteousness* bore this title because it distinguished the civil righteousness of the non-Christian from the faith-driven but externally similar pious righteousness of the believer. This treatise discussed these two forms of the "active righteousness" of human performance in the horizontal relationships with other creatures along with the "passive righteousness" of the human relationship with God. After the fall into sin, true human righteousness can be restored to sinners only on the basis of what Christ has done to meet the Law's claim for the death of the sinner and to claim life for forgiven sinners through His resurrection. The work of Christ refashions sinners into God's children in the action of God's Word, parallel to His original creation in Genesis 1, as that word of forgiveness, life, and salvation comes in oral, written, and sacramental forms.

Luther defined the righteousness which Christ gives the sinner through the forgiveness of sins as a righteousness as free and unconditional as the humanity given to Adam and Eve at creation, before they had had a chance to perform any deeds of love. This righteousness is comparable to the identity that a person has because it has been bestowed by birth, a total gift (*natalis*). It is a righteousness that is essential, that is, that determines the core identity of a person (*essencialis*). It is determined by the person's origin by the power of God's re-creative Word, and therefore it cannot be separated from who the person is (*originalis*). It comes as a gift from someone else, from God, and thus it comes to the person from outside (*aliena*). This righteousness, Luther points out, comes from being born of water and the Spirit (John 3:5). It is received by God's power to make sinners His children (John 1:12). Therefore, because God has given new birth to believers, they are no longer identified as sinners (1 John 3:9) because Christ has given them His righteousness (Rom. 5:18-19).[26] This righteousness of pure gift, of new birth, brings with it, however, divine parental expectations. The gift of identity as creatures and children of God issues naturally into the performance of what God created human creatures to do, into the good works that actively express the core identity of human passive righteousness.[27]

This distinction of two kinds of righteousness functioned as a presupposition for all that Luther said about the human being and the human relationship with God. As a presupposition rather than a dogmatic topic in itself, it did not become a standard part of the list of teachings in Lutheran dogmatics because the form for presenting Biblical teaching that Philip Melanchthon bequeathed his students did not have a place for the presentation of presuppositions. Using the best linguistic theories of their time, those of the Biblical humanists) Melanchthon adapted rhetorical forms from that movement, chief among them the organization of material to be taught in categories or topics, called *loci communes* (commonplaces) in the academic Latin of his day. In many details the Wittenberg theologians left behind the model of Peter Lombard's *Sententiae*, which had provided the configuration for Western public rendering of the Biblical message since the eleventh century (though Lombard's outline of topics did shape Melanchthon's organization of his own topics to some extent).[28] However, Melanchthon's second and third editions of the *Loci* did follow Lombard's model in simply beginning with the topic, "On God." The communication theory of the time did not recognize any need for laying down the conceptual framework of its way of thinking-although in at least one preface to the work, Melanchthon did sketch the framework of distinguishing Law and Gospel.

Nonetheless, within the Wittenberg practice of theology there is a place for modern interpreters to make certain that its presuppositional framework is made clear. The Wittenberg team sometimes called the whole of Biblical teaching a *corpus doctrinae*, a "body of doctrine," and the individual topics were members, or *articuli*, of that body.[29] Even though the Wittenberg theologians did not have a way to describe it, it is true that presuppositions run like a nervous system or a circulatory system through the entire body, shaping a number of the specific topics. Therefore, we can recognize the critical role of the distinction of two kinds of righteousness—the two dimensions of humanity—as a critical anthropological presupposition for the exposition and proclamation of a number of topics of Biblical teaching even if this is not made explicitly clear in the tradition.

As a presupposition this concept is not dealt with in detail in most of Luther's works, but nonetheless, it surfaces as the clear framework for his thinking, for instance, in his Genesis sermons of 1523 and 1527. This is true in other works of the period following the publication of the sermons on two kinds and three kinds of righteousness as well.[30]

God the Creator in Luther's Genesis Sermons

Humanity in its vertical dimension, its relationship with its creator, consists of God's gift of life as the creature He shaped in Eden. He has given dominion to that creature within the created order. When the Creator reclaims human life through Christ's death and resurrection, He bestows a new or restored identity as His chosen child and the human response of trust in the God who gives this identity through Christ. This definition of being human presumes the person of the Creator, who is almighty and whose will it is to fashion for Himself human creatures. The first two chapters of Genesis teach that and provide a natural basis for conveying this idea to other Christians. Luther did just that in his sermons on the Genesis account of creation.

He identified God as the almighty Creator, the Lord, who is responsible for the origin of everything that exists and everything that happens in the course of human history. That was clear, for instance, in the Flood. God's will determines everything, including His manner of caring for His people.[31] He both promises the goodness He wills for His people and has the power and might, as well as the wisdom, to deliver His promises.[32]

Luther defined this Creator as a God of conversation and community. He fashioned the world through His creative Word, and He designed human beings to be in community and conversation with Him and with each other. This creative Word not only set God's creation in place or in motion; it continues to sustain all things that exist. God has made Himself responsible for the sustenance of His creation. From his Ockhamist instructors Luther had learned that the Creator, who could do anything He pleased according to His absolute power (*potentia absoluta*), had actually pledged Himself to act in the ways His covenant promised. Thus, His interaction with creatures, according to His "ordained" or "ordered" power (*potentia ordinata*, His power as He had limited and prescribed it), was not arbitrary but rather faithful to His covenantal promises.[33] Reflecting on this instruction, the Wittenberg exegete proclaimed to his congregation that "Everything proceeds out of God's order, and nothing has its own essence of itself; nothing is in charge of its own existence. Rather, everything proceeds from God's hand, counsel, and will, so you should see God in all creatures if we open our eyes or ears and then give him thanks."[34] The reformer commented on Genesis 22:16-18, "When God pronounces a blessing, speaking and doing are one thing."[35]

On the basis of God's revelation of Himself in the cross of Christ, Luther identified the essence of God as love and mercy, and the Creator has consistently displayed this disposition toward His creatures since creation, he argued. "What a kind, fine God he is, nothing but sweetness and goodness that he feeds us, preserves us, nourishes us."[36] The preacher reinforced his text with words from Christ: "My Father is at work until now, and I am at work" (John 5:17).[37] That fundamental divine disposition of mercy and grace continued in His attitude and actions toward sinners. Adam had deserved nothing from God after his fall (as was the case before the fall as well), but God showed mercy, and His Gospel created a new faith and love in Adam.[38]

Luther captured the Biblical presupposition that the almighty Creator acts in His creation through His Word, in its various forms. "God created [the essence of each individual created person or thing] through the Word so that it grows without ceasing and we do not have any idea how. . . .It is an eternal Word, spoken from eternity, and it will be spoken always. As little as God's essence ceases, so little does his speaking cease."[39] Luther asserted that God has the whole world on His lips: "[T]he earth has its power only from God's Word," for "you see soil on which nothing grows, it is still soil and dry earth, empty, for God is not giving his word or command that it bear and that something can grow. Therefore, the reason that not all land bears fruit in the same way is due not to the ability of the land but to God's Word, for where it is, there is the power to be fruitful. The entire world is full of the Word that drives all things and bestows and preserves power."[40]

Therefore, it is no wonder that Luther described sin in terms of Adam and Eve being torn away from God's Word.[41] To be human is "to have God's Word and cling to it in faith."[42] Restoration of life with God comes to sinners by a creative act of God's Word, just as Isaac was given to Abraham and Sarah as a result of such an act of the Word. "The divine majesty pours out the power with the Word. Therefore he is a child of the divine Word even though produced by flesh and blood. . . . Therefore, they are not God's children apart from being born through the Word."[43]

Restoration to a proper, righteous relationship with God takes place through the action of God in His Word, through its re-creative power. Already in 1523 Luther employed the Sacrament of Baptism as described by Paul in Romans 6:3-11 and Colossians 2:11-15 as a model for God's justifying activity. Sinners die when baptized into Christ, and the children of God are brought to new life through the mystery of God's working in this sacramental form of the Word, Luther told the Wittenberg congregation.[44]

All depends on the gracious disposition of God, Luther asserted in treating the sins of the patriarchs in Genesis 34.

> If works made us righteous in God's sight, these patriarchs must have been rejected, since only such terrible things are found in the stories of them. Therefore, it must be that in God's sight nothing has worth apart from pure grace and favor. . . . Those are the secret and wondrous works of God, that he wishes to make sinners holy, so that all our boasting of our own righteousness and good works be destroyed. This is what it all means: as long as he regards us as righteous, we are righteous. When he withdraws his hand and lets us go our own way, we are desperate scoundrels. Indeed, no one should despair, even if we fall. We should just not lose God's Word. For his Word and grace are greater and more than all human sin.[45]

The sinner is completely dependent on the unconditional mercy of the Creator.

The Passive Righteousness of the Human Creature in Luther's Genesis Sermons

Luther's view of the human being is sometimes caricatured as an extremely negative opinion that focuses only on sin and rebellion against God. In fact, Luther defined the human situation not only out of its sinfulness but also out of its creatureliness, and in that creatureliness he found both a positive assessment of God-given human potential and an appreciative affirmation of human dependence upon a loving Creator. "Creatures do not have their essence from themselves, and even when their essence has been bestowed, they do not have any power of their own."[46] God built Adam's world before He made Adam. Adam earned nothing. He simply inherited and received the beneficence of the heavenly Father. Human beings can only receive what God gives in faith and trust, and from that faith and trust they live.[47]

Luther went into some detail discussing what it means that human beings are created "in the image of God" (Gen. 1:27) without arriving at a simple, definitive answer. He avoided the speculation involved in trying to equate human memory, understanding, and will with the Trinity and instead posited with Paul that there is an "earthly" and a "heavenly" human being on the basis of 1 Corinthians 15:48-49 and Ephesians 4:22-24. The "earthly" is the sinner, that is, the human creature who in Adam has become blinded and perverted, living in unbelief, false faith, and doubt. That is not the human being God created. The "heavenly" image is that of Christ: "He was a human being full of love, mercy and grace, humility, patience, wisdom, light, and everything good. His whole essence was dedicated to serving everyone and harming no one. We must bear this image and conform to it. In this image belongs also his death and suffering and everything attached to it, his resurrection, life, grace, and power...."[48] Christ reveals not only who God is but also what it means to be human. Luther believed that sinners had lost this image of God because it is centered in true faith in God. Nonetheless, elements of the original humanity remained in the ability to practice God's will outwardly, for instance, in married life.[49] For without faith no one can understand God and His work; unbelief deprives the descendents of Adam of their ability to enjoy life as God made it.[50]

The account of the creation of Adam and Eve and the giving of the command not to eat of the tree of the knowledge of good and evil (Gen. 2:15-17) gave Luther the opportunity to spell out precisely what he meant by "passive righteousness." Adam did not earn God's favor by keeping that command. He already possessed God's love and favor from the moment God breathed into the dust the breath of life and created him.

> God gave him this command as a sign,. . .for he had to know and remember that he had a lord over him. He could not become upright through obeying the command, but he could become a sinner. This is an important proof that no law can make a person upright, but rather it is given to him so that he can keep it and prove that he is already upright and lives hearkening to God. The law does not bestow uprightness but those who are already upright practice the law.[51]

Since the fall into sin, the law of God functions as an accusation and indication of our sinfulness, but obedience to it, even before the fall, was always the result of God's favor, not a cause of it.[52] This remains true after the fall, since God promised rescue and absolution immediately after Adam and Eve's sin.[53]

Sin consists in doubting God's Word and therefore straying from God and His plan for human life. Although some sinners take away from the Word, Eve's breakdown of trust led her to add to it. The story of sin is the continuation of the doubt and denial engendered from the devil's questioning of what God had said. "As Eve stood there wavering back and forth and the devil had maintained that it was not against God, he had won already. Faith was gone, it was suffocated. She had lost the Word."[54] The consequences of losing the Word of God and faith in Him are clear: "When faith and God's Word are gone, you cannot think that you can hold off the evil lusts and loves. The passion is there and is nothing but sinful, evil inclinations."[55] Finally, Adam tried to turn God's Word against God, the ultimate mark of a blasphemer (Gen. 3:12).[56] The restoration of faith through the promise of redemption in Christ in Genesis 3:15 demonstrated for Luther that in His goodness God called sinners out of their doubt and focused their lives, that is, their trust, upon His Word once again.[57] Forgiveness of sins came for Adam's and Eve's sins only through the promise of the Seed (Gen. 3:15). Faith blots out sin, for God does not accept recompense for sin through works."[58]

The righteousness which God bestows upon His chosen children constitutes itself in the human creature as trust in the Creator.[59]

Therefore, the preacher told his hearers that it was not Abel's sacrifice which pleased God but rather his faith, whereas "Cain was not condemned because of his works but because of his unbelief. . .God looks first at the person, the man, and then at the works that he does, not vice versa."[60] Luther cited Hebrews 11:4 to affirm to his hearers that Abel was upright because of his faith. For "the almighty God had given Adam his Word and promise and has it proclaimed to us" that Christ would come to destroy the devil and make his children his own.[61] This faith is created by and demonstrates the power of the Word of God. Luther's imagination often flared when he contemplated the trials of the patriarchs, and he visualized for his hearers how Noah and his family must have felt when God's wrath descended upon their world in the Flood. Tossed about in their little ship, they were dependent on God's promise alone.

> What a faith it must have been, to be able to remain upright in the face of such dreadful wrath. For it was real battle between faith and unfaith, and their hearts must have suffered many a strong blow. . . . They had to cling to this mere word and fight against all their senses and reason with faith. So you see what mighty power the Word has when it is grasped by faith, as they had death unceasingly before their eyes for five months and were able to disregard all that.[62]

Luther followed Paul in seeing in Abraham the greatest example of the righteousness of faith. The patriarch was a true example of both faith and love because he held to God's living Word.[63] His life proves that "if someone is converted and becomes upright, a Christian, we do not initiate that. No prayer, no fasting helps. It has to come from heaven, from grace alone, when God hits the heart through the promise of the Gospel so that it feels this Word and has to say that it never before occurred to him or came to his mind that such grace should fall upon him."[64] And so, the preacher proclaimed, "Those who want to become righteous should just not say, 'I want to begin this matter and do good works, so that I can attain grace,' but rather, 'I will wait until God wants to give me his grace and his Spirit through his Word.'"[65] "For Abraham lived from the naked Word of God to which he clung and in which he remained."[66] "Everything depends on God's Word. If

God speaks, even about a stalk of straw, his is nevertheless an eternal word, and the person who believes it will be righteous and upright and has God and has enough for eternity." So Luther affirmed, "The gospel is an everlasting treasure."[67] For, as he commented in treating chapter 17, "God is truthful, faithful, and almighty, and therefore I do not ask whether it is impossible if I have his Word and promise. Nothing can go amiss then even if everything else deceives. For the Gospel is a light which leads us and lightens the darkness when reason is blind and becomes foolish. When according to nature it is impossible, but with God it is possible."[68] Righteousness in God's sight came to Abraham as an undeserved and unexpected gift through God's activity in His Word, Luther assured his hearers.

In preaching on Genesis 16, Luther contrasted the people of the promise—Isaac's descendents—with the people who have not received the promise. The preacher pointed out that it is not said of "coarse, insolent people" but of "the very best, most upright and wisest people on earth that none of that has any worth before God unless at the same time they have been born of the Holy Spirit and become a new human creature."[69]

Always concerned about the smoldering wick and broken reed, Luther used the example of Sarah in Genesis 18 to remind his hearers that even when faith is weak, God remains faithful. Sarah doubted whether she would receive the promised child (18:12). "Nevertheless, God did not reject her because of that but treated her gently because of her earlier faith, and he cherished her although her faith was not as strong as Abraham's."[70]

Therefore, the preacher could also make practical application of the example of Noah's faith as the tossing of the waves in the midst of the Flood made life seem very fragile. In the midst of trials and temptations in the throes of death, the believer is thrown into despair, saying,

> "I am dying and do not know when I will depart and to which place." Luther answered, "Then you must close your eyes and shut off all your senses and not want to know or hear anything but that which God's Word says. Don't pay attention to what you feel, or try to overcome those feelings yourself. May the Word grasp you and do not let it be taken from you, so you can say, 'Here I am in the agony and anxiety

of death, but I know that I am baptized and that God has promised me this and that.' However strong and intensively death may be attacking, throw the Word in its face." For, the preacher continued, it is not a matter of how much you have served God and how many good works you have done. That is the devil's nonsense, designed to arouse despair. Instead of talking about works, confess your sins, he told the congregation, and then confess, "But you are the kind of God that does not examine how pious or how evil a person has been if that person looks only to your goodness and trusts."[71]

Such is the righteousness of faith. The presumption that works do not belong in the most intimate of conversations of the believer with God reveals how the distinction of the two kinds of righteousness is designed to work in the life of the Christian.

The Active Righteousness of the Human Creature in Luther's Genesis Sermons

This trust and its righteousness produce the active righteousness that meets God's expectations for the performance of those to whom He has given a new identity as redeemed and restored children of God. Luther understood that God has planned daily human living in relationship to the rest to creation as obedience to God's commands for individual human actions. This obedience takes place within the context of God's calling of each person to specific roles and functions that are integral to the warp and woof of society as the Creator designed it. Believers practice the virtues or works God commands within the framework of the vocations to which He calls them. The example of Abraham demonstrates that "you must not be idle but must perform works. But you do not create an inheritance for yourself through your works. . . . We have it completely through faith. But we do good works so that God's kingdom expands. We preach and bring other people to it through our words and works, so that our life is dedicated to other people, to helping them."[72] "When God has restored a human being, he does not let him be idle but brings him into continuing practice" of new obedience even though the devil's attacks do not end, and the Christian life goes on in the midst of the struggle he imposes upon God's children.[73]

Luther posited it as a general rule in Moses' writings that

> every person should so conduct himself in his walk of life and produce appropriate works so that he is certain that they please God, and thus live so that we are always prepared for death. . . . We do not create certainty regarding this with works, but faith does so. It makes people pleasing to God and gives the heart assurance that everything pleases God, and that even if something is done that does not please him, as often happens, he nevertheless regards that person as good.[74]

For the Gospel does not alter the human nature that God created in the first place. That means that in relationship to God, Christians live by faith, but on earth they assume the responsibilities of loving one another. "God does not want to tear our nature out of us through the Gospel, but he lets remain what is natural, directing it, however, along the proper lines. It is natural that a father love his child, that a wife love her husband, and is happy when he prospers."[75] Therefore Christians act as true Christians when they hearken to God in everything and show concern for other human beings in need.

God's commands and callings, on the one hand, and the welfare of other human beings, on the other hand, constituted two poles between which believers practice new obedience. In preaching on Abraham's military rescue of his nephew Lot (Gen. 14:13-16), Luther answered the question of whether a Christian may raise the sword in violence against others. Not in his own behalf, the preacher instructed: "If God had not commanded this, he [Abraham] would under no circumstances have done this nor undertaken to proceed against such mighty kings. . .But because God commanded it, and precisely to rescue his brother, he did it and went forth in faith."[76] What military action accomplished in behalf of Lot was balanced by Abraham's prayers for the people of Sodom. "As an upright man, Abraham was so disposed to have a heart full of love toward everyone as he had toward God, and so he afterwards prayed so assiduously for the Sodomites that he probably would have even died for them."[77] The story of Abraham demonstrates, Luther concluded, that "Abram continued to love his neighbor, but he submitted that love to God, for faith and love toward God is to govern love for the neighbor since we do not love human beings more than we love God."[78]

From the pulpit Luther was concerned to cultivate good works. He praised Abraham for living on the basis of his faith as one who demonstrated the love of God, for instance, through his hospitality in Genesis 18.[79] The example of Esau and Jacob reminded the reformer of God's ability to work such miracles of reconciliation as was reported in Genesis 33:417: "It is God's essence and way of working that he can make the worst enemies into friends."[80] At the same time, Luther commended the humility and desire for peace that Jacob displayed to his hearers. The people of Wittenberg received both the admonition to do good works and specific instructions about which works were good and which were not from Luther's preaching. They also received encouragement to endure in times of trial, for active righteousness included both obedience to God's commands and patient suffering in the face of evil. What Jacob and his family suffered at the hands of his father-in-law Laban illustrated how faith is prepared to show love and bear the cross of persecution and maltreatment.[81] Luther personally had experienced a wide range of spiritual and physical suffering, and so had his hearers. He met that part of their lives with the promise of God's presence in the midst of tribulations.

Luther knew, like Paul in Romans 6:1-3, that the Gospel of passive righteousness bestowed through the work of Christ can be misheard as an invitation to licentiousness. So he reminded the Wittenberg listeners, "Why are good works commanded if faith suffices? It is true that faith alone is enough before God, so that we need to do no works. Nonetheless, a person must do works to prove our faith before the world, so that God is praised and my neighbor is aroused to faith. I may not do them in my own behalf but in behalf of others, for the praise of God and the service of my neighbor so that others come to us."[82] The distinction of active and passive righteousness correlated with the distinction of Law and Gospel. Luther registered his opposition to both the failure to perform active righteousness and also to despair or arrogance regarding the believer's relationship to God.

Conclusion

This concern for both obedience to God's commands and trust in God as the center of human life reflected Luther's fundamental perception of the reality between God and His human creatures. This perception presumed that God acts through His Word which both bestows human identity as a child of God and sets forth God's expectations for living as His human creature. This distinction of Law and Gospel found its anthropological corollary in the distinction of two kinds of righteousness, the presupposition that shaped Luther's understanding of what it meant to be human as a creature of the almighty Father and Creator of all things. The Wittenberg reformer defined the human creature on the basis of his belief that God is that Creator, responsible for all things in His creation. At the same time, Luther insisted that the Creator had so designed and fashioned His human creatures that they exercise total responsibility for all that God has made them to be and to do. This mystery of the relationship between God and human creatures reflects the fact that for Luther it is not possible for God's creatures to grasp fully who He is and to understand completely who they are as the products of His creative imagination and grace.

To explain and proclaim all that God says about Himself and His human creatures, Luther believed that, Christians must recognize that human life takes place in two dimensions or that what it means to be human takes form in a completely different way in relationship to God than it does in relationship to God's creatures. Like human parents, God has given life to His creation, and He restores life to those dead in sin through His Word of absolution. It conveys the gift of new life in and through the death and resurrection of Jesus Christ. This aspect of Luther's anthropology provides unshakable comfort for the people of God, for the identity of believers as children of God rests solely on His gracious will and loving disposition toward them. No human effort or merit could possibly be responsible for the personal identity of Christ's people. At the same time Luther's anthropology frames the daily life of believers in their living out of the expectations of their Creator and Father in the performance of the love which constitutes who they are in relationship to their neighbors. Bound together in God's creative and re-creative action, both the identity and the performance of His human creatures, once lost through sin, have been restored through the work of Jesus Christ. Although human performance, under the mystery of the continuation of sin and evil in the lives of the baptized, attains only imperfect restoration, the identity of the sinner as a forgiven child of God is complete and unshakable because it rests alone on God's disposition and His Word.

Notes

1. See the introduction to the printed edition in *D. Martin Luthers Werke* (Weimar: Bohlau, 1883-1993 [henceforth WA]), 24:XIII-XLVII, and to the notes taken on the sermons as they were delivered, WA 14:92-96. The text of notes from Georg Rörer and Stephan Roth are found in WA 14:97-488. See J. P. Boendermaker, "Heet eerste word blijft gelden. Luthers preken over de vijf boeken van Mozes, 1523-1525 inleiding en enkele teksten," in *Luther na 500 jaar, teksten, vertaald en beproken*, ed. J. T. Bakker and J. P. Boendermaker (Kempen: Kok, 1983), 99-123. Sabine Hiebsch, in her study of Luther's use of the interpretive method of "figura," also treats this sermons series (*Figura ecclesiae: Lea und Rachel in Martin Luthers Genesispredigten* [Münster: LIT, 2002]).

2. Robert Kolb, "Luther on the Two Kinds of Righteousness: Reflections on His Two-Dimensional Definition of Humanity at the Heart of His Theology," *Lutheran Quarterly* 13 (1999): 449-466; David Lumpp, "Luther's 'Two Kinds of Righteousness': A Brief Historical Introduction," *Concordia Journal* 23 (1997): 27-38. See also Charles P. Arand, "Two Kinds of Righteousness as a Framework for Law and Gospel in the Apology," *Lutheran Quarterly* 15 (2001): 417-435.

3. Scott H. Hendrix, *Recultivating the Vineyard: The Reformation Agendas of Christianization* (Louisville/London: Westminster John Knox, 2004).

4. This is not true of all his uses of the term, but, for example, see "Ein Sermon von Ablass und Gnade" 1517, WA 1:243-246; "Sermo de poenitentia," 1518, WA 1:319-324, and "Ein Sermon von der Bereitung zum Sterben," 1519, WA 2:685-697.

5. A comprehensive study of Luther's postils does not exist. The introductions to the editions of the work in WA serve as the best orientation to it. See WA 7:458-462,10.1.2: IX-LXXIX, 17.2:IX-XXVI, 21:IX-XXV, 22:XI-LXXXIX, 52:VII-XXXV.

6. WA 14:1-91.

7. WA 9:416,420,422-423,427,428,430,431,459-461,471-475,482-498,500, 503-505,507-512,535-537,540-544,547,551-554,558-562,575-581,583-587,593 -597,601-606,612-616.

8. See Hans Rost, *Die Bibel im Mittalalter* (Augsburg: Seitz, 1939), 133-140.

9. WA 24:112,25-113,17. Cf. Robert Kolb, "God Kills to Make Alive: Romans 6 and Luther's Understanding of Justification (1535)," *Lutheran Quarterly* 12, 1 (1998): 33-56.

10. WA 24:121,21.

11. He informed readers that the Hebrew word for "wind" can also mean "spirit," and in Genesis 1:2 he preferred "wind" since he believed that the Holy Trinity presents Himself in proper order in this chapter. That means that God the Father is present from the beginning, God the Son appears as the Word in verse 3, and the Holy Spirit follows in verse 4, as the divine "being well-pleased" in person, God taking His new creation under His wings like a hen. Luther did not want to insist on his interpretation but made his preference for it quite clear (WA 24:27.16-28). Luther expanded on this interpretation of God's seeing that His creation is good as the indication of the person of the Holy Spirit, WA 24:30.20-29. He carefully differentiated the usual German understanding of "soul" (as the spiritual part of the human being that temporarily is separated from the body at death, he said) from the Hebrew meaning which used the term for "everything that constitutes human life in the five senses" (WA 24:67,11-68,16).

12. WA 24:64,24-65,16.

13. WA 24:81,18-22. Cf. 24:116,34-35.

14. WA 24:176,20-180,9.

15. E.g., at 3:8-13 in the Latin, WA 24:93,6-7, 93,28-94,35. Cf. 24:106,18-2 6,288,6-11,693,13-14.

16. WA 24:112,25-113,17.

17. WA 24:17,11-12.

18. WA 24:17,29-18,25.

19. Preface to the Genesis sermons, WA 24:18,26-33.

20. Preface to the Genesis sermons, WA 24:27-22.8; cf. On Gen. 1:1, WA 24:21,31-22,7.

21. On Gen. 1:1, WA 24:22,21-22.

22. To be sure, Luther later insisted that nothing in this Hidden God contradicts what He has revealed of Himself in the Revealed God; see his lecture on Genesis 26 a quarter century later, WA 43:459,24-32; Luther's Works ed., 5:45. Luther was most concerned to assure the believer that God's promise of salvation in Jesus Christ, delivered through the means of grace, is absolutely trustworthy.

23. "Heidelberg Disputation, 1518," WA 1:362,15-19. (*Luther's Works* (Saint Louis and Philadelphia: Concordia and Fortress, 1958-1986; henceforth LW)) 31:53. See Gerhard O. Forde, *On Being a Theologian of the Cross: Reflections on Luther's Heidelberg Disputation, 1518* (Grand Rapids: Eerdmans, 1997), 39-43, 69-102.

24. These ideas are more fully developed in Robert Kolb, *Bound Will, Election, and Wittenberg Theological Method from Martin Luther to the Formula of Concord* (Grand Rapids: Eerdmans, 2005).

25. WA 40,1:45,24-27; LW 26:7.

26. Sermo de triplici iustitia, 1518, WA 2:44,32-38. Cf. the similar definition in the Sermo de duplici iustitia, 1519, WA 2:145,9-146,35; LW 31:297-299. See J. T. Bakker, "De tweevoudige gerechtigheid. Luthers 'Sermo de duplici Iustitia', 1518," in *Luther na 500 jaar*, 30-57.

27. WA 2:46,1-4; cf. WA 2:146,36-147,23; LW 31:299-300. Luther uses the description of Christ as both *sacramentum* (gift) and *exemplum* (example) to describe His relationship to the creature's two dimensions or kinds of righteousness. See Norman Nagel, "*Sacramentum et exemplum* in Luther's Understanding of Christ," *Luther for an Ecumenical Age*, ed. Carl S. Meyer (St. Louis: Concordia, 1967), 172-199.

28. Robert Kolb, "The Ordering of the *Loci Communes Theologici*: The Structuring of the Melanchthonian Dogmatic Tradition," *Concordia Journal* 23 (1997): 317-337.

29. Irene Dingel, "Melanchthon und die Normierung des Bekenntnisses," in *Der Theologe Melanchthon*, Günter Frank, ed. (Stuttgart: Thorbecke, 2000), 195-211.

30. See also, for example, Robert Kolb, "Mensch-Sein in Zwei Dimensionen: die Zweierlei Gerechtigkeit und Luthers De votis monasticis Iudicium," forthcoming.

31. On Gen. 6:17-22, WA 24:180,29-34.

32. On Gen. 22:18, WA 24:397,18-30.

33. Heiko A. Oberman, *The Harvest of Medieval Theology: Gabriel Biel and Late Medieval Nominalism* (Cambridge: Harvard University Press, 1963), 30-47.

34. On Gen. 1:14-19, WA 24:42,22-25.

35. On Gen. 22:18-19, WA 24:398,13-14.

36. On Gen. 1:9-13, WA 24:39,23-25. Cf. 24:57,28.

37. On Gen. 2:1-3, WA 24:61,21-29.

38. On Gen. 3:9, WA 24:111,23-112,8.

39. On Gen. 1:9-13, WA 24:37,12-14,23-25.

40. On Gen. 1:9-13, WA 24:38,11-18. This idea is repeated in detail at 24:44, 20-45.13.

41. On Gen. 3:1-6, WA 24:85,26.

42. On Gen. 3:1-6, WA 24:86,9-10.

43. On Gen. 17, WA 24: 322,34-323,11. The study of Juhani Forsberg, *Das Abrahambild in der Theologie Luthers Pater Fidei Sanctissimus* (Stuttgart: Steiner, 1984), helpful in many ways, is marred by its presumption that "union

with Christ" rather than the righteousness of faith granted by the word of absolution is Luther's fundamental definition of what justification produces.

44. On Gen. 23, WA 24:411, 18-35. On Luther's use of Romans 6:3-11 in his formulation of his doctrine of justification in the Galatians commentary of 1535, see Robert Kolb, "God Kills to Make Alive." Cf. Jonathon D. Trigg, *Baptism in the Theology of Martin Luther* (Leiden: Brill, 1994), 92-99.

45. On Gen. 34, WA 24:593,21-34. Cf. On Gen. 38:1-7, WA 24:623,16-32, on the story of Thamar, Genesis 38.

46. On Gen. 1:9-13, WA, 24:36,22-24.

47. On Gen. 1:29-30, WA, 24:58,8-59,9.

48. On Gen. 1:24-27, WA 24:49,23-51.8. Luther continued by asserting that the human creature is either in God's image or the image of the devil; see also WA 24:153,15. Such statements anticipate his later comments on Genesis in his lectures (1535-1545) and the view of Matthias Flacius Illyricus. See Lauri Haikola, *Gesetz und Evangelium bei Matthias Flacius Illyricus. Eine Untersuchung zur lutherischen Theologie vor der Konkordienformel* (Lund: Gleerup, 1952), 97-192.

49. On Gen. 1:28, WA 24:52,12-53,15.

50. On Gen. 1:28, WA 24:57,18-19,28-35.

51. On Gen. 2:15-17, WA 24:72,15-23.

52. On Gen. 2:15-17, WA 24:73,19-32.

53. On Gen. 2:25-17, WA 24:74,14-30.

54. On Gen. 3:1-6, WA 24:86,24-88,33.

55. On Gen. 3:1-6, WA 24:89,19-21.

56. On Gen. 3:11, WA 24:96,14-97,29.

57. On Gen. 3:14, WA 24:99,27-101,15.

58. On Gen. 5, WA 24:154,25-28.

59. On Gen. 9:18-29, WA 24:211,24-33.

60. On Gen. 4:3-5, WA 24:127,29-128,12. The Latin text ascribes to Abel the thought, "I am not an acceptable person, but you, God, nevertheless accept what I offer by your mercy since you owe nothing to me, WA 24:128,1-3.

61. On Gen. 4:3-5, WA 24:129,24-130,18.

62. On Gen. 7:1, WA 24:183,17-27.

63. On Gen. 12:1-2, WA 24:243,23-26.

64. On Gen. 12:1-2, WA 24:244,21-26.

65. On Gen. 12: 1-2, WA 24:244,29-30.

66. On Gen. 12:4-6, WA 24:249,21-22.

67. On Gen. 12:7-9, WA 24:254,5-14.

68. On Gen. 17, WA 24:318,36-319,16.

69. On Gen. 16:12, WA 24:315,27-31.

70. On Gen. 18, WA 24:34,29-335,34.

71. On Gen. 7:1, WA 24:184,10-29.

72. On Gen. 17:5, WA 24:327,14-20.

73. On Gen. 3:9, WA 24:110,36-111,22.
74. On Gen. 8:15-19, WA 24:195,12-26.
75. On Gen. 23, WA 24:409,22-410,9.
76. On Gen. 14, WA 24:273,6-35.
77. On Gen. 14, WA 24:274,18-20.
78. On Gen. 14, WA 24:275,19-23.
79. On Gen. 18, WA 24:336,12-29.
80. On Gen. 33, WA 24:585,27-587,31.
81. On Gen. 31, WA 24:554,18-29,556,8-22.
82. On Gen. 17, WA 24:330,20-26.

8

The Two Kinds of Righteousness!: What's a Preacher to Do?[1]

Timothy Saleska

Preaching and the Righteousness of Faith

How do you make someone into a *tsaddik* (a righteous man)? This was a question Reb Saunders needed to answer. Reb Saunders was the spiritual leader of the Russian Hasidic Jewish community in Chaim Potok's bestseller, *The Chosen*.[2] He was a man of wisdom and compassion who had endured unimaginable suffering for his people during World War I. When the war ended, the rabbi had moved his family and the Hasidic community to America. Here he had a son, whom he named Daniel. As Reb Saunders's firstborn son, everyone in the community expected Daniel to succeed his father as leader of the community. He was "the chosen one."

One day, when Daniel was just four years old, he picked up a book and read it. Then he repeated it from memory, word for word, back to his father. On that day, Reb Saunders realized that God had given Daniel a brilliant mind, "a mind like a jewel." Daniel started devouring books like they were food and water. But as proud as Reb Saunders was, he soon realized something else about Daniel as well. He realized that even though Daniel had been blessed with a great mind, God had not given him a *heart*. And a heart was the most important thing for a *tsaddik*. Daniel had a magnificent mind, but he did not have the heart of a *tsaddik*. What would the father do? How could he raise Daniel to be a *tsaddik*? How could he give Daniel a heart?

The father wrestled with the problem and finally came to a decision: he would raise his son *in silence.* In other words, the father stopped talking to Daniel and rarely even looked directly at him. From age four until Daniel graduated from college, the father never again had a normal conversation with his son. Through most of his youth, Daniel carried this awful burden of a silent father.

What kind of way is that to raise a son? Near the end of the story, Reb Saunders tries to explain it to Reuven Malter, Daniel's closest friend. But as Reb Saunders talks, Reuven realizes that he was not talking only to him, but *through him* to his son, Daniel. At one point, Reb Saunders, full of emotion, says, "One learns the pain of others by suffering one's own pain. . . . And it is important to know of pain. . . . It destroys our self-pride, our arrogance, our indifference toward others. It makes us aware of how frail and tiny we are and of how much we must depend upon the Master of the Universe."

The Father's Problem

How do you make someone a tsaddik (a righteous person)? For the Christian, a *tzaddik* is someone who is "right" with God, that is, someone who is in a right relationship with Him. A *tsaddik* is also someone who fulfills God's plan for human life—someone who lives in the relationship that God intended not only with the Creator Himself but also with His creation.[3] *How do you make someone a tsaddik?* That is the problem for our heavenly Father as well. And our heavenly Father, for now, has chosen silence as His way too. In an insightful observation, Reuven's father says to his son, *"It is, perhaps, the only way to raise a tsaddik."*

And so we suffer the silence of the almighty God every day of our lives. In our world it is evil that does all the talking. Disease and poverty and violence and disaster bluster away. But God remains silent. He is supposed to be in control, but He lets it all go by without a word. What are we to think? One minute God plays the world's tyrant, and the next minute its benevolent king. He is kind to some and cruel to others. *What are we to think?* God does not answer for any of it.

At critical moments in our lives—moments of anguish or grief—God's silence gets personal and painful. God keeps terribly silent when *I* want answers!

"Why?" I wonder. What's the point? Does this God even exist? And what does He think about me? What is in His heart when He looks at me? When I die, then what? Sooner or later I might meet up with this God. What is He going to say? What if He knows my thoughts?

God's silence becomes painful when it gets personal because *unavoidably* we interpret His silence in the face of our suffering as disapproval of us—and agreement with the punishment. We all know that in the face of an atrocity, if someone with the power to stop the insanity keeps silent, such silence signals assent. If a *king* stands silent while soldiers beat his servant, the king is an accomplice. Does God's silence in the face of suffering signal His assent to it? Does it signal His wrath against our sin and His immanent judgment? Moses had such fears, and so should we:

> For all our days pass away under your wrath;
> We bring our years to an end like a sigh.
> Who considers the power of your anger,
> And your wrath according to the fear of you? (Ps. 90:9, 11)

What can you do about a God who doesn't speak? Job asked that question as well (Job 23).

But at those times when the silence is most deafening, that is when we must realize that the silence is not total. God is not *completely* silent. Neither was Reb Saunders. Near the end of the book, in a startling revelation to Reuven, the great rabbi thanked him for the blessing he had been to his son, Daniel. Then he said, "The Master of the Universe sent you to my son. He sent you when my son was ready to rebel. He sent you to listen to my son's words. *He sent you to be my closed eyes and my sealed ears* (italics added)."

In other words, Reb Saunders saw Reuven as an extension of himself. He carried on the relationship that the father could not. And indeed, throughout the book we learn how Reuven functioned as Daniel's friend against the background of that awful silence. He brought joy and hope to Daniel, and so *in concert with the silence of the father* Reuven had a big hand in giving Daniel the heart of a *tsaddik*.

But in a much more profound way (and here the analogy that I have been making fails to fully capture the nature of the reality) God has sent us a Friend, a final Word on the subject, "begotten of His Father before all worlds, God of God, Light of Lights, Very God of Very God. . .who for us men and for our salvation came down from heaven". . . . A *Word from God against the background of that awful silence.* It is in Christ alone that God Himself speaks to us (John 1:1-14; Heb. 1:1). In Christ we see what is in God's heart and what his intentions are towards us: "No one has ever seen God; the only God, who is at the Father's side, he has made him known" (John 1:18).

This Word is a gift from God to us across the silence. It is the gift of *righteousness.* Jeremiah says it well: "Behold, the days are coming, declares the Lord, when I will raise up for David a righteous Branch. . . . In his days Judah will be saved, and Israel will dwell securely. And this is the name by which he will be called: The Lord is our righteousness" (Jer. 23:56). In Christ, God speaks the word of reconciliation. He shows us His favor and restores the relationship with Him that He intended us to have. God solves the problem of our righteousness by giving us the righteousness He wants us to have.[4] In the person and work of Christ He has restored our identity as His children and given us peace with Him. This means that in Christ we are the righteousness of God.[5]

The Preacher's Task

The preacher is honored to serve Christ and His gift of righteousness to the people who come to hear him. People who are having identity crises come to hear the preacher. They may not be sure who they are anymore or to whom they belong. They may have forgotten, or they may never have known. They may be crushed by God's silence towards the facts of their lives, or they may be ready to rebel against it. In these cases, the silence has done its work. People feel frail and tiny and are looking for a voice, a word of hope, a Light in the darkness!

Others come feeling pretty self-confident. They have done well. They live well. They are not particularly compassionate or interested in the plight of others. They are not worried about themselves. And they are not at all worried about God. So the preacher reminds them. He interprets the silence and brings it to the forefront of their lives so that they begin to think about God like Moses did—and Job and St. Paul and Martin Luther. *What is the preaching of the Law but a proper interpretation of the silent God?*

It confirms our suspicions that God is angry over our sin, that we do not and cannot measure up, and that there is no escape from His clutches. What does the Holy Spirit do as His alien work through the preaching of the Law but terrify the heart so that it feels frail and tiny and dependent? *"God resists the proud but gives grace to the humble"* (Ps. 138:6; Is. 66:2; James 5:6; 1 Pet. 5:5). Only then, because God wills it, can a person become a *tsaddik.*

A *tsaddik!* A righteous person! A person who is right with God and whose relationship with the Creator is as the Creator intended. This is what the preacher aims at. He is not so interested in *talking about* Christ or explaining "how things work," but in *giving the blessing of Christ,* the good Word of their righteousness, to people who feel the burden of a silent Father. That is, in proclaiming the blessings of Christ, the preacher acts on God's behalf to bring His Word to people, giving them a new identity, a new name: "the Lord is our Righteousness."

Through the preacher's proclamation of forgiveness, people are actually killed and raised up. The old is stripped away to make place for the new. Hearts are strengthened and renewed! And the Word served by the pastor does that killing and raising over and over again in the Christian life, in the Absolution and in the Sacraments. Preaching the Word is a joyous occasion like the birth of a baby, like a resurrection, because Christ brings life in the midst of death. If preaching brings the resurrection of dead hearts, how can you have too much resurrection going on? Against the crushing silence of God, which screams anger and death, the preacher brings a Word from the heart of God, which announces righteousness and life to sinners living in God's silence.

Because of this understanding about the function of the preached Word, Luther describes preaching in sacramental terms. To preach the Word is to do the same thing as the Sacraments—to give Christ

and all His blessings.[6] Luther had in mind that a sermon was "a manifestation of the incarnate Word from the written Word by the spoken
word."[7] The preacher bears witness to the Word as flesh in the word
as written by the word as spoken. Preaching is the Word of God in
the same way as the word spoken at creation.[8]

Preaching and the Righteousness of Works

From Identity to Practice

But this is not where all talk about being a *tsaddik* ends for a Christian!
Christians are not invited to sit back and wait passively for the parou-
sia. Reb Saunders was not interested in that either. When Daniel
finally told his father that he was not going to take his father's place
as the leader of the Hasidic community, Reb Saunders let him go. He
knew that Daniel had the heart of a *tsaddik*. It was his identity. But he
still wondered if Daniel would *live as a tsaddik*. Would his activities
show others what he was at heart? Daniel told his father that he would
live as a *tsaddik*. And Daniel knew how to do that because throughout
his life his father had instructed him in the teachings of the rabbis. In
fact, the only time he *did* talk to Daniel was when they were studying
the Talmud together, when the father was teaching the son what it
meant to live as a *tsaddik*.

As Christians—people who have been given righteous hearts—
we also live out our lives in this world, not separate from it. Christians
fill various roles in society, and we use our God-given reason, gifts,
and abilities like everyone else. In carrying out our tasks as human
beings, are we going to live as the righteous people we are? That is,
are our works going to reflect our identity? In the joy that Christians
have over the gift of righteousness that is ours in Christ, we do not
forget about the other side of being a *tsaddik* in this world—the life of
righteousness lived for our neighbors and the rest of humanity. The
first kind of righteousness—the passive righteousness that is a free
gift—does not abolish the second kind of righteousness—the good
works we pursue in our daily lives.[9]

The two dimensions of righteousness are, of course, connected.
They together make up what it means to be a human creature as the

Creator intended. Robert Kolb well describes the Christian life in its two dimensions:

> Human life is cruciform—eyes lifted to focus on God, feet firmly planted on his earth, arms stretched out in mutual support of those God has placed around us. Having the focus of our lives directed toward Christ inevitably extends our arms to our neighbors. Human beings are truly human, that is, right or functioning properly (according to the design for human righteousness that God made) when their identity does express itself in the activities that flow from that identity.[10]

As Luther described it, this active righteousness is the fruit and consequence of the first type (Gal. 5:16-26).[11] God gives us a new name and reconciles us to Himself. We actively respond to His gift of righteousness by putting away the works of the flesh and actively producing the fruit of the Spirit: "If we live by the Spirit, let us also walk by the Spirit," Paul writes (Gal. 5:25).

The Preacher's Task

Faith sends Christians back out into the world to serve their neighbors. The apostle James stresses that this is an important aspect of our Christian life:

> What good is it, my brothers, if someone says he has faith but does not have works? Can such faith save him? If a brother or sister is poorly clothed and lacking in daily food, and one of you says to them, "Go in peace, be warmed and filled," without giving them the things needed for the body, what good is that? So also faith by itself, if it does not have works, is dead (James 2:14-17).

Christians are responsible to live a life that reflects God's love to other humans and also to the rest of God's creation. God also assumes that Christians are to serve God according to His will and not their own. Therefore, Lutherans teach good works and how they are to be done. That means that part of the preacher's job is *to instruct* his people as to what the life of a Christian *tsaddik* "looks like" and *to exhort* them to live as the righteous people God has called them to be.

This task is as important as it has ever been because the culture in which we live is also forming our thinking about morality and the lifestyle choices that we make. What do our children learn everyday? The culture instructs them at every turn that moral principle, the difference between right and wrong, is not a given. It makes one lesson particularly clear: we are all free to "make up our own minds" as we go along and as our feelings dictate.

As Lesslie Newbigin explains, in our modern culture the world of beliefs and values, the world of "right and wrong" is a private world, a world of personal choice. When it comes to morality—questions of right and wrong—our culture teaches that we are free to follow our own preference. Personal conduct and lifestyle, as long as we are not hurting anyone else, ought not to be judged. There are no "right" or "wrong" styles of life.[12]

Because Christians still have sinful hearts, those who come to hear a word from the preacher come, to one degree or another, with these assumptions in mind. They may be confused or unclear about certain issues. They may be facing certain decisions and are relying only on their feelings to guide them. They may have problems in their relationships but do not know what they ought to do. They may have no clue about how to live as a Christian, a *tsaddik*, in the morally ambiguous world. *There is one thing the preacher knows: his people are being shaped every day in ways that negate the "way of the Lord," that is, in ways that deny what it means to be human as God intended.*

The Christian faith has a very different view of what it means to be truly human: "For we are his workmanship, created in Christ Jesus for good works, which God prepared beforehand, that we should walk in them" (Eph. 2:10). At creation, God designed us with our nature to do the works that He foreordained for us to do. He "hard-wired" us to know the difference between right and wrong. He gave His human creatures a "moral compass" to guide them in their behavior and in the treatment of their fellow humans. This is part of what it means to be a human being, to live as a *tsaddik* in God's creation.

Our sin, of course, has clouded our judgment and dulled our conscience. Even though Christ has delivered us from sin and death, sin remains in us, which keeps tempting us to think that we are our own gods and can make our own lifestyle decisions as we see fit. In effect, our sinful nature is always tempting us to deny our status as human creatures created by God. As a result, we often do what we know we should not, what we know is wrong (Rom. 7:7-25).[13] To get rid of the guilt that comes from going against what we are and what we know, we try denial or self-justification or rationalization. Ultimately, every strategy fails.

Only the gift of the righteousness of Christ can take that guilt away. Through that Word, the Holy Spirit comes to us and dwells in us. He assures us that through Christ we are forgiven (Rom. 8:9; 1 Cor. 3:16; Eph. 5:18; John 14:17). Because of Him we are new creatures—a new creation. Old guilt is gone; new freedom has come!

But as Paul says, we are created in Christ Jesus *for good works*! That means that in Christ, God (re)creates us to be the creatures He originally intended, and that is how He wants us to live in this world. We have put on the new man, which is renewed in knowledge after the image of Him who created Him (Col. 3:10).

This new reality, the reality of the Holy Spirit and Christ in us (Gal. 2:20), means that in our heart of hearts, as forgiven sinners, we also love the will of God for our lives. Now the "real I" wants to obey God's will even while the sinful flesh wars against it and works disobedience (Rom. 7:7-25). God's will for human life, the good works that He foreordained for us, and the sense of morality which He built into us, are something that we want to follow because our mind and heart have been transformed. We have the mind of Christ (Phil. 2:5). Therefore, while the Law continues to accuse and threaten us because of our sinful conscience, the Law does not *only* threaten and accuse our conscience. It is also a delight because it shows us what God wants us to do, and it echoes the delight of our new hearts!

The Law as we read it in the Bible is a reflection or elaboration of the will of God for His creatures. It is in our hearts because God created us that way and recreated us that way in Christ. In the Bible this includes the Ten Commandments, which are a summary of God's will for our lives, but it also includes such material as Proverbs, which has the Ten Commandments as its foundation and builds upon them so that we learn how to live wisely (as true *tsaddikim*). It also includes the paraenetic material in the Epistles where Paul gives instruction in many areas of human life on the basis of the moral teaching God has put in us all (Rom. 1-2, for example). This is why the psalmist can say that God's people love the Law that God has given and meditate on it (Ps. 1). We meditate on it because we know that it is the *truth* (Ps. 119:151)! It is good and praised by God who promises certain blessings to those who keep it.[14]

Therefore, the preacher not only delivers to people the righteousness of Christ, so that by His Word they become *tsaddikim*, he also urges, beseeches, and instructs them in how to live as *tsaddikim* in this world.[15] The preacher operates in both dimensions. People need and want to hear how Christians are supposed to live. And because their sinful flesh still wars inside of them, even though they have a new identity in Christ, they need both negative and positive exhortation to do so.[16] It is so easy to forget, and people hear so much "advice" from other sources. They want help with difficult decisions. Now more than ever Christians need to hear what it means to have a Christian marriage, how a Christian husband and wife are supposed to treat each other, and how they are not. They need reminding of how Christians ought to conduct themselves in their places of work and in their relationships with their neighbors, reminding of what is actually "right and wrong," "good and bad," and the list goes on.

In this horizontal dimension—the righteousness of works—the pastor must be aware that he is operating mainly within the sphere of "Law." In his speaking within this dimension, the Law will function to accuse *(lex semper accusat)*, but it will also instruct, urge, encourage, and so on, according to the condition of the hearer's heart and the Spirit's work. This is what the Law does. This dimension has its place in the formation of a *tsaddik* and in proper relationship to the vertical dimension. "[The two dimensions] come into conflict only when the righteousness of works becomes the basis for our righteousness before God or when the righteousness of faith is used to eliminate the need to do good works."[17]

When good works are kept in their proper relationship, a pastor will recognize that he is speaking to the conscience as well as the reason and intellect of his hearers to help them learn how God wants them to live. He wants to give appropriate direction for their footsteps in life's walk.

The pastor approaches this task, then, with the understanding that the written Law is a reflection of the natural law, which God put in the hearts of us all, and which is created anew in those in whom the Spirit lives. The pastor, then, in his preaching in this dimension, elaborates in various ways on the implications of God's instruction for the Christian life. He is interested in properly interpreting it and applying it in relevant and practical ways to a Christian's life. At times he will warn of the dangers of neglecting God's will for their lives. At other times he will positively encourage.[18] He is interested in persuading his hearers to act in God-pleasing ways. For example, Paul talks about the roles of husbands and wives in Ephesians 5 (cf. Col. 3:18-4:1; 1 Pet. 2:13-3:7). Here he deals with family relationships, a topic that is the source of much confusion today, and also great relevance. What does Paul say about the relationship between husband and wife? As he reflects on the God-given institution of marriage, what guidance does he offer for families today? A pastor will seek out others who have thought through what Paul is saying and what other parts of Scripture say on this topic so that he can help his people to embody in their behavior what God intended for the male and female whom He created to be in partnership with each other in the first place. What does that "partnership" mean? What does it not mean? What should it look like? The material in Paul's epistle gives us the opportunity to approach this topic in a God-pleasing way.

In fact, the Epistles in general are the obvious texts for this kind of preaching. As others have pointed out, Paul bases his paraenesis on the Gospel promises. He grounds his exhortations on the work of Christ and on promises about the coming salvation that awaits God's people.[19] At that time, the two kinds of righteousness will become "one" in our fully realized identity as God's creatures. In the meantime, it is clear that Paul is interested in both identity and performance.

Pastors might take advantage of this by leading their people through an Epistle as a sermon series. Following Paul's method, in this kind of expository preaching, he would be able to proclaim to people "the righteousness of faith" and give them the comfort of the Gospel. He could also speak of the implications of this for their lives, encouraging, warning, and instructing them to live as the people that they have been called out of darkness to be: God's *tsaddikim* in identity and practice.

Notes

1. The author would like to thank colleague Joel Biermann for his helpful critique of this paper.

2. Potok, Chaim, *The Chosen* (New York: Ballantine Books, 1967).

3. Kolb, Robert, "Luther on the Two Kinds of Righteousness: Reflections on His Two-Dimensional Definition of Humanity at the Heart of His Theology," *Lutheran Quarterly* 13 (1999): 450-452, 455-456; Charles Arand, "Two Kinds of Righteousness as a Framework for Law and Gospel in the Apology," *Lutheran Quarterly* 15 (2001): 420-421.

4. This is the "righteousness of faith" of which Melanchthon, for example, writes: "Since we receive the forgiveness of sins and reconciliation on account of Christ by faith alone, faith alone justifies. This is because those who are reconciled are regarded as righteous and children of God, not on account of their own purity, but through mercy on account of Christ, as long as they take hold of this mercy by faith" (Ap IV, 86). All quotations from the Confessions are taken from *The Book of Concord: The Confessions of the Evangelical Lutheran Church*, ed. Robert Kolb and Timothy J. Wengert (Philadelphia: Fortress, 2000).

5. Already here, then, the two dimensions of the Christian life are implied. First, the righteousness of faith gives us our identity as God's children. But also, if in Christ we really are the *righteousness of God* as Jeremiah suggests, it is also our mission to embody and manifest that righteousness in our lives—in the way that we serve those around us. In a parallel way, Christ calls Himself the "light of the world" in fulfillment of the Servant described in Isaiah 49:6. But Paul also asserts that he and fellow Christians fulfill that role as they bring the Gospel to the nations (Acts 13:47; cf. Acts 1:8). In Christ we are "the servant" who is the light to the nations. In Christ we are "the righteousness of God" who reflect Christ's righteousness in the world. So the Lord also says to us, "I am the Lord; I have called you in righteousness; I will take you by the hand and keep you; I will give you as a covenant for the people, a light for the nations, to open the eyes that are blind, to bring out the prisoners from the dungeon, from the prison those who sit in darkness" (Is. 42:6-7).

6. G. Forde, "Preaching the Sacraments," *Lutheran Theological Seminary Bulletin* 64 (1984): 3-4.

7. A quote by Bernard Lord Manning cited by David Steinmetz, "Luther, the Reformers, and the Bible," in *Living Traditions of the Bible*, ed. James E. Bowley (St. Louis: Chalice Press, 1998), 169.

8. Ibid., 169.

9. Arand, "Two Kinds of Righteousness," 433.

10. Kolb, "Luther on Two Kinds of Righteousness," 455-456.

11. Ibid., 458.

12. Lesslie Newbigin, *Foolishness to the Greeks: The Gospel and Western Culture* (Grand Rapids: Eerdmans, 1986), 19.

13. J. Budziszewski, *What We Can't Not Know* (Dallas: Spence Publishing, 2003), 66-67. For a succinct treatment of natural law see also C. S. Lewis, *The Abolition of Man: How Education Develops Man's Sense of Morality* (New York: McMillan, 1947).

14. "Morever, we willingly give this righteousness of reason the praises it deserves, for our corrupt nature has no greater good than this, as Aristotle rightly said: 'Neither the evening star nor the morning star is more beautiful than righteousness.' God even honors it with temporal rewards. Still, it ought not be praised at Christ's expense" (Ap IV, 24).

15. P. Raabe and J. Voelz, "Why Exhort a Good Tree?: Anthropology and Paraenesis in Romans," *Concordia Journal* 22 (1996), 160, write about Paul's exhortation: "Fifth, it should be noted that Paul's intent in paraenesis is not to accuse the Romans as sinners. He does that in chapters 1-3, where the tone is notably different. Paraenesis uses the language of urging, appealing, and beseeching rather than that of harsh demanding and condemning. Can Christians as sinners still hear paraenesis as accusatory? No doubt they can. If the addressees were not paying taxes, presumably they would have felt accused by 13:6-7. But there were probably other hearers in the church in Rome who saw the rightness of Paul's appeal and gladly embraced it."

16. Many years ago, my father-in-law, who is a dedicated Christian businessman, lamented to me about the lack of this kind of speaking from the pulpit. He said, "Every once in a while I need to hear, 'Don't cheat on your taxes! That's wrong! Don't steal! Don't lie!'" and so on. Rightfully so, he sought that kind of guidance for daily living as a Christian.

17. Arand, "Two Kinds of Righteousness," 427.

18. Raabe, Voelz, "Why Exhort a Good Tree?," 159.

19. Ibid., 158.

9

The Ministry of the Church in Light of the Two Kinds of Righteousness

Charles P. Arand

The expectations on pastors have greatly expanded over the last generation. At times, the increased responsibilities brought with them shifts in the "job descriptions" of pastors. Much of this was due to a renewed emphasis on the importance of mobilizing the priesthood of the baptized for that mission of the church. In the process, pastors came to be seen less as "curers of souls" or mouthpieces for God and more as counselors, managers, coaches, leaders, administrators, spiritual guides, and the like. The need for pastors to function in these capacities brought about curriculum revisions in seminaries that supplemented courses on preaching, catechesis, leading worship, baptizing, and presiding at the Lord's Supper with courses that focused on other skills like administration, conflict resolution, leadership, management, and counseling. Acquiring competence in these areas is a good thing, even a necessary thing, in a society in which shepherding congregations has become analogous to running medium to large size nonprofit organizations.

Just as the twentieth century saw increased attention given to the human and sociological aspects of the church, the last few decades have seen similar attention given to the person, personality, entrepreneurial, and leadership skills of a pastor. At times it has occurred at the expense of the theological definition of the pastoral office in which the pastor serves as the one who delivers the gifts of Christ to God's people. In any event, we need to rethink the office of the public ministry and the priesthood of the baptized within the framework of the two kinds of righteousness in order to do justice to the Biblical and confessional understanding of the pastoral office as well as the contemporary mission needs of congregations in twenty-first century America. Like the church, the office of the public or pastoral ministry rests upon the presupposition that the believer lives in two distinct but inseparable relationships. God's Word of forgiveness establishes our relationship with God; God's design for human action regulates the horizontal sphere of life. The understanding of this ministry rests also upon the nature of God's Word in Lutheran theology, for the church as church is created and identified by that Word. The public ministry of the church is ultimately a ministry of the Word.

The Ministry of the Church *Coram Deo*

In the early days of the Reformation it was necessary to stress, in light of the doctrine of justification, that there was no distinction *coram deo* ("before God") between the spiritual estate and the secular estate. The confusion of the two kinds of righteousness during the Middle Ages had resulted in the development of a hierarchical relationship between the socalled spiritual and secular estates in at least two ways. First, the spiritual estate was ranked as a higher order than the secular estate, thereby creating a distinction between first-class and second-class Christians. The Christian could best achieve righteousness in the eyes of God by dedicating himself or herself fulltime to the pursuit of sanctification. In other words, to attain full godliness it was necessary to dedicate oneself to God twenty-four hours a day, seven days a week, three hundred sixty-five days a year. Such dedication required that one be in a situation that was freed of external distractions or temptations that would attach a person to this world. Only by entering one of the spiritual orders could a person climb up the ladder beyond the Ten Commandments to the "evangelical counsels" in order to attain the angelic life *(vita angelica)*. Those who entered the "holy orders" thus entered into a state of existence whereby they could acquire a higher level of perfection than ordinary Christians. Luther's distinction of two kinds of human righteousness stressed that those who entered one of the spiritual estates were no closer to God than those who labored on the farm or in the mill. The relationship with God was established only by faith in Jesus Christ.

Second, the confusion of the two kinds of righteousness in the Middle Ages gave rise to a job description for those who lived in the spiritual estate as priests that empowered them to dispense the *habitus* of grace to the people through the Sacrament. If a priest's standing before God gave him special standing over his parishioners, his power to dispense God's grace gave him special power over them. It was argued that the priest had been given a special quality through his ordination that enabled him to do things no others could do. In a sense, they "controlled" God's grace to the people, turning it on and off like a faucet. Early on, however, Luther came to realize that the power of God is expressed through the Word, not through priests who had attained a special spiritual status. All are justified on the basis of Christ's work. The priest could not control God's dealing with believers or dominate the life of the believer. Luther insisted that all hold in common the gifts that flow from justification. "Rome said ordination separated. The Lutherans said baptism is our common base. Thus they promoted something of a baptismal egalitarianism."[1] All Christians, whether ordained or not, have the same Baptism, the same Gospel, and the same faith. There is no spiritual distinction among the people of God.

The Ministry of the Church *Coram Mundo*

So does this mean that Luther abolished the office of the ministry in favor of an egalitarian or democratic view of the work of the church? Not at all. Although there are no distinctions among people *coram deo* when it comes to the matter of justification, Luther did not deny that God established different roles and tasks for people *coram mundo* ("before the world") when it comes to the matter of carrying out the work of the church. The two kinds of righteousness not only allowed Luther to break through the secular-spiritual estate distinction *coram deo* but also allowed him to recover the value of vocation for life here on earth. This led him to emphasize that in our horizontal relationships (*coram mundo*) God has established distinct estates or walks of life within which people serve. In these walks of life people are given "offices" or responsibilities that Christians recognize as callings or vocation from God. On the eve of the Reformation, many believed that God had structured the human life to be lived in three situations: home (both family and economic activities), the political realm, and the church. By virtue of their creatureliness, people are commissioned to discharge complementary tasks in these offices for the good of creation and human society. By virtue of their Baptisms, Christians are given the task of confessing the name of Christ within every walk of life. All Christians bring the message of repentance and forgiveness of sins in ways appropriate to their walks of life.[2] In other words, Luther stressed that by virtue of Baptism, every Christian had the responsibility and privilege to share the Word of God with others.

That every Christian had the responsibility to share the Word with their neighbors did not mean that there was no need for a public office of the ministry nor that every Christian automatically held that public office. For Luther, it simply meant that every Christian had the responsibility and privilege of taking that Word to others within his or her divinely appointed walk of life. They were to be prepared to give reason for the hope that was within them. To that end, the Lutheran reformers placed a renewed emphasis upon the responsibility of parents to keep the Word of God before their household—a household that would include not only the children, but farmhands, maids, servants, etc. Within this role, Luther was not even averse to speaking of the husband and wife as the bishop and bishopess of the household.[3] Indeed, Luther prepared his Small Catechism and addressed each "chief part" to the head of the house in order to help him carry out his responsibility of witness and discipleship.[4] In a similar way, Luther frequently gave instruction to governmental leaders regarding their responsibilities for maintaining community chests and for establishing schools.[5]

As God has ordered each of the horizontal spheres of human life (governmental official or ruler and subject or citizen, parent and child), so he has ordered the church (pastor and parishioner). Unlike his medieval predecessors, Luther did not see this as an ordering *coram deo*, but as an ordering of the church *coram mundo*. Particularly as the Reformation moved into its second and third decades, it became necessary to stress this aspect against the spiritualists and fanatics who relegated God to work simply within and through some kind of internal word. Over and against the radicals, Luther stressed that the public ministry was not optional.[6]

> I hope, indeed, that believers, those who want to be called Christians, know very well that the spiritual estate [the pastor] has been established and instituted by God, not with gold or silver but with the precious blood and bitter death of His only Son, our Lord Jesus Christ. From His wounds indeed flow the Sacrament. . .He paid dearly that men might everywhere have this office of preaching, baptizing, loosing, binding, giving the Sacrament, comforting, warning, and exhorting with God's Word, and whatever else belongs to the pastoral office. . .Indeed, it is only because of the spiritual estate that the world stands and abides at all, if it were not for this estate, the world would long ago have gone down to destruction.[7]

Robert Rosin points out that Luther is not saying here that either the church or the world depends on the office of the ministry for its existence, but because things go wrong, pastors must be the line of defense. "True preaching—the Word—will set things right again."[8]

The Wittenberg reformers stressed that for the proper ordering of the church *coram mundo*, God has established the special priesthood within the midst of the common priesthood. Luther viewed it as a gift from God in the horizontal sphere of human relationships, a particular position to which some are called to make possible the formal and public use of God's saving Word. The pastor possesses no spiritual superiority or special holiness *coram deo*. Instead, God created the office of the pastoral ministry for the well-being of all the priests of God (even as He gave parents for the sake of children, governors for sake the of citizens). And so it exists as a place of service for others. For this reason, the church has the command to appoint ministers.[9]

So for Lutherans, the ministry of the Word has been entrusted to the common priesthood and the special priesthood. Each uses the Word, but in different settings. Even though the offices of spouse or parent or public official are not dedicated exclusively to the delivery of the Word (also serving creation), this does not mean they are inferior offices *coram deo* or that the pastoral office is of superior status *coram deo*. Both belong together, but each has a different sphere of activity. To play them off against each other is to confuse the two spheres of relationship and the mutual service in and through the Word.[10] This most often occurs when personal authority and talk of rights dominate the conversation about the ministry, be it common or special. Then problems only get worse.[11] The pastor is a servant of God's command and of God's people's needs. The people respect the office on account of God's institution and the Word delivered to them.

Called from Common Priesthood into Special Service

In addition to telling people about Jesus within their vocations, the common priesthood carries out its responsibility of the keys by calling someone from its midst to serve in the special priesthood. In one sense, all Christians are priests in that they are born of water and the Spirit, and any could carry out the public functions—to baptize, preach, celebrate the Lord's Supper, to bind and loose sins, to sacrifice (offer up praise in worship), pray for others, and judge doctrine.[12] Yet they are not to usurp the tasks delegated to the special servants of the congregation by claiming the public use of God's Word for themselves without consideration for the community. "Publicly, one may not exercise a right without the consent of the whole body or of the church."[13] This is the point of the fourteenth article of the Augsburg Confession concerning the proper placement of pastors into their office. The common priesthood has the responsibility by virtue of Baptism to fill the public office of the special priesthood. Luther put it well:

> You should put the Christian into two places. First, if he is in a place where there are no Christians he needs no other call than to be a Christian, called and anointed by God from within. Here it is his duty to preach and teach the Gospel to erring heathen or non-Christians. . .even though no one calls him to do so. . . . Second, if he is in a place where there are Christians who have the same power and right as he, he should not draw attention to himself. Instead, he should be called and chosen to preach and to teach in the place of and by the command of others.[14]

All Christians serve the Word in one setting (in private or out in the world); a pastor serves the Word in another setting (in the public assembly, for all to see).[15] Thus pastors do not exercise their office in their own right and of themselves but because they have been asked to do that by and for the community of believers. Those who are pastors, in the public office, were chosen to be there by others with whom they share that common priesthood by virtue of Baptism. The pastor serves with the approval of the congregation.

Therefore, the reformers stressed that pastors must be "rightly called" (*rite vocatus*). The reformers generally insisted that three things occur for one to be rightly called: examination, call, and ordination. Examination signaled to the congregations that candidates were aligned with evangelical theology. Those who are called to serve in the special priesthood must above all else "be apt to teach" (1 Tim. 3:2). That is to say, they must be competent to proclaim the Word. This was especially important for the reformers who saw the church as a creature of the Word and defined the office of pastor in terms of delivering the Word. The call signaled to the candidate that a congregation was willing to receive him as its pastor. Ordination was a rite celebrated to mark the coming of one called.

While the reformers tended to regard the three moments, examination, call, and ordination, as non-negotiable components of being *rite vocatus*, precisely *how* that took place could vary according to human wisdom *(de jure humano)*. There was not one "proper method" for how a man might be placed into the public office. Luther was prepared to use whatever established procedures were in place so long as the Gospel was being proclaimed. Procedures for doing so could always be revamped if necessary. But it *will* be done, and the ministry of the Word *will* happen. That is to say, how much education and how that education is delivered in order to be apt to teach could vary. Often it has occurred by way of university education. In other cases it was by on-site continuing education. That training in the Word culminated with the examination (certification). It, too, could take place in a variety of ways. Often it took place through a lengthy examination before a panel of three professors at Wittenberg. In other cases, the local superintendent bore the responsibility. Similarly, the procedures for calling, whether by the superintendent, the congregation, or a placement board, could, and did vary during the era of the Reformation. Ordination was a rite by which the wider church celebrated a man called to a particular congregation. Thus the bishop or superintendent normally performed the ordination. But pastors could ordain where a superintendent was unavailable.

Although the Confessions place a strong emphasis on the importance of filling the office of pastor, they recognize certain "emergency" situations can occur when a pastor cannot be obtained. Two situations stand out. First, it may be that a pastor cannot be obtained because the established authorities refuse to provide pastors to congregations. In the 1530s Roman bishops refused to ordain Lutheran candidates as pastors of congregations. So what are the churches to do when bishops refuse to give them pastors? Melanchthon gave an answer in 1537 when he wrote "On the Jurisdiction of Bishops" in his Treatise on the Power and Primacy of the Pope. The church cannot be without pastors. The people cannot be denied God's Word. Thus churches must ordain pastors for themselves. Second, emergency situations may arise when a pastor cannot be obtained because there are no candidates available. That may require any believer to step in and carry out the responsibilities of the office.[16] The "Treatise on the Power and Primacy of the Pope" also affirms that in cases of necessity each Christian has the right to baptize and publicly to declare the forgiveness of sins. It is important to note in both emergency situations the issue has to do with *how* the pastoral office was filled, not whether it is optional to fill the office.

The common priesthood (the priesthood of the Baptized) has been given three tasks *de jure divino:* (1) as individuals they share the Word within the mission assignments of their vocations, (2) collectively as a congregation they call an individual to serve as pastor within their midst; (3) in an emergency, the common priesthood temporarily takes on the tasks of ministry, serving publicly until the office can be properly filled.

Distinguishing a Pastor's Duties
De Jure Divino and *De Jure Humano*

As the office of pastor was established by God for the proper ordering of Christ's church *coram mundo*, it is further necessary to distinguish between those responsibilities given by God and those assigned to the pastor by the common priesthood.

When titles were chosen for the first seven articles of the Augsburg Confession, the title "the office of the ministry" (German) or the "office of the church" (Latin) was chosen for the fifth article, which flowed from the central teaching of the document, found in the fourth article on justification. The article opens by stating, "To obtain such faith God instituted the office of the ministry." Melanchthon uses the word ministerium as a "verbal noun."[17] In other words, Melanchthon regarded the medieval term for the office of the ministry, "ministerium," as a word that describes both the thing and the action that constitutes the thing and gives it its purpose—in the case of the ministerium, serving. Even as the confessors stressed that God had instituted a specific office for conveying the power of God's Word into the lives of sinners, they emphasized that the pastor who filled that office did so by serving in a specific way: as the agent for releasing God's forgiving and re-creating Word.

Augsburg Confession V defines the nature of the service rendered by the office of the ministry with the phrase, "that is, [through it God] provided the gospel and the sacraments as means through which the Holy Spirit ignites faith within the human heart."[18] The public ministry of the church is inextricably linked with God's tools for creating faith. "Pastor and Word are like horse and carriage; the church does not have one without the other."[19] Melanchthon especially stresses this in Augsburg Confession XXVIII, where he distinguishes between those tasks that God has authorized and those tasks that other humans (especially ecclesiastical or secular leaders) authorize. He repeatedly argues, "The power of the keys or the power of the bishops is the power of God's mandate to preach the gospel, to forgive and retain sins, and to administer the sacrament."[20] Even though pastors are responsible for conveying the Word of God into the lives of people, this does not mean that pastors can convert anyone. The Spirit does that through the Word, and He creates faith "when and where he pleases."

What God has given the pastor to do (*de jure divino*) must be distinguished from what human beings assign the pastor to do (*de jure humano*). This is in part the burden of article XXVIII of the Augsburg Confession, where Melanchthon deals with the confusion and the damage done to the pastoral office by having bishops fill a formal political role in secular society. Today, there is little danger of a man serving simultaneously as a pastor and a governor. Still, the church as a non-profit human organization within God's left hand realm may ask the pastor to exercise certain secular tasks. That is to say, the congregation as an empirical community of people asks the pastor to carry out left hand kingdom responsibilities alongside the right hand kingdom responsibility of proclaiming the Word. In calling a pastor, a congregation (as non-profit organization) may authorize a pastor to lead its members in strategic planning, administration, counseling, vision setting, hiring, budgeting, and the like. This is only an authority given by human right *(de jure humano)*.

Similarly, distinctions that might be made within the public ministry, such as that between pastor and bishop, are *de jure humano*. The confessions of the Lutheran church consistently affirm that these are not distinctions *coram deo*. Whether they are called bishops, pastors, or presbyters, they all belong to the singular ministry of the word. This became an important point to make in the 1530s over against Rome. During that time Roman bishops increasingly refused to ordain Lutheran candidates for the ministry, thereby depriving evangelical congregations of pastors. Medieval theologians had contended that priests could conduct five of the seven sacraments (Baptism, absolution, Lord's Supper, marriage, and last rites) while bishops carried out the additional tasks of confirmation and ordination. In "Treatise on the Power and Primacy of the Pope," Melanchthon argued that such distinctions were humanly devised. By divine right, all the tasks of the one office belonged to all those who served in that office. Thus, when bishops refuse to ordain, the church should have its pastors ordain men into the ministry. And so throughout the course of the sixteenth century, Lutheran churches did not in any way regard themselves as less church than Rome because they lacked bishops.

Case Study 1: The Pastor's "Job Description"

The tasks found in a pastor's job description have expanded greatly over the past several decades. As a result, many pastors have become increasingly specialized. For example, a congregation may ask a pastor to be a church planter. Others may call a pastor to develop and expand the youth program. A congregation may call a pastor to serve as counselor. Or they may call a pastor to be the administrative pastor or the director of ministries. All of these specialized tasks are not intrinsic to the office of the ministry in such a way that one is not a pastor if one is not engaged in these particular specializations. Consider the topic of strategic planning.

In a sense, strategic planning has no direct or immediate connection to the well-being of the church as an assembly of believers *coram deo*. Nor is it an activity that Christ has explicitly given to those who hold the office of the ministry. He has given them the mandate to proclaim the Gospel and administer the Sacraments. Planning does have to do, however, with building those human support structures in the left hand realm for the proclamation of the Gospel and the administration of the Sacraments. That is, it deals with how we go about carrying out the mission of God as a congregation. It deals with how we can best accomplish that task given the challenges and opportunities that we have. To that end, it requires the use of brains and imagination in the service of the Gospel.

Inasmuch as strategic planning involves finding ways to carry out the mission God has given His church, it is of interest to the pastor. The Gospel and the theology of the church (as an assembly of believers) must provide the basis and direction for everything that the church (as an empirical sociological reality) does here on earth. Inasmuch as strategic planning involves a specific process it may well (and often does) go beyond the particular skills, experience, and training of the pastor. That is to say, it involves activities in which lay people may be far more skilled, for strategic planning is itself a process that has grown out of non-theological disciplines. So a pastor certainly has a vested interest in the outcome of strategic planning and how it contributes to the proclamation of the Gospel among the lost. On the other hand, it is a process and activity with which those in the corporate world may have more experience and skills.

To be sure, a pastor can certainly go out and acquire the training and skills necessary to lead a congregation through a process of strategic planning. But as he engages in that process, it should be recognized that he is carrying out an activity that is not intrinsic to the pastoral office. That is not to say that it is an unimportant activity by any means. But it belongs to the *bene esse* (well-being) of the church and not to the *esse* (essence) of the church. Thus it cannot simply be equated with the *de jure divino* activities of the office by which the church as an assembly of believers is built up. Instead, it provides the context, structures, and direction needed for a congregation to use every resource and opportunity it has to bring the Gospel to those living in unbelief.

Case Study 2: The Pastor's Creaturely Gifts

The particular direction that a pastor takes in his ministry may depend in part upon his first article gifts. Indeed, many of the tasks given to a pastor are not rooted in the pastoral office itself, but are assigned on the basis of an individual's first article creaturely gifts. Some pastors are gifted with a charismatic personality, an entrepreneurial spirit, organizational abilities, and leadership abilities. These gifts and skills can be a tremendous asset for a congregation. The downside is that they can overshadow the Gospel or build a congregation upon the unique talents of the individual.

At their best, pastors will develop and utilize their first article gifts to serve the third article proclamation of the Gospel. For example, learning Greek assists in interpreting the Scriptures. The Bible is inspired by the Holy Spirit and was originally written in Hebrew and Greek. Yet we do not learn Greek grammar and syntax from the Bible. The Bible is neither a dictionary nor a grammar. Instead, we use lexicon and grammars produced through first article gifts and then utilize them to interpret the Scriptures, which were written in human language. Similarly, learning the first article gift of rhetoric or communication can assist in the construction of a sermon that effectively conveys the Gospel into the lives of people. Developing first article people skills can greatly assist a pastor in breaking down barriers for finding entrance into people's lives for sharing the Gospel. Developing analytical and thinking skills through the study of philosophy can help pastors diagnose intellectual obstacles within our culture that prevent people from giving a hearing to the Gospel. Developing first article leadership principles and financial management skills can assist in organizing the church so as to get the Gospel out to a wide variety of people. For these reasons, Lutheran seminaries have traditionally placed a strong emphasis on a good liberal arts background for seminary students as preparation for the study of the theology and the proclamation of the Gospel.

At their worst, first article gifts can be used unintentionally to replace or supplant the Gospel in a way that shifts our focus from growing the church as a fellowship of the faith to growing the church as a first article non-profit organization. This can occur when we unconsciously come to regard first article gifts as key to the growth of the church more than third article preaching and teaching. These first article gifts have a tremendous impact upon the establishment and growth of the church as a first article creation. Indeed, a pastor who has been endowed with extraordinary first article gifts such as charisma, people skills, or administrative skills could grow any organization, be it a business, a company, a church, or, for that matter, a cult. First article gifts alone can create large communities or institutions.

Pastors' creaturely gifts also differ greatly from one person to another. Not everyone has been endowed with the same charismatic personality or gifts for organization. Not everyone shares the same willingness for risk taking that is a prerequisite for entrepreneurial types. This is not to say that each should not develop to the fullest the particular gifts that God has given us. There is no excuse for not developing and using the gifts that God has given us. At the same time, Lutherans are skeptical about the idea that if one only follows "this particular program" or "these proven principles," then all churches will grow. Much depends upon the God-given abilities of each person to carry out these things.

Case Study 3: Delegation of Tasks

The core of the pastoral office is the proclamation of the Gospel and the administration of the Sacraments. With regard to the first, it involves at the very least, preaching and teaching. He is responsible both for his own teaching as well as the doctrinal content of all those who are engaged in instruction within the congregation. The administration of the Sacraments involves acting as gatekeeper in terms of those who are admitted as well as the actual ministration of the Sacraments. Herein lies the core. Now does this mean that *only* the pastor can teach? Or *only* the pastor can administrate the Sacraments, especially to shut-ins? Does it mean that *only* the pastor carries out hospital calls? After all, it is very possible that the load of hospital and shut-in visits is beyond the scope of a single pastor, or even several pastors, given the size of the congregation. Can these be delegated to lay staff or elders without undermining the pastoral office? The answer is yes and no.

Consider shut-in communions. The pastor's task involves not only the actual administration of Communion but also especially the matter of acting as a gatekeeper. That is, he has the responsibility to determine who is admitted to the table and who is not. It seems to me that a good solution is to do the following. When the Lord's Supper is celebrated in the congregation on Sunday, the pastor not only hands the elements to elders for distribution to members who are present that morning, but he also hands the elements to elders who immediately take them to shut-ins that very morning. In a sense, then, the entire congregation joins together in Communion, both those who are present and those who are homebound. But, if in the course of distributing the elements to the homebound, the shut-in reveals a particular spiritual problem that requires pastoral discernment and care, then the elder has the responsibility of getting in touch with the pastor who can then come and deal with that person.

Something similar can take place for the hospitalized. Trained lay people can certainly visit the sick and offer a devotion or prayer. That it is seen as an exclusively pastoral task is more a matter related to the culture of the congregation than the theology of the church. At the same time, if the hospitalization involves a serious illness or the parishioner is experiencing a spiritual crisis of some kind, the pastor must be notified that he may administer care for the soul. People will want the pastor not only because he is ordained, but also because as such he has more training and experience in the care of souls than the average person.

We can use the example of a physician's assistant. Very often, when I am ill, my wife will call the doctor. She will not actually speak with him. Instead, she speaks with the physician's assistant to whom she describes my symptoms. The physician's assistant then phones in the appropriate prescription to the pharmacy. Now that works as long as we are dealing with such recurring things as allergies, flu, bronchitis, sore throats, etc. Generally, my wife and I are okay with that. But if there is something more serious going on, something out of the ordinary, then we want to speak with (or see) the doctor himself. Why? Because he is the doctor. It is his role. He has the training and experience for such matters. I think that something similar would apply to the pastor-parishioner relationship.

Conclusion

Many of the challenges confronting the church lie within the horizontal realm of life. The reason for this is that the Christian foundation that shaped society for the last two millennia continues to crumble. For much of that time, the church could rely on the wider society to support its efforts and do much of its work. As Jim Bachman has noted, "We are living through a painful transition from congregational dynamics governed by what I call the 'hidden hand familial and of ethnic social structure' to dynamics that are today much more in need of 'visible hands' to build, shape, and guide our church communities. And how we. . . argue to build, shape, and guide." The same applies to the pastoral office. "The hidden hand of ethnic social dynamics no longer constructively shapes and supports congregational life. Pastors and those who prepare them are scrambling to think through how pastors along with other congregational leaders must be community creators, builders, and sustainers, as well as stewards of the Word and Sacrament."[21]

Notes

1. John F. Johnson, "The Office of the Pastoral Ministry: Scriptural and Confessional Considerations," *The Collected Papers of the 150th Anniversary Theological Convocation of the Lutheran Church-Missouri Synod*, eds. Jerold Joersz and Paul McCain (Saint Louis: Lutheran Church-Missouri Synod, 1998), 88.

2. Johnson, "Office of the Pastoral Ministry," 88.

3. "Ten Sermons on the Catechism," LW 51:57; WA 30, 1:57, 26-58, 22.

4. Small Catechism, Household chart, *Book of Concord*, 365-367, BSLK, 523-527.

5. For example, in his "Ordinance of a Common Chest, Preface," published along with the regulations for social welfare in the Saxon town of Leisnig,

1523, LW 45: 169-194; WA 12:11-30; and his "To the Councilmen of All Cities in Germany That They Establish and Maintain Christian Schools," 1524, LW 45:347-378; WA 15: 27-53.

6. "Confession Concerning Christ's Supper," 1528, LW 37:364; WA 26:504, 30-35.

7. "A Sermon on Keeping Children in School," 1530, LW 46:219-220; WA 30, 2:526, 33527, 25.

8. Robert Rosin, "Luther on the Pastoral Ministry, the Biography of an Idea," unpublished paper delivered for the ILC Theology Professors conference in Erfurt, Germany in 2004.

9. Apology of the Augsburg Confession, XIII, 12, *Book of Concord*, 220, BSLK, 294; Treatise on the Power and Primacy of the Pope 69, *Book of Concord*, BSLK, 491.

10. Robert Kolb, "Ministry in Martin Luther and the Lutheran Confessions," in *Called & Ordained: Lutheran Perspectives on the Office of the Ministry*, eds. Todd Nichol and Marc Kolden (Minneapolis: Fortress, 1990), 52.

11. Rosin, "Luther on the Pastoral Ministry, the Biography of an Idea," 12.

12. "Concerning the Ministry," 1523, LW 40:33-34; WA 12:189, 5-190, 31.

13. "Concerning the Ministry," 1523, WA 12:189, 26-27.

14. "That a Christian Congregation or Assembly has the Right and Power to Judge All Teaching," 1523, LW 39: 310; WA 11:412, 30-34.

15. Rosin, "Luther on the Pastoral Ministry, the Biography of an Idea," 11.

16. "Concerning the Ministry," 1523, LW 40:34; WA 12:189, 15-16.

17. Peter Fraenkel, "Revelation and Tradition: Notes on Some Aspects of Doctrinal Continuity in the Theology of Philip Melanchthon," *Studia Theolgica* 13 (1959): 97-133.

18. Augsburg Confession, V, *Book of Concord*, 40-41, BSLK, 58.

19. Kolb, "Ministry," 56.

20. "This jurisdiction belongs to the bishops as bishops (that is, to those to whom the ministry of Word and sacraments has been committed): to forgive sins, to reject teaching that opposes the gospel, and to exclude from the communion of the church the ungodly whose ungodliness is known—doing all this not with human power but by the Word" (Augsburg Confession, XXVIII, 21, *Book of Concord*, 94 BSLK, 123-124.

21. James Bachman, "The Communion of Saints: The Church's Unique Contribution to the Changing Moral Landscape," *Issues in Christian Education*, 35: 2 (Fall 2001), 1819.

Conclusion

Charles P. Arand

The church has often drawn upon the resources it has inherited from those who have gone before into order to help its members think through how best to address the questions that they face in their particular age. This is not to say that the church does so blindly without regard for the distances in time or without regard for the different questions that each age faces. Nor does it mean that it does so simply by appropriating the theological formulations and terminology of the past with little regard for the way they may be heard in the present. Instead, the church freshly appropriates the insights of previous generations for a its own day. At times this requires the task of translation. At other times it may involve applying those insights creatively to new questions that could not have been envisioned at that time.

These resources that the church freshly appropriates for the issues of its day include both the dogmas of the church as well as various theological distinctions. And in both cases, they serve the cause of Christian witness, that is to say, they function in such a way as to keep our speaking of the story and promises of God a *Gospel* story and *Gospel* promises.[1]

For example, with regard to the dogmas or doctrines of the church, we might consider the Trinitarian and Christological confession as set forth in the Athanasian Creed. They addressed problems the church faced about how to speak of the Son's relation to the Father and the Son's relation to creation, especially human creatures. These arose out of questions raised by the Gospel narratives and inadequate answers to those questions that had been provided over the course of the third, fourth, and fifth centuries. The Athanasian Creed sets forth the answers by providing a grammar—or perhaps better yet—grammatical boundaries—for how one talks about God so as to speak in the way that Scripture speaks.

Consider the Athanasian Creed's confession of the Trinity. It urges that, however we talk about God, we should tell the story so as not to give the impression that it is a story about three Gods. And however we tell the story, we should tell it so as not to give the impression that there is no distinction between the Father, Son, and Spirit. In other words, we dare not speak of them in such a way as to obscure their distinctive identities or confuse their persons. Beyond that, it does not seek to probe the mystery. Instead, it seeks to speak in a way that is faithful to the way that Scripture speaks about such matters.

Similarly, consider the Athanasian Creed's confession of Christology. Here also, it sets boundaries for how we speak about Jesus or tell the story of Jesus and the promises he made to us so as to speak in the way that Scripture speaks. As in the case of its confession of the Trinity, it again sets boundaries within which we speak faithfully. Should one go outside those boundaries, one no longer is speaking in the way that the Christians speak as set forth in the Scriptures. In the case of Christology (as was the case with its confession of the Trinity), the Athanasian Creed sets two boundaries for our speaking. It is as if to say, "however, you talk about Jesus, do not talk in such a way that sends the message that Jesus is two different persons rather than one integral person who is at once completely divine and completely human." And at the same time, "do not talk in such a way as to speak of his personhood in such a way that conflates or absorbs his human nature into his divine nature" (in other words, don't emphasize one nature at the expense of the other nature).

The Athanasian Creed concludes its summary of the Trinity and Christological dogmas from the fourth and fifth centuries by reciting the narrative elements of Jesus' life as typically found in baptismal creeds such as the one with which most of us are familiar, namely, the Apostles Creed. In other words, having set forth these guidelines for the Christian discourse about God, one now has a framework for telling the story of God and his story of creation and new creation in a way that is faithful to the Christian account set forth in the Scriptures.

The Athanasian Creed would not, however, be the last time that the church would have to revisit and reexamine the way in which it tells the story on the basis of which it proclaims the promises of God.

Roughly a thousand years later, the meaning of that Gospel narrative—Jesus' incarnation, life, death, and resurrection—had moved to the foreground with the topic of justification. A young friar named Martin Luther struggled to find a gracious God in the face of a stern Christ who sits on his throne as a judge waiting for Luther to appear before him on the last day. And with this question of justification, we may say that anthropological question, moved to the foreground. In other words, if Jesus is the Lord (true God begotten of the Father from eternity and true man begotten of the virgin Mary—SC), what does it mean for our salvation and how do we come under his gracious rule so live with him in "everlasting innocence, righteousness, and blessedness" (SC)?

The heart of Luther's discovery in which he drew out the meaning of Jesus' death and resurrection lay in drawing a distinction between the righteousness that God demands from us and the righteousness that God bestows upon us. On the one hand, this distinction served to maintain the story of Christ as a Gospel story and not allowing it to become little more than a moralistic story. That is to say, the Gospel tells a story from which a promise of God's favor and forgiveness flow and with it, the role of faith by which we trust God to keep his promises. Martin Luther's reformation and theology soon yielded other distinctions that further served to keep the gospel story of Christ a *Gospel* story, that is a story that issued in a promise to be received by faith.

The most well-known of those theological distinctions among Lutherans is the distinction between law and Gospel. On the one hand, the distinction between law and gospel as the *verba dei* provided a way to read the Scriptures so as not to equate the Old Testament with law and the New Testament with Gospel. Thus Melanchthon writes,

> "All Scripture should be divided into these two main topics (*duos locos preaecipuos*): the law and the promises. In some places it communicates [or teaches, "*tradit*"] the law. In other places it communicates the promise concerning Christ, either when it promises that Christ will come and on account of him offers the forgiveness of sins,

justification, and eternal life, or when in the gospel itself, Christ, after he appeared, promises the forgiveness of sins, justification, and eternal life." AP IV, 5.

On the other hand, the distinction of law and Gospel as topics (*loci*) served the proclamation of repentance in which the words of God (*verba dei*) become the works of God (*opera Dei*). Law and Gospel bring produce repentance (contrition and faith) in which we are brought to a dependence upon the promise of Christ rather than a dependence upon human works and piety.

"For these are the two chief works of God (*duo praecipua opera Dei*) in human beings, to terrify and to justify the terrified or make them alive. The entire Scripture is divided into these two works." (Ap XII, 53).

In the centuries following the Reformation, the church appropriated these distinctions for questions that it faced in a new day. For example, in the nineteenth century, a theologian in America named C. F. W. Walther addressed the misguided notions of Christian piety in his book *A Proper Distinction between Law and Gospel*.

The late nineteenth and early twentieth centuries saw questions being asked related to matters of revelation and epistemology. How do we know about God in an age in which our scientific understanding of how the world works seems to leave little room for God's activity? Or how do we reconcile the God's love and power in a world that has witnessed the holocaust, the killing fields, not to mention countless individual tragedies? In that context, Luther's Heidelberg Disputation (1518) came to the foreground as a helpful resource. Though Luther had in view mainly the issue of faith and good works in the matter of justification, he addresses the question of theological method that could be used for addressing new issues related epistemology. In theses 19 and 20 he distinguishes between a theologian of glory and a theologian of the cross.

Thesis #19. "That person does not deserve to be called a theologian who perceives the invisible things of God as understandable on the basis of those things which have been made [Rom. 1:20]." Roots, 83.

Thesis #20. "That person deserves to be called a theologian, however, however, who understands the visible and the "backside" of God [Exod. 33:23] seen through suffering and the cross. Roots, 84?

In brief, Luther cautions against the use of inferential reasoning by which we draw speculative conclusions about God (especially about God's attributes) from what we observe in the creation that are then used by human creatures to get a handle on God (about what God can and can't do or must do) and God's thinking. These then drive our theology of God and shape our telling of the story and promises of God so as to make God appear reasonable and manageable. Instead, Luther urges us not to "clamber" up to Mt Olympus for a God's-eye view of things and instead content ourselves with the "this-ness" of God's revelation that involves the "backside of God," that is, the suffering, humiliation, and weakness on display with the cross.

About the same time, Luther's distinction between the two kingdoms/realms of God came into play in a culture that wrestled with issues regarding the relationship between church and state. Early in the twentieth century it was misused for malevolent ends by some in Nazi Germany, even those who counted themselves as devout Christians, Germany for which reason it became discredited in the eyes of many. But by the end of the twentieth century Lutheran scholars were revitalizing it in line with Luther's thought for an American context.[2] To be sure, Luther's two realms are not identical with the American distinction between church and state in as much as the church exists in both realms. As an institution the church exists in the left hand realm under the reign of the law. As a spiritual entity (the body of Christ) the church exists in the right hand realm under the reign of the Gospel. Nevertheless, Luther's two realms provided a way by which Christians may think of their lives within creation and especially within the political sphere. Here one recognizes that the created world in which we currently live is a penultimate realm in which we must work with non-Christians. Thus we don't seek to establish utopia. We live by reason. We work for compromise by not letting the perfect become the enemy of the good.

Finally, with the close of the twentieth century and in the first couple decades of the twenty-first century, the church finds itself in a culture in which questions about what it means to be human have been growing in importance for several centuries. All one has to do is consider the proliferation of fields or disciplines in the twentieth century that explore and answer such questions. The fields of politics economics, psychology, sociology, genetics, astrobiology, artificial intelligence (not to mention the various fields in the humanities) all provide a particular take the question of what it means to be human. With that question comes questions about identity (who/what) am I? Questions of about purpose (why am I here?), and questions about meaning and significance (what is the purpose of my life?). And now in the twenty-first century, such questions are gaining greater urgency in light of cosmology, technology, and artificial intelligence.

It is in this context that the two kinds or righteousness has proven to be a rich resource for the church. Although the question of what it means to be human continues to grow with increasing urgency, it is not necessarily a new question. In some ways, one could say that the Reformation marked an anthropological turn in theology. Martin Luther's question about how one finds a gracious God was a question about his identity, value, and status before God. And it raised questions about how one appropriates the work of Christ. Other anthropological questions swirled around this central question. All one has to do is take a glance of the topics covered in the Augsburg Confession to get a sense of this. The topics include original sin, free will, faith, good works, the church, confession, repentance, the civil realm, practices and rituals—all of which in their own way deal with specific issues related to anthropology.

The distinction between the two kinds of righteousness provides a fairly comprehensive framework for considering the question about what it means to be human. It does so by speaking of the human creaturely relationally and holistically rather than compartmentally or substantively (in terms of intrinsic characteristics). It considers the human creature in relation to God (*coram deo*) and in relation to the world. Both relationships need to be considered in order to take into account the fullness of what it means to be human biblically. The distinction between the two kinds of righteousness recognizes that human identity, purpose, and meaning cannot be considered by an exclusive concentration on only one of those relationships at the expense of the other (e.g., my relationship to God apart from the world or my relationships within the world apart from my relationship to God). The confusion of the distinctive features of either relationship runs the risk of diminishing our full humanity. . .at least as God created and recreated us to be.

The medieval church fell into the trap of confusing the two kinds of righteousness by making our righteousness of works before the world become the basis for our righteousness in the eyes of God. Thus they were accused of confusing philosophical righteousness with divine righteousness or the righteousness of works with the righteousness of faith. This confusion in turn led to a quantification of works in which some works were deemed as having a greater value than others for making our way up to God. This in turn resulted in a two-class Christianity or stratification between the sacred and the secular (the *perfecti* and *carnali*), in which the former moved one higher up on the rungs of the ladder. In the end, this diminished our life in the world and the value of the world by instrumentalizing our neighbor. I help my neighbor because it really helps me to work my way up to God..

The Reformation church at times ran into the opposite risk with a form of antinomianism that confused the two kinds of righteousness by ignoring or downplaying the need for teaching/exhorting active righteousness within the world. All one needs is faith and faith does the rest spontaneously and automatically. In our own day, such a view has at times led to a disparagement of making use of such things as the social sciences (for example) for helping us to build good relationships within human society or how to care for the the wider creation. Thus it runs a similar risk of disparaging the "secular" or the "worldly," that is, the creaturely/creation even as did the medieval church. The Gospel does transform us and produces good fruit. Embracing the horizontal realm creates space for recapturing the importance of reason in figuring out how best we can live according to God's law given the needs around us as well as our own particular capacities and abilities.

At this point, it might be worth saying a word about terminology. The language of *two kinds* of righteousness has at times caused a little confusion. Timothy Wengert has suggested that we speak of a "twofold righteousness" in order to highlight that there is but one righteous person whose identity before God as a child of God flows into his life as one who lives as a child of God among siblings.[3]. It might be helpful to think of it in the following way.

First of all, the language of righteousness implies conformity to a standard or a blueprint. In a sense, to be righteous means that one meets one's "design specifications." In this case, we might say that righteousness involves being the human creature that God envisioned us to be when he created with fear, love, and trust in our Creator at its center. In that regard, there is one standard for righteousness, namely, God's will for what we and our lives are to look like. And that means our *entire* being and *entire* life, not simply one aspect or another.

Second, the standard of righteousness that God has for us to be fully human takes on different features or characteristics within our different relationships.[4] Put another way, one might say that our righteousness looks different in our relationship with God and our relationship with others in the world. Different features of righteousness come into play (e.g., faith with regard to God and love with regard to neighbor). In this sense, one speaks of two kinds or righteousness.[5]

It is worth noting in this regard that the Bible speaks in both ways. For example, our righteousness depends upon what God promises me ("not having a righteousness of my own that comes from the law, but that which comes through faith in Christ, the righteousness from God that depends on faith"—Philippians 3:9). On the other hand, my righteousness is something that I should cultivate as Paul himself exhorts ("Pursue righteousness, godliness, faith, love, steadfastness, gentleness"—1 Timothy 6:11).

In any event, the point of the distinction between two kinds of righteousness acknowledges that our relationship/identity with God rests upon a fundamentally different basis than does our relationship with the world (and all of its inhabitants). That is to say, our identity with God rests upon what he has done and says about us while our relationship, identity, and worth (*coram mundo*) depends upon me living as the creature that God has created and re-created me to be). Either way, the key is the two different relationships have difference foundations or bases even as they are related (with active righteousness dependent upon passive righteousness). That is to say, righteousness in each relationship has its own distinct features.

In the end, as Christians we seek both kinds of righteousness simultaneously, but for different purposes. I seek the righteousness of Christ alone as the basis for my identity as a child of God. Because of this righteousness, I seek a righteousness in the eyes of the world for purpose of maintaining and restoring the relationships into which God has called us. Ultimately, righteousness is righteousness. And to be righteous (the human person God created and recreated us to be) and embraces the entire person and thus the distinctive features of righteousness in both relationships.

The two kinds of righteousness provides Christians in the twenty-first century one more tool to include in their theological tool belt. Like the other tools (law-gospel, two realms, etc) it serves the of helping us communicate the Gospel faithfully. But like various tools, each also serves to help us carry out a specific task well (screwdriver versus pliers). For example, Law and Gospel deals with God's ways of talking with us, while twofold righteousness deals with anthropology—who we are as his human creatures. So each of these theological distinctions helps us to address the various needs or problems that we encounter as theologians and proclaimers.

Notes

1. See for example, George Lindbeck, *The Nature of the Doctrine: Religion and Theology in a Postliberal Age* (Westminster John Knox Press, 1984) and Timothy Luke Johnson, *The Creed: What Christians Believe and Why it Matters* (Image, 2004).

2. See Robert Benne's *Paradoxical Vision: A Public Theology for the Twenty-first Century* (Fortress Press, 1995). And more recently, see Joel Biermann, *Wholly Citizens: God's Two Realms and Christian Engagement with the World* (Augsburg Fortress, 2017).

3. See Timothy J. Wengert, Human Freedom, Christian Righteousness: Philip Melanchthon's Exegetical Dispute with Erasmus of Rotterdam, Ocford Studies in Historical Theology (Ocford University Press, 1998).

4. Thanks to Joel Okamoto for his insights on this.

5. In this regard, Joel Biermann will speak of three kinds of righteousness as a way of distinguishing the active righteousness of Christians that bears the feature of faith from civil righteousness in which the active righteousness of non-Christians may look outwardly similar but is performed without faith. Biermann's distinction stems from Luther's *On Three Kinds of Righteousness*, 1518, a sort of practice run at the more mature expression of his understanding of righteousness in *On Two Kinds of Righteousness* the following year. He did

not explain why he moved from a schema of threefold righteousness to that of twofold righteousness, but it may be that in his society, where almost all were baptized, he expected the active righteousness of the believer from his readers. Throughout his life Luther held to his concept of "civil righteousness."

Contributors

Charles P. Arand is the Eugene E. and Nell S. Fincke graduate professor of systematic theology and director of the Center for the Care of Creation at Concordia Seminary, Saint Louis, USA.

Joel Biermann is Waldemar A. and June Schuette professor of systematic theology at Concordia Seminary, Saint Louis, USA.

Robert Kolb is professor emeritus of systematic theology and retired director of the Institute for Mission Studies at Concordia Seminary, Saint Louis, USA.

David A. Lumpp is professor emeritus of theology and retired dean at Concordia University, Saint Paul, USA

Timothy Saleska is professor of exegetical theology and dean of ministerial formation at Concordia Seminary in St. Louis, USA.

William W. Schumacher is Buehner-Duesenberg Professor of Missions and Historical Theology and Director of the Institute for Mission Studies, Institute for Mission Studies at Concordia Seminary, Saint Louis USA

The editor and 1517 Publishing are grateful to the following journals for their original essays and the permissions to republish them:

1. David A. Lumpp, "Luther's 'Two Kinds of Righteousness". A Brief Historical Introduction," Concordia Journal 23 (1997), 27-39.
2. Robert Kolb, "Luther on the Two Kinds of Righteousness. Reflections on His Two-Dimensional Definition of Humanity at the Heart of His Theology," Lutheran Quarterly 13 (1999): 449-466, and Harvesting Martin Luther's Reflections on Theology, Ethics, and the Church, ed. Timothy J. Wengert (Grand Rapids: Eerdmans, 2003), 38-55.
3. Charles P. Arand, "Two Kinds of Righteousness as a Framework for Law and Gospel in the Apology," Lutheran Quarterly 15 (2001): 417-439.
4. William W. Schumacher, "Civic Participation by Churches and Pastors: an Essay on the Two Kinds of Righteousness," Concordia Journal 30 (2004): 165-177.
5. Robert Kolb, "'The Chief Controversy between the Papalists and Us': Grace, Faith, and Human Righteousness in Sixteenth-Century Ecumenical Exchange," in: 2001. A Justification Odyssey, Papers Presented at the Congress on the Lutheran Confessions, ed, John A. Maxfield (Saint Louis: The Luther Academy, 2002), 62-82.
6. Charles P. Arand and Joel D. Biermann, "Why the Two Kinds of Righteousness?" Concordia Journal 33 (2007): 116-135.
7. Robert Kolb, "God and His Human Creatures in Luther's Sermons on Genesis: The Reformer's Early Use of His Distinction of Two Kinds of Righteousness," Concordia Journal 33 (2007):166-184.
8. Timothy E. Saleska, "The Two Kinds of Righteousness: What's a Preacher to Do?" Concordia Journal 33 (2007): 136-145.
9. Charles P. Arand, "The Ministry of the Church in the Light of the Two Kinds of Righteousness," Concordia Journal 33 (2007): 344-356.

Apology of the Augsburg Confession (Melanchthon)

Article II, 40
Article II:11-13, 43
Article II:12, 45
Article II:26, 43
Article II:27-30, 47
Article II:42, 43
Article II:43, 45, 47
Article IV, 35, 37, 40, 43
Article IV: 5, 38
Article IV:2-3, 45
Article IV:10, 46
Article IV:12-16, 45
Article IV:14, 40, 41
Article IV:18, 42
Article IV:21, 45
Article IV:24, 42, 45
Article IV:43, 45
Article IV:48, 43
Article IV:48-60, 44
Article IV:58+, 44
Article IV:121-183, 51
Article IV:134, 50
Article IV:142, 50
Article IV:152, 53
Article IV:157, 45

Article IV:159+, 50
Article IV:165, 45
Article IV:183, 50
Article IV:184, 48
Article IV:185, 50
Article IV:188, 48
Article IV:213, 45
Article IV:215, 45
Article IV:241, 52
Article IV:243, 52
Article IV:252+, 44
Article IV:257, 45
Article IV:269, 45, 48
Article IV:283+, 40, 42, 43
Article IV:285, 45
Article IV:317, 45
Article VII:34, 37
Article VII:37, 37
Article XI, 48
Article XII, 35, 37, 44, 48
Article XII:51, 109
Article XII:53, 109
Article XV:50, 41
Article XVI, 40

Article XVI:3, 41
Article XVIII, 40
Article XVIII:4, 40
Article XVIII:5, 50
Article XVIII:7, 50
Article XVIII:9, 50
Article XX:4, 45
Article XXI, 44
Article XXII, 35, 36
Article XXIII, 35, 36, 49
Article XXIII:37-39, 49
Article XXIII:38-39, 49
Article XXIII:40, 49
Article XXIV, 35, 36
Article XXV, 35, 36
Article XXVI, 35, 36
Article XXVI:14, 52
Article XXVII, 35, 36
Article XXVII:8, 51
Article XXVII:21, 42
Article XXVII:27, 51
Article XXVII:49, 41
Article XXVII:55, 52
Article XXVIII, 35, 36, 48

Subject Index

A Proper Distinction between Law and Gospel (Walther), 182
Abel, 138, 147n60
Abraham, 42, 83–84, 93, 135, 138–39, 140, 141–42
active righteousness, 186, 187–88n5
  conscience and, 22, 104
  coram mundo (relation to world), 102
  forensic justification on, 8
  in Genesis sermons, 140–42
  and Law with Christian life, 112
  Luther on, 2, 83, 155
  Melanchthon on, 83
  merit theology and, 8
  public square and, 115
actual righteousness, 4, 26
Adam, xviii, 26, 28–29, 31, 32, 102, 128, 131, 134, 136–38
Adrian VI, Pope, 81
Against Latomus (treatise) (Luther), 5
Agricola, Johann, 13n4
alien righteousness, 4, 5, 26, 44
"aliena" concept, xiii, xviii, xix, 5, 131
alienation, 64
Althaus, Paul, 117, 123n57
American public life
  American Evangelicalism, 66
  as post-Constantinian age, 64
  religion aspects in, 62–63
  separation of church and state, 63–64, 69–70

Ansbach Proposal, 117, 123n57
anthropology
  Aristotelian, 45–46, 46
  of Luther, xvi, xviii, xx, 181
  of Melanchthon, 39, 40, 43, 46–47
  twofold righteousness and, 187
antinomianism, 13n4, 111, 121n36, 185
Apology of the Augsburg Confession (Melanchthon)
  analysis of opponents' position, 50
  Confutation of the Augsburg Conference, xiv, 36–37, 47, 82–83
  on glory of Christ, 45
  on Holy Spirit, 43
  as judicial genre, 36–37
  Law/Gospel distinction and, 35–36
  on obedience, 39–41, 42, 43–44
  relating two kinds of righteousness, 44–50
  rhetorical character of, 36–37
  on righteousness of faith, 38, 39, 43, 44, 45, 50–53
  on righteousness of works, 38, 39, 42, 44–45, 50–53
  theme and framework of, 36–38
  thoroughness of, 35
  on two dimensions of human life, 38–44
  on two kinds of righteousness, 36–37, 100
Apostles Creed, 112, 180

Arand, Charles P., 35–57, 99–119, 163–77, 179–88, 189
Aristotle
  anthropology of, 45–46
  conceptual framework, 77, 82, 94
  on ethics, 39–40, 40, 41
  on fairness, 52
  Melanchthon on, 39, 41, 42, 49–50
  Nichomachean Ethics, 39, 45
  on obedience, 41
  on righteousness, 42, 45, 47, 161n14
Athanasian Creed, 38, 179–81
Athaus, Paul, 117
Augsburg Confession (1548). *See also Confutation* of the Augsburg Conference
  Charles V and, 81–82
  defining human righteousness in, 81–84
  defining righteousness in, 88–90
  doctrine of justification by grace through faith, xiv, 81
  Luther's *Galatians Commentary* and, 100
  ministry and, 171–72
  on pastors, 168
  on religious life, 59–60
  on secular society, 61
  topics covered in, 184
Augsburg Interim, 88–91
Augustine of Hippo, Saint, xvii–xviii, 3, 64–65, 86–87, 91, 115
Augustinian theology, 3, 6, 91, 92, 107

Bachman, Jim, 177
Baptism
  baptismal creeds, 180
  common priesthood and, 168–70, 171
  disposition for justice and, 91
  egalitarianism of, 165–66
  Paul on, 30, 135
  Pentecostals on, 56n52
  regeneration of, 7, 9

righteousness of grace and, 4, 5, 47
saving action of, 30, 135
Barmen Declaration, 117
Barth, Karl, 108, 110
beatification, 47
Benne, Robert, 73, 116, 119n7
Biel, Gabriel, 107
Biermann, Joel, 99–119, 187–88n5, 189
bridegroom metaphor, 11, 26
Bucer, Martin, 84–85, 86–87

Cain, 138
Calvinism, 108
carnal righteousness (*iustitia carnis*), 38
Carter, Stephen L., 63–64
Charles V, Emperor, 81, 82, 84–86, 88, 90. *See also Confutation* of the Augsburg Conference
Chemnitz, Martin, xv, xvii, 76–78, 92–95
The Chosen, 149–50, 151, 154
Christian Coalition, 66, 116
Christian righteousness (*iustitia Christiana*), 38, 45, 120n19
Christians. *See also* civic participation
  hierarchical distinction between, 46
  options open to, 114–15
  seeking of righteousness by, 186–87
Christological confession, 179, 180
churches. *See also* civic participation
  politics and, 70–73
  separation of church and state, 63–64, 69–70, 71, 122n44, 123n55
City of God (Augustine), 65
civic participation
  about, 59–61
  living civil life and religious life, 70–73
  Missouri Synod, 67–69
  religion in American public life and, 61–67
civil authority, 51–52
civil righteousness (*iustitia civilis*), xix, 4, 38, 42, 49, 187–88n5

civil sin, 4
common priesthood, 167–68, 168–70
Confutation of the Augsburg Conference, xiv, 36–37, 47, 82–83
conscience
    active righteousness and, 22, 80
    the Law and, 157
    passive righteousness and, 8, 9–10
    terrors of, 104
Constantine, Emperor of Holy Roman Empire, 64, 65
Contarini, Gasparo, 86–87
coram Deo (relation to God), 13n4, 46, 101–3, 104, 107, 108, 110–11, 112, 120n17, 172, 184–85, 186–87
coram hominibus, 13n4, 120n17
coram mundo (relation to world), 101–3, 112, 120n17, 170–71, 186–87
Council of Nicaea, 66, 122n47
Council of Trent, xv, 76–78, 91–95
Cruciger, Caspar, 125

David, 93, 152
de jure divino, 170, 171
de jure humano, 169, 171
Declaration of Independence, 71
Dedel, Adrian, 81
"Disputation on Faith and Love" (Melanchthon), 41
divine righteousness. *See also* righteousness of faith
    philosophical righteousness and, 185
    two kinds of, 17–18
Dominicans, 91
duplex iustitia, 87

Ebeling, Gerhard, 104
ecclesiastical authority, 51–52
Eck, Johann, 86–87
Eden, 28, 32, 133
Elements of Rhetoric (Melanchthon), 37
Elert, Werner, 108, 117, 123n57
emotions, Melanchthon on, 41
Enlightenment, 114

Epistle to Diognetus, 64–65, 65
Erasmus, 47, 78, 81, 84, 88
Esau, 142
eternal life, 47, 182
eternal righteousness (*iustitia aeterna*), 38, 120n19
ethics
    Aristotle on, 39–40, 41–42
    Biermann on, 101
    Judeo-Christian, 109
    law and, 42
    Luther's theology of, 3, 10–12
    Melanchthon on, 39
Evangelicals, 56n52, 66, 99, 111, 115, 169
Eve, xviii, 28–29, 32, 128, 131, 135, 136–37
Examination of the Council of Trent (Chemnitz), xv, 76–78, 77
exchange imagery, 3, 6–7, 9–11, 11
exile, 64

faith
    antinomianism and, 185
    as determining identity, xiii
    as determining righteousness, xiii
    Holy Spirit and, 102
    Melanchthon on, 43, 84
    personal faith and politics, 66
    service and, 155–56
    similarities and differences with Papalists on, 81
First Amendment, 63, 69
Flood, 133, 138, 139
Forde, Gerhard, 108
forensic justification, 8. *See also* Melanchthon, Philip
Formula of Concord, 95
The Freedom of a Christian (Luther), 7, 10–11
French Revolution, 116
Friedrich Wilhelm III, King of Prussia, 69
Fritz, J. H. C., 67–69, 70, 74n12

frölicher Wechsel (happy exchange), 3, 6–7, 9–11, 11

Galatians commentary
exchange imagery and, 7–8, 9–11
Luther's lectures and, xiii–xiv
preface, xiv, 17, 19
Two Kinds of Righteousness (sermon) (Luther) and, 6
Galatians lectures of 1531-1535, 7, 9, 12, 78
Genesis sermons, 100
about, 125
active righteousness of human creature in, 140–42
God the Creator in, 133–35
hermeneutical and homiletical methods in, 127–29
importance of, 126–27
passive righteousness of human creature in, 135–40
two kinds of righteousness and, 130
George, Duke of Saxony, 84–85
Giertz, Bo, 108
Gnosticism, 112
God. *See also* righteousness of God *(iustitia Dei)*; Trinitarian confession
anger of, 153
chief works of, 182
as Creator, xvi, xviii, 21, 32, 60–61, 105, 111–12, 133–35, 145n11, 180, 186
human's relation to, 125–44, 184–85, 186
intentions of, 47
judgment of, 22
living according to law of, 185
Luther on righteousness of, 2
power of, 133
righteousness bestowed by, 181, 186
righteousness demanded by, 181
golden mean, 41
good fruit, 185

Gospel. *See also* Apology of the Augsburg Confession (Melanchthon); Law/Gospel distinction
confession of the, 35
distinction between law and, 112, 181
faithful communication of, 187
as God's ways of communicating, 187
Luther's proclamation on message of, xvii
Luther's rediscovery of, 2, 60
passive righteousness and, 9–11
preserving and promoting the, 35
righteousness of grace and, 4
righteousness of the Gospel *(iustitia evangelii)*, 38, 120n19
saving righteousness of, 7
transforming aspect of, 185
Gospel and Law (Barth), 108
grace
Augustine on, xvii–xviii
Chemnitz on, 92–95
as healing, 3
initial grace *(gratia prima)*, 47, 48
Luther on, 9
Melanchthon on, 47, 81
passive righteousness as, 22
prevenient grace, 22
Regensburg on, 87
Roman Catholic theologians on, 91–92
similarities and differences with Papalists on, 76, 77, 81, 82
Gropper, Johannes, 88
guilt, 157

habit *(habitus)*
Melanchthon on, 39–40
of righteousness, 5, 39–40, 47, 48, 49
Hagenau, 85
Hammer of God (Giertz), 108
Hauerwas, Stanley, 66, 114
Hebrews, xviii, 44

Heidelberg Disputation (Luther), 100, 130, 182
Helding, Michael, 88
Hidden God (*Deus absconditus*), 130
historical overview
    on ethics, 3, 10–12
    evangelical development of, 2–8, 11
    Galatians lectures of 1531-1535, 7, 9, 12, 78
    on Incarnation, 3, 9, 10–12
    on soteriology, 10–11
    on theology of Luther, 1–2
Holl, Karl, 3
Holy Spirit. *See also* Trinitarian confession
    delivery of benefits of Christ through, xvi
    faith and, 102
    forgiveness and, 157
    iustitia activa and, xix
    as moving/directing actions, xiii
    sinners and, 32
    work of, 153
    works apart from, 40, 50
    works of, 155
horizontal dimension of life, xvii, 21, 27, 46, 49, 50, 79–80, 101, 129, 131, 158, 164, 166–68, 177, 185. *See also* righteousness of reason
human creatures
    active righteousness of, 140–42
    as in image of God, 135–36
    in Luther's sermons, 125–44
    "On the Manner by Which the Human Creature Receives Justification," 89–90
    passive righteousness of, 135–40
human identity. *See also* identity
    in 21st century, 183–84
    Luther's concept of, xiii, xx, 131–32
    two kinds of righteousness and, 60, 184–85
human life. *See also* horizontal dimension of life; vertical dimension of life

distinct between two kinds of righteousness and, 26–28
    Luther on two kingdoms of, xvi
    morality and, 157
    righteousness in relationships of, 20–21
    two dimensions of, 38–44, 155
    of two kinds of righteousness, 23–26
    two spheres of relationships, 79–80
human righteousness
    similarities and differences with Papalists on, 81–82
    two kinds of, 19–20, 101–3

identity
    as child of God, 21, 187
    as children of God, 39
    as determined by faith, xiii
    Luther's doubts on, 33
    righteousness of, 22–23
Incarnation, 3, 9, 10–12, 130
indulgence controversy, 78
initial grace (*gratia prima*), 48
internal/external concepts, xiii. *See also* "aliena" concept; "propria" concept
Isaac, 135
iustitia activa, xix
iustitia aeterna (eternal righteousness), 38, 120n19
iustitia carnis (carnal righteousness), 38
iustitia Christiana (Christian righteousness), 38, 120n19
iustitia civilis (civil righteousness), 38
iustitia cordis (righteousness of the heart), 38, 120n19
iustitia Dei (righteousness of God). *See* righteousness of God (*iustitia Dei*)
iustitia evangelii (righteousness of the Gospel), 120n19
iustitia evangelit (righteousness of the gospel), 38
iustitia fidei (righteousness of faith), 38, 120n19
iustitia legis (righteousness of the law), 38

iustitia operum (righteousness of works), 38
iustitia passiva, xix
iustitia propria (one's own righteousness), xix, 38
iustitia rationis (righteousness of reason), 38
iustitia spiritualis (righteousness of the spirit), 38, 120n19

Jacob, 142
James the Apostle, Saint, 155
Jeremiah, 152
Jesus Christ. *See also* Christological confession; righteousness of Christ; Trinitarian confession
    bridegroom metaphor, 11
    death and resurrection of, xix, 181
    as *Deus revelatus*, 130
    exchange imagery and, 7–8
    forgiveness and, 157
    on fulfilling the law, 78
    glory of, 45
    on human identity, xviii
    Incarnation of, 3, 9, 10–12, 130
    personhood of, 180
    righteousness in and through, 29–32, 30–32, 44
    similarities and differences with Papalists on, 76
    trust in, 32, 145n22
Job, 153
Johann Friedrich, Prince of Saxony, 88
John the Baptist, Saint, 82
"Joint Declaration on the Doctrine of Justification" and, 95–96
judgment of God, 22
justification
    in Apology of the Augsburg Confession, 35
    Augsburg Interim, 88–90
    Council of Trent on, 91–95
    as distinct from sanctification, 99–100

forensic justification, 6, 8
    initial grace and, 47
    inner renewal and, 3
    Luther's concept of, xix–xx, 3, 60, 147n43, 181
    Melanchthon on, 48–49, 81, 82, 83
    promise of, 182
    similarities and differences with Papalists on, xv, 76–77
    through faith, 26
    vocations and, 51

Kant, Immanuel, 111
Kittelson, James, 1
Kolb, Robert, xiii–xx, 8, 13n5, 17–34, 39, 75–98, 125–44, 155, 189
krinomenon, 37

Laban, 142
Large Catechism, xiii, 51, 61, 112
Law. *See also* Law/Gospel distinction
    Christ as the end of the, 31
    civil authority, 51–52
    comprehension of the, 38
    divine-human relationship and, 8
    as ending in Jesus Christ, 9–11
    external conformation to God's, xviii
    before God, 104–5
    as God's ways of communicating, 187
    horizontal dimension of life and God's, 185
    in human courts, 42
    Luther on righteousness of the, 2
    Melanchthon on, xiv–xv, 40–41
    natural law, 109
    pastors and the, 12
    righteousness of the law (*iustitia legis*), 38
    sinful conscience and the, 157
Law/Gospel distinction
    Apology as framework of, 35–36
    exchange imagery and, 7
    similarities and differences with Papalists on, 76

as theological distinction, 2, 119n7, 181, 182, 187
two kinds of righteousness and, 106–12
two realms and, 113–14
twofold righteousness and, 101
lectures of Luther, 1, 7. *See also* Galatians commentary
Lectures on Galatians (Luther), 1
Leipzig conference (1539), 84–85
"Leipzip Interim," 89–90
Lincoln, Abraham, 62–63
Loci communes (Melanchthon), xiv–xv
Lombard, Peter, 132
Lord's Supper, 86, 168
Lot, 141
love
    creation and, xvi
    God's righteousness as, 18, 80
    God's unconditional love, 22
    grace and, 47
    Melanchthon on, 51
    parent/child analogy, 79
    righteousness/identity as establishing, xiii
Lumpp, David A., 1–12, 189
Luther, Martin. *See also* Genesis sermons; sermons of Luther; theology of Luther
    on active righteousness, 2, 187–88n5
    anthropology of, xvi, xviii, xx, 181
    on boundaries, 2
    on civil righteousness, 187–88n5
    death of, 90
    on distinction of righteousness, 1–2
    evangelical development of, 3–12, 19
    on faith, 2
    on forgiveness, 18
    The Freedom of a Christian, 7, 10–11
    on governance, 122n44
    on grace, 2
    on Hidden/Revealed God, 145n22
    on human creation, 33

on justification, xix–xx, 3, 181
    Kolb on, 101
    Against Latomus (treatise), 5
    Lectures on Galatians, 1
    letters of, 6
    monastic life of, 4, 19, 23, 100
    on morality, 2
    on original sin, 29
    Papalist controversy and, 77–80
    on passive righteousness, 2
    on preaching, 153–54
    Preface to the Complete Edition of Luther's Latin Writings (Luther), 2
    reformational period of, 9
    on religion, 2
    on secular society, 2
    soteriology of, 2, 4
    On Three Kinds of Righteousness, 26, 131, 187–88n5
    on Trinity, 145n11
    Two Kinds of Righteousness (sermon), 4, 10–11, 26
    uses of the Law, 2, 13n4
    vocation doctrine of, 2
    volume of writings by, 1
    on works, 2
Lutheran Church
    in 20th century, 110
    in 21st century, 110
    in America, 114–17
    in Germany, 116, 117
    humanity and, 33
    importance of Apology to, 35
    "Joint Declaration on the Doctrine of Justification," 95–96
    in Prussia, 69
    resources of, 179
    similarities and differences with Papalists, 75–77
    theologians of, 108–10

Martens, Gottfried, 75–77
Masaki, Makito, xvii

Melanchthon, Philip. *See also* Apology of the Augsburg Confession (Melanchthon)
  Arand on, 101
  on Aristotle, 39, 41, 42, 49–50
  assistance of, 3
  Chemnitz on, 95
  critique of Augsburg Interim, 90
  critique of theologians, 47
  "Disputation on Faith and Love," 41
  Elements of Rhetoric, 37
  on justification, 48–49, 81, 82, 83
  in Leipzig, 84–85
  loci communes rhetoric forms of, 132
  on ministry, 171–72
  on ordination, 170
  at Regensburg, 86–87
  on righteousness distinctions, xiv–xv, 120n20
  on righteousness of faith, xiv–xv
  on righteousness of the law, xiv–xv
  on Scripture, 181–82
  Wengert on, 13n4
mercy
  God's righteousness as, 18, 19, 42, 80, 135
  passive righteousness as, 22
  similarities and differences with Papalists on, 76
merit (*meritum de congruo*), 47, 48, 81, 83, 91, 92, 107–8
ministry. *See also* civic participation; pastors; preachers
  coram Deo (relation to God), 164–65
  coram mundo (relation to world), 165–68
  Luther's call to pastoral care, 33
  Melanchthon on, 171–72
  special service, 168–70
Missouri Synod, 67–69
morality, 156–57, 157
Moses, xv, 7, 93, 127, 141, 151, 153
Mueller, J. T., 114
Muslims, 104

natural law, 40, 109, 110, 118, 121n34, 158–59
Neuhaus, Richard John, 67
New Testament, 93, 181
Newbigin, Lesslie, 156
Nichomachean Ethics (Aristotle), 39, 39–40, 45, 56n50
Noah, 128, 138, 139
Noll, Mark, 115
non-Christians
  active righteousness of, 112, 187n5
  approaches to, 115–20
  working with, 183

obedience
  as form of discipline, 42
  Melanchthon on, 39–41, 42, 43–44
Ockhamist theology, 91, 92, 133
Old Testament, 18, 93, 94, 128, 181
"On the Jurisdiction of Bishops" (Melanchthon), 170
"On the Manner by Which the Human Creature Receives Justification," 89–90
On Three Kinds of Righteousness (Luther), xviii, 100, 131, 187–88n5
On Two Kinds of Righteousness (Luther), xviii, 187–88n5
one's own righteousness (*iustitia propria*), 38
opera Dei (works of God), 107, 182
ordination, 169
original righteousness, 4, 26, 28–29
original sin
  as Augsburg Confession topic, 184
  Luther on, 4, 26, 28–29
  Luther's definition of, 29
  Melanchthon on, 43, 47
  original righteousness and, 26, 28–29
Osiander, Andreas, 94–95

Papalist controversy
  about, 75, 95–96
  defining human righteousness in Augsburg, 81–84

defining righteousness in Augsburg, 88–90

defining righteousness in Leipzig, 84–85

defining righteousness in Regensburg, 85–88

defining righteousness in Trent, 91–95

Luther's two kinds of righteousness, 77–80

similarities and differences, 75–77

parent/child analogy, 79

passive righteousness, 186

  coram Deo (relation to God), 102, 106

  as dependent on Christ, 60

  as external, 8

  forensic justification on, 8

  as forgiveness of sins, 22

  in Genesis sermons, 135–40

  as grace, 22

  Law/Gospel distinction and, 9–11

  Luther on, 2, 20

  Melanchthon on, 83

  as mercy, 22

Pastoral Theology (Fritz), 67

pastors. *See also* ministry

  challenges of, 177

  in civic realm, 59, 67, 70, 72–73, 74n12

  creaturely gifts of, 174–75

  distinguishing duties, 170–72

  expectations on, 163–64

  job description, 172–74

  task delegation, 175–77

Paul the Apostle, Saint

  baptismal model of, 30, 31, 135

  Chemnitz on, 93–94

  on Christian life, 155, 157, 157–58, 159, 186

  on faith, 43, 83, 138

  on human creation, 135–36

  Luther on, 4, 9, 18, 19–20, 27

  on servant role, 160n5

Peasants' Revolt of 1525, 105

Pedro de Malvenda, 88

Pelagians, 46, 82

Penance, 48

perfecti/carnali stratification, 185

Pflug, Julius, 88

Philip, Prince of Hesse, 88

philosophical righteousness, 42, 45, 185. *See also* righteousness of works

Pietism, 104, 108, 109, 116

piety

  on continuum of virtue, 46

  established acts of, 48

  obedience and, 42

  Walther on, 182

  works apart from, 82

politics

  Christians in, 116

  misuse of religion for, 71–72

  separation of church and state, 63–64, 69–70, 71

post-Constantinian age, 64–65, 114

Potok, Chaim, 149–50, 151, 154

prayer, 49

preachers

  from identity to practice, 154–55

  preaching and the righteousness of faith, 149–50

  preaching and the righteousness of works, 154–59

  silence of God, 150–52

  task of, 152–54, 155–59

  two kinds of righteousness and, 149–59

Preface to the Complete Edition of Luther's Latin Writings (Luther), 2

proper righteousness, 5

"propria" concept, xiii, xviii, xix, 38, 120n20

Prussian Union, 69

reason(ing)

  importance of, 185

  Luther's cautions on, 183

Melanchthon on, 40, 43, 46, 50
righteousness of reason (*iustitia
    rationis*), 38
righteousness of works *(iustitia ope-
    rum)* and, 38
redemption, Wingren on, 110
Reformation
    as anthropological turn in theology,
        184
    antinomianism risk of, 185
    on distinction of righteousness,
        103–4
    pastors during, 170–71
    Penance and, 48
    preaching during, 126
    public ministry after, 166–67
    secular life after, 60
    teaching and, 81
    theological distinctions after, 182
    writings of, 35
Reformed church, 69
Regensburg Conference (1541), 85–88
relationships. *See also coram Deo*;
    coram mundo
    with God, 21, 28–29, 111–12, 186
    horizontal, 21
    with others, 21, 159, 186
    vertical, 21
religion
    in American public life, 61–67
    political misuse of, 71
repentance
    indulgence controversy, 78
    Law/Gospel distinction and, 113
    Melanchthon on, 107
    proclamation of, 182
    vocations and, 166
revelation
    Barthian understanding of, 110
    Luther on God's, 128, 134, 183
    questions on matters of, 182
Rhau, Georg, 125
righteous man *(tsaddik)*, 149–50, 152,
    153, 154–59

righteousness
    in 21st century, 183–84, 187
    bestowed by God, 5, 186
    Biermann on, 187–88n5
    conformity and, 186
    cultivation of, 186
    definitions of, 20, 187
    as determined by faith, xiii
    as gift from God, xvii
    internal/external concepts applied
        to, xiii
    Luther's concept of, xiii
    Melanchthon on, xiv–xv
    as obedience, xv
    reasons for two kinds of, 99–119
    relating two kinds of, 44–50
righteousness in the world (*coram
    hominibus*), 60
righteousness of Christ
    as alien righteousness, 5, 26
    guilt and, 157
    imputation of, 8–9
    Luther on, 4, 5–7, 30
righteousness of faith
    Melanchthon on, 39, 44, 48
    shalom (state of peace) and, 44
righteousness of faith (*iustitia fidei*)
    medieval church on, 185
    Melanchthon on, 38, 120n19
    mystery of, 8
    as passive righteousness, 20
    passively received, xviii–xix, 8, 42
    as serving good works, 50–53
    teaching of, 48
righteousness of God (*iustitia Dei*)
    definitions of, 17–18
    Jesus Christ and, 160n5
    Luther's concept of, 2–3, 4–5, 6,
        17–18, 19, 27
    Melanchthon on, 38, 120n19
    mercy and, 42
    as passive righteousness, 8, 19, 118
    as redemptive, 3, 7–8, 27
righteousness of grace, 4

righteousness of identity, 22–23

righteousness of law/righteousness of faith relationship, xiv–xv

righteousness of performance, 22–23

righteousness of reason (*iustitia rationis*), 38, 39, 44, 45, 48, 50

righteousness of the Gospel (*iustitia evangelii*), 38, 120n19

righteousness of the heart (*iustitia cordis*), 38, 120n19

righteousness of the law (*iustitia legis*), 38

righteousness of the spirit (*iustitia spiritualis*), 38, 120n19

righteousness of works (*iustitia operum*), 38, 39, 48, 80, 185

Roman Catholicism. *See also* Papalist controversy

    16th century theologians on justification, 75–77

    Augsburg Interim and, 88, 90–91

    Confutation of the Augsburg Conference, xiv, 36–37, 47, 82–83

    "Joint Declaration on the Doctrine of Justification" and, 95–96

    Regensburg, 85–88

    similarities and differences with Lutheran Church, xv, 75–77

Rorer, Georg, 125

Rosin, Robert, 167

sacraments

    Melanchthon on, 48

    pastors and the, 175

sacred/secular stratification, 46, 185

Saleska, Timothy, 149–59, 189

salvation

    Chemnitz on, 78

    Luther on, 10–11, 77–78, 145n22, 181

    Melanchthon on, 47

    Muslims and, 104

    obtaining of, 104

    Regensburg on, 87–88

    rejection of Luther's theology on, 91

sanctification

    as distinct from justification, 99–100

    Luther's concept of, xix–xx

    vocations and, 51

Sarah, 135, 139

Schumacher, William W., 59–73, 189

Scotist theology, 91, 92

Scotus, John Duns, 75

Scripture

    Athanasian Creed and, 179–80, 181

    creation-redemptive narrative of, 109

    Luther's interpretation of, xvi, 81

    Luther's study of, 32–33

    reading of, 181

secular world. *See also* civic participation

    Christian life and, 59–60, 112, 115–20

    disparagement of, 185

    early Church on, 64–65

    problem of religion within, 61–67

Sententiae (Lombard), 132

separation of church and state, 63–64, 69–70, 71

Sermon on Monastic Vows (Luther), 100

sermons of Luther

    On Three Kinds of Righteousness (Luther), xviii, 4, 100, 131, 187–88n5

    Two Kinds of Righteousness, 4, 10–11, 100

shalom (state of peace), 39, 44

Siemon-Netto, Uwe, 114, 123n56

Sihler, William, 123n55

sin

    as abolished, 27

    forgiveness of, 9–11, 18, 22, 81, 182

    grace and, xvii–xviii

    healing from, 3

    laws' condemnation of, xvi

    Luther on, 4, 26, 29, 135–37

    Melanchthon on, xv, 44

    morality and, 157

non-imputation of, 8–9
of patriarchs, 135
rescue and restoration from, xvii, 30
similarities and differences with
    Papalists on, 76
will and, 46–47
Smalcald Articles (Luther), 48
Smalcald War, 91
Small Catechism, 166
social Darwinism, 110
Sodom, 141
soteriology
    historical overview on, 10–11
    of Luther, 2, 4, 77
    of Roman Catholic theologians, 77
special priesthood, 167–68
Spenlein, George, 6
spiritual righteousness (iustitia spiritu-
    alis), 38, 120n19
standard of righteousness, 186

temperance, Melanchthon on, 41–42
Ten Commandments, 112, 157, 164
    law of first three, xvii
    Melanchthon on, 40, 49–50
    posting of, 109
    righteousness of works and, 51
Theodosius I, 122n47
theologians
    Luther on methods of, 182–83
    of Lutheran Church, 108–10
    Melanchthon's critique of, 47
    Roman Catholic theologians, 75–77,
        91–92
    Wittenberg theologians, 125–33
theological distinctions
    after Reformation, 182
    law/Gospel, 181, 182, 187
    Luther on, 183
    Melanchthon on, xv, 45–46
    two kinds of righteousness, 187
    two realms, 187
theology of Luther
    development of, 2–8, 19

divine righteousness and, 17–18
Law/Gospel distinction, 2, 181, 182,
    187
methods, 182–83
three interpretive pillars of, xvi–xvii
two governments distinction, 2,
    14n22
two kinds of righteousness and, 1–2
Thesis #19, 182
Thesis #20, 183
Thomas Aquinas, Saint, 22–23, 76
Thomist theology, 91, 107
"Treatise on the Power and Primacy of
    the Pope" (Melanchthon), 170, 172
Trinitarian confession, 76, 145n11, 179,
    180. See also God; Holy Spirit; Jesus
    Christ
trust, 32
tsaddik (righteous man), 149–50, 152,
    153, 154–59
two kinds of righteousness
    antinomianism and, 185
    as coming from God, xix
    defining righteousness in, 101–3
    in Galatians Commentary, 100
    as indispensable to Luther's theol-
        ogy, 1–2, 100
    as inseparable but distinct, 23–26,
        101–3
    Luther's early use of distinction of,
        125–44
    preachers and, 149–59
    in recent Lutheran thought, 100–
        101, 118–19
    relationship of, 103–6
    roots of distinction between, 26–28
    term usage, 185–86
    two realms and, 113–18
Two Kinds of Righteousness (sermon)
    (Luther), 4, 10–11, 100
two kingdoms
    Luther's distinction between, 183
    Schumacher on, 101

separation of church and state and, 69–70
term usage, xvi
two realms
 coram Deo (relation to God), 101–3
 coram mundo (relation to world), 101–3
 life within, 70–73
 as theological distinction, 187
two-dimensional humanity, 17–34
twofold righteousness, defined, xix

unionism, 67–68

values
 personal choice and, 156
 in post-modern society, 111
 value scale, 46
verba dei (words of God), 107, 181, 182
vertical dimension of life, xvii, 21, 46, 48, 49, 50, 79–80, 101, 132, 158. *See also* righteousness of faith
via antiqua, 47–48

via moderna, 47–48
virginity, 49
virtue
 Aristotle on, 41
 Melanchthon on, 39–40, 41–42, 52
 will and, 46–47
virtue continuum, 46
vocations
 justification and, 51
 Melanchthon on, 41
 sanctification and, 51

Walther, C. F. W., 107, 108, 182
Washington, George, 62–63, 63
Wengert, Timothy, 13n4, 36, 185–86
will
 Eramus controversy over, 78
 Melanchthon on, 40, 43, 46
Wingren, Gustav, 110, 120n24
Wisconsin Synod, 68
Wittenberg theologians, 125–33
Witzel, Georg, 84
Worms, 85

Scripture Index

OLD TESTAMENT

Genesis
1, xvi
1:27, 136
2, 28
2:4-6, 127
2:15-17, 136
2:21-22, 128
3:12, 137
3:15, 137
4:7-8, 83
14:13-16, 141
15:1, 83
16, 139
18, 139, 142
18:12, 139
22:16-18, 134
33, 142
34, 135

Job
23, 151

Psalms, 7
1, 158
51:10, 89
51:14, 18
90:9, 11, 151
119:151, 158
138:6, 153

Isaiah
40:10, 83
53:6, 7, 27
58:7-8, 83
64:8, 28
66:2, 153

Jeremiah
23:56, 152
31, 52

Habakkuk
2:4, 4

NEW TESTAMENT

Matthew
20:8, 83
22:34-40, xviii
22:37, 39, 20, 78
22:37-39, 21

Luke
7:47, 53

John
1:1-14, 152
1:12, 131
1:17, ix
1:18, 152
1:29, 31

3:5, 131
3:14, 31
5:17, 134
6:37, 25
6:44, 83
6:55, 25
14:17, 157
16:10, 30

Romans
1-2, 158
1:16, 4
1:17, 4
4, 93
4:3, 44
4:6-8, 95
4:25, 31
5:18-19, 131
6:1-3, 142
6:3-11, 7, 30, 135
6:9, 27
7:7-25, 157
8:9, 157
8:18-23, 118
10:4, 9, 31
13, 116

1 Corinthians
3:8, 83
3:16, 157
4:7, 83
15:48-49, 136

2 Corinthians
  3.5, 83
  5:10, 83
  5:17, xvi
  5:19-21, 95
  5:21, 7, 9

Galatians, 20
  2:20, 157
  3:13, 7
  5:16-26, 155
  5:25, 155

Ephesians
  2:10, 156
  4:22-24, 136
  5:18, 157

Philippians
  2:5, 157

3:4-7, 93–94
3:9, 186

Colossians
  2:11-15, 30, 135
  3:10, 157
  3:18-4:1, 159

1 Timothy
  6:11, 186
2 Timothy
  4:7-8, 83

Titus
  2:12-13, 89

Hebrews
  1:1, 152
  11:4, 138
  11:8-10, 93

James
  1:17, 83
  2:14-17, 155
  5:6, 153

1 Peter
  2:13-3:7, 159
  4:8, 52
  5:5, 153
2 Peter, 126

1 John
  3:9, 131

Jude, 126

Lightning Source UK Ltd.
Milton Keynes UK
UKHW012018250123
415976UK00012B/185/J